HIDDEN IN THE HYMNS

ENDORSEMENTS

I suppose it has become somewhat of a reflex to groan and stare at the ceiling any time I hear of anyone purporting to make something of hymns or psalms "more accessible" in some way or another to the uninitiated. In the main, these attempts are more of a dumbing down—an attempt to short-cut a process of learning that ought to be anything but expedient. Rivers Houseal does nothing of the kind in *Hidden in the Hymns*. Rather, she has produced what amounts to a gracious, intelligent, labor of love. Her regard for the beauty of words is evident, as well as her regard for the truths they contain as sourced in the Word of God. Her translations (almost commentary) are smart, lovely to read, and accessible in the best sense of the word. *Hidden in the Hymns* would be a lovely companion to hymn singing at home, a great study for personal devotion, or a great reference for those moments when curiosity or wonder demand an answer. I wish I had this book when my children were little!

KENT YOUNG
Music Teacher, The Oaks Classical Christian Academy
Director, The Oaks Conservatory for the Arts
Chief Musician, Christ Church (Spokane, WA)

Rivers has done the fabulous job of making the words and phrases in older hymns very accessible for the Church. When I was a song-leader in another church decades ago, we always sang contemporary praise choruses because we thought there were just too many words in those old hymns and were stymied by what they actually were trying to say. But we lost the poetic beauty and richness of thoughtful truth-tellers who led us down deep paths of devotion and truth that needs to marinate in one's mind and soul for years and decades. This book helps young and old alike appreciate the meaning of many familiar (and almost familiar) hymns so that one can then sing with understanding and join in on the devotion and worship of God. This is a great aid to personal and family devotions and will bolster one's preparation for singing to the Lord with the whole body of Christ.

DAVID HATCHER
Pastor, Trinity Church, CREC (Woodinville, WA)

Rivers Houseal is amazing! She has created a beautiful, Spirit-filled teaching tool about "Psalms, hymns, and spiritual songs" that will make all ages want to sing aloud and "make melody in their hearts to God" (Ephesians 5:18-21 and Colossians 3:16-17). As a worship leader since the age of 15 years (1954), I find that this book resonates with my life-long desire to teach everyone in the church, unashamedly, to sing praises to God. No Christian is exempt from singing praise (Psalm 100:1-2). Everyone is commanded to sing with understanding (Psalm 47:7, NKJV). I marvel that Rivers is far beyond her years in spiritually understanding these beautiful hymns and putting her thoughts so clearly on paper.

DR. JAMES D. WHITMIRE
Minister of Music Emeritus, Bellevue Baptist Church (Cordova, TN)
Teacher Emeritus, Mid-America Baptist Theological Seminary (Memphis, TN)
Worship Leader, Crossroads Baptist Church (Eads, TN)
Served on five Hymnal Committees

Opening up the rich inheritance we have received in the church's hymnody for our covenant children is both a great privilege and a great responsibility. This delightful book will prove to be a vital tool in the arsenal of parents, teachers, and pastors as we take up that privilege and responsibility with joy.

DR. GEORGE GRANT
Pastor, Parish Presbyterian Church (Franklin, TN)

Aside from the Bible itself, one of the richest sources of Biblical truth is the hymnal we use in the worship of our glorious God. Children learn the words to "Amazing Grace" and "Holy, Holy, Holy" at an early age, and senior citizens still recall those lyrics long after they have forgotten almost everything else! But how many of us have truly plumbed the depths of the hymns we sing? How many of us are more captivated by a catchy tune than a powerful lyric? How often have we sung, "Here I raise my Ebenezer" without any idea of the Old Testament context? *Hidden in the Hymns* invites you to reflect on the rich truth contained in the great hymns of the church. It's a dinner bell for the soul—calling us to enjoy a banquet of rich blessing that will thrill your heart, strengthen your faith, and give wings to your worship.

REV. WILLIAM SPINK, JR.
Pastor (1981-2020), Riveroaks Reformed Presbyterian Church, PCA (Germantown, TN)

Kudos to Rivers for noticing the need (poetry can be challenging!) and then generating such a suitable solution! Rivers takes the most elegant verses ever penned in the English language and unpacks them so even a child can comprehend and appreciate these cherished lyrics. As Christians, we are commanded to sing with understanding (1 Corinthians 14:15), and thus this book is essential for children, parents, Christian school teachers, Sunday schools, small group leaders, music pastors, pastors, and any other persons I happened to not mention. I have been teaching hymns to churches and schools for many years and as I look over each of River's renderings I continue to have two thoughts: 1) I couldn't have said it better. 2) I wish I had this sooner.

JORDAN DOOLITTLE
Chief Musician, Cornerstone Reformed Church, CREC (Carbondale, IL)

What Rivers accomplishes in this work is a translation from the sung word to the devotional word. As we seek to rebuild a generation who cherishes the great hymns of the Church, we also need to educate them in the devotional language of these hymns. The authors of these congregational masterpieces were not mere professionals, they were saints with deep piety that reached the apex of theological orthodoxy in their compositions, but also pierced deeply the human heart. A robust faith is both orthodox and orthopraxis. In explaining these hymns, the author brings these truths nearer to our minds and hearts. I commend this labor as a song of love for the Church.

REV. DR. URIESOU BRITO
Senior Pastor, Providence Church, CREC (Pensacola, FL)

Miss Houseal has assembled a very handy little companion to the hymnal, and not just for the benefit of children but adults, too. Use her summaries as a tool for learning, understanding, and memorizing hymnody, or use them in devotions as a guide to prayer how we might address our Glorious Heavenly Father. Her summaries are succinct, accurate paraphrases of the hymn texts, and are saturated with scripture references and quotations. Miss Houseal knows the Bible well to be able to assemble such a compendium of scripture references.

MARK REAGAN, DMA
Director of Music, Christ Church, CREC (Moscow, ID)

Hidden in the Hymns is both informative and fun. It explains and brings to life many great songs of the church and provides another valuable resource for Christian families. This is a rich treasure to be mined and used regularly in family worship. To sing, and to sing with understanding, is one of the most powerful ways to establish, inculcate, and transmit our faith to the next generation of believers.

RANDY BOOTH
Pastor, Grace Covenant Presbyterian Church, CREC (Nacogdoches, TX)

Modern thinking says look to the New, Cool, and Sensational. In *Hidden in the Hymns,* Rivers Houseal seeks to meditate on the True, Good, and Beautiful in the time-tested hymns of the Christian faith. This book is a product of loving and living with a rich hymnody and a call for young people to find the same encouragement and refreshment that Rivers has found in these hymns. May more Christian young people see the same encouragement from the rich legacy of hymnody given to God's people through history.

JARROD D. RICHEY
Director of Music & Choir, Church of the Redeemer and Geneva Academy (West Monroe, LA)

A treasure for generations of believers to come, Rivers Houseal has woven the history behind our great hymns with poignancy and grace. Such knowledge lifts the Christian's spirit from lethargy to passionate adoration of our most Glorious Savior. These tales of unfolding grace are sure to inspire the reader as they carry on the love and truth of Christ sung through the ages.

ROBERT L. SHACKELFORD, D.C.
Elder, Grace Covenant Church, CREC (Fontaine, AR)

The Lord delights in the praises of our little ones, and he gloriously enlists their songs to cause his enemies to cease. With a view to how the Lord has ordained his strength and in honor of the Church's best hymns, *Hidden in the Hymns* equips children with a good understanding of the biblical truth in Church hymnody. Our hymns are laden with doctrinal riches. Get this book to disciple your children in their truth, and they will sing a new song to the Lord.

PHILLIP BOZARTH
Pastor, Grace Covenant Church, CREC (Fontaine, AR)

HIDDEN IN THE HYMNS

RIVERS HOUSEAL

NOGGINNOSE
PRESS

HIDDEN IN THE HYMNS

ISBN 978-1-956611-01-4

Cover design and content layout by Houseal Creative
Edited by Rachel Nix

Cover image: *The Village Choir* by John Watkins Chapman (1832-1903)

Nogginnose Press
PO Box 96
Smithville, AR 72466 USA
nogginnose.com

To the congregants of
Grace Covenant Church,
who taught me to love hymns
by singing them with me
every Lord's Day.

I'll walk through life with
a rooted understanding of
what "Church family" means
because of each one of you.

What a delight it will be to sing
with you for eternity!

"Your statutes have been my songs in the house of my sojourning." — PSALM 119:54 (ESV)

CONTENTS

HYMNS

HYMNWRITERS

TRANSLATORS

DEAR CHILDREN

I wrote this book for you.

At the time I'm writing this, I'm not much older than you are, most likely, so I remember what it's like to be your age. I grew up in a Christian family. As far back as I remember, I've believed that Jesus is my Lord. But when I was younger, I would hear the grown-ups, and even some of my friends, talking about the love they had for Jesus... and I realized I didn't completely understand what they meant. I didn't quite feel this love, joy, and comfort they were always talking about—at least not as much as they apparently did. What was I missing? "Jesus is my Savior, too," I thought to myself. "So why don't I feel about Him like they do?" Have you ever asked yourself that question?

I wondered about this especially when our church sang hymn lines like this one: "*Thou, O Christ, art all I want.*" Truly? Nothing else? I couldn't honestly say that, I realized.

But I knew I wanted to be able to say it. Don't you? I wanted to truthfully say that Christ really is "*all I want*"! I wanted all the rival "wants" weeded out of my heart until there was nothing left to grow there but love for my King Jesus. And the Holy Spirit has been showing me that He is doing that weeding for me. It's slow work, but every day He is helping me understand *how* to love Jesus.

He has used two things in particular to teach me: God's Word, and hymns.

Now, we must be very clear: hymns are not Scripture. They are man's words, not God's. But good hymns *are* true—and that's the sort of hymns I've collected into this book. Good hymns come from hymnwriters who see what God's Word teaches, then sing about it.

Would you like to know how to sing about Christ as if He is truly the most precious thing to you? These hymns remind you over and over again what Jesus Christ has done for you (and what He's still doing). So they fill you up with gratitude and love for Him, and at the same time they give you the words to tell Him about it.

So sing these hymns like you mean them, my friends! Let's practice filling the air with our joyful praises now, because we will be singing together for all eternity.

DEAR PARENTS

I was four years old when I first met a hymnal. I proceeded to grow up on it. Those hymns, the ancient and the new, have played in my head while I played with dolls, or was supposed to be doing long division, or was building my next fort in the woods. I have loved those hymns as long as I've known them, and it sure feels like they have loved me.

But that does not mean I've always understood them.

Picture a six, eight, or even ten-year-old me standing in front of a pew. Red hymnal in hand, I'm belting out, "*All hail the pow'r of Jesus' name! / Let angels prostrate fall / Bring forth the royal diadem / To crown Him Lord of All.*"

Such richness! But eight-year-old me was thinking, "The hail is gonna do what to the angels? And what's a diadem? Huh ... catchy tune, though."

Here's another example. "*The earth with its store of wonders untold / Almighty, your pow'r has founded of old / Has 'stablished it fast by a changeless decree / And 'round it has cast, like a mantle, the sea.*"

"Stablished ... mantle ... you mean like the thing over our fireplace?"

The hymns of old are rich, and drip Scripture from every corner. What better to be playing on repeat in a child's head? But in order for a child to love these hymns as they really deserve to be loved, he or she will need to know *what the hymn is talking about.* It's hard to appreciate what you don't understand. But if a few generations go by paying scanty heed to these hymns, they're in danger of going the way of cuneiform.

My intention is *not* to rewrite the old hymns, to make them "new," nor "relevant and contemporary." Bede the Venerable wrote a hymn in the mid-7th century saying that Christ will return again in the same way the Apostles saw Him go, and that He is worthy of all praise and glory. Is that not still true? If it is (and it is), how could anyone possibly argue that this hymn is not relevant *and* contemporary—even if it is now over 1,300 years old? One might argue that the Venerable Bede's hymn is outdated because it's archaic in language. Very well...then let's learn to read archaic English, shall we? We don't stop teaching Latin or Koine Greek just because you can't order french fries with them.

And other than reading the Word of God itself, how could a child better grasp the concept of our God being the God of Ages than by singing something true that his brother or sister in Christ penned 1,000 years ago?

To that end, I wrote this book. I want to help children understand these hymns, so that they will be enriched by them as I have been. Each hymn in this book comes with a paraphrase, presented stanza by stanza. I'm not trying to add meaning to these hymns; I'm simply peeling away the archaic layer for a moment so that a child can understand what they see when I put it back. And I do put it back. I give the vocabulary "translation" of a stanza first and then give the original stanza, because I don't want anyone to walk away with my words in their head. Know and understand the ideas you will be meeting, and then hear Paul Gerhardt or Isaac Watts or Augustus Toplady say it better than I can.

I expect someone will ask me, "Why didn't you include [fill in the blank with a beloved hymn]?" There are two possible reasons: first, there's a good chance I simply wasn't aware that particular hymn existed. My apologies; I'll get duly acquainted with it post haste. Second, perhaps I left it out on purpose—not necessarily meaning I don't like it. I took many hymns off my list because I realized they were clear without any paraphrase at all.

I trust that a number of these hymns will be familiar to Christians across most denominations, but I also fully expect that the average evangelical hasn't heard of half these hymns. (Confession: many of them *I* hadn't heard of until recently, even though they had been living in the hymnal beneath my nose for years.) These forgotten hymns made the cut because they have been *wrongly* ignored. I hope to have the privilege of introducing you to new friends.

It is my hope that whenever you set this book down, you walk away with poetry running between your ears, even if you don't know its tune. You can find recordings online for many of these hymns, so listen to them if you can... or better still, find an old hymnal and learn them yourself. With each hymn, you will see a list of tunes the hymn has been set to over the ages. I've provided wee biographies for some of the hymnwriters and hymn-translators, too.

If you're new to old hymns, then prepare yourself. You will be challenged; you will be comforted. But watch the effect on your children: the young souls in your home will be trained and molded by the repetition of truth, beautifully stated. Their vocabulary is going to grow by an oxgang. Young wordsmiths-in-the-making will soak up all sorts of goodness from the stellar poetry of these hymns that will grow them up into better writers, poets, and songwriters... maybe even *hymn*writers.

I am not one to say that Christians should only be singing old hymns. New and wonderful hymns are being written even now. There was a day when "Jesus, Lover of My Soul" was new. But there is a reason these old hymns have survived the centuries, and the frank truth is that they offer a theological depth (and therefore, a comfort) that Christian pop radio does not.

We'll be singing for all eternity, so I propose that we start now. Get thee busy.

A NOTE ON SOURCING

Aggravatingly, there is no "master text" (at least, one that I could find) for most of these hymns. Oh, how I've wished I could ask Isaac Watts for the original manuscript of a hymn so I could see how he wrote it, not how some denomination altered it two hundred years later. Some hymnals exclude this stanza or that. Some show subtle text changes. Others alter a hymn beyond recognition.

I make no claims to have included every extant stanza of every hymn. This is no academic study of *hymnology*—it is a celebration of *hymns*, and yes, there is a difference. In each case, I have simply tried to include as many stanzas of a hymn as I could find. If the wording of that stanza differed from one version to another, I usually chose the one I was most familiar with or whichever was more archaic. So you'll probably never find a hymnal that shows every hymn exactly as I've presented it. I haven't cited my sources even once... apologies, but that much citation and source-checking is about a mile beyond the scope of this book. (But I can tell you that most of these hymns I know from my childhood with the *Trinity Hymnal*.)

The sourcing I *have* focused on is Scripture referencing. I meant it when I said these hymns drip Scripture from every corner. I don't claim to have caught and cited all of it, but I have done a fair bit. Look and see how much credibility and truth laces through these hymns. It's astounding, and it only answers any questions of why these hymns have survived. Truth has a tendency to do that.

You know, this does raise a question... If the old hymns are so chocked with truth and worthy of our attention, why do so many churches have boxes in their basements marked "Hymnals"?

FOREWORD

BY DOUGLAS BOND

I am thrilled to discover this new book celebrating the greatest hymns throughout the centuries! As the contemporary church has so feverishly supplanted the majesty, reverence, and awe of God for the latest trends in popular musical entertainment, this book of hymns shines as a beacon on the pathway back to biblical singing in congregational worship. Let me explain more specifically why I feel this so strongly.

A dear pastor friend of mine, lamenting the loss of hymnals in so many churches, refers to lyrics projected up on a screen as "off-the-wall songs." He's not a fan. But the popular trend is definitely against him. Most churches see it as a giant step forward to leave their hymnals moldering in the basement of the church, relics of a bygone era, and good riddance.

The rationale is that people are looking up, not fumbling with the pages of an old book. And what about the visitors, unbelievers that come to church? It's way easier for them to just look at the words up on the screen. No hunting for the right page number. No confusing musical score to distract them. It's huge progress to leave those hymnals behind us.

Still more, it is argued that the old hymnal doesn't include all the cool new songs. We're stuck singing lyrics written hundreds of years ago by a bunch of old dead guys. *Ewww*. The new way lets us add new songs any time we want. Just get the lyrics to the tech guys; they can plunk them into PowerPoint slides, and we can sing the latest new thing next week.

NO GATEKEEPERS

But what have we lost by giving up our hymnals? We surrendered scrutiny. Publishing a hymnal is an enormous task, requiring careful organizing of the hymns by themes and biblical texts, also requiring an editorial committee of people chosen because of their literary and theological training and experience. Hymnal editors spent years compiling the best hymns for congregations to sing.

Giving up our hymnals takes all that scrutiny away and leaves us at the mercy of the latest new songs. We need more scruples about the new material. It's way too easy to fabricate a worship song and introduce it next Sunday; no vetting, no scrutiny, no gatekeepers, no hymnal editors.

When we abandoned our hymnals we also abandoned literary and theological standards of orthodoxy and excellence. All too often, emotional nonsense, however well-intentioned, supplants a timeless hymn like Bernard of Clairvaux's "O Sacred Head, Now Wounded," which every Christian needs to sing in corporate worship several times a year and in family worship at least as often. Instead, we endure the singing of vacuous, repetitive lyrics that fall far beneath what is appropriate and well-pleasing to God—that is, the kind of lyrics that used to be in our hymnals because they had undergone the rigor of the centuries.

Without that rigorous scrutiny we may find ourselves joining in a catchy Disneyland song about the world singing God's love, "*And we'll all join hands / every woman, every man / we'll sing His love.*" This sounds like it was penned by a universalist Unitarian worship leader. True, every knee will bow and every tongue confess that Jesus is Lord to the glory of God, but unbelievers won't be joining hands and singing His love. They will be weeping and wailing and gnashing their teeth at His wrath.

The hymnal helped us learn our theology, and get it not only into our heads, but into our hearts. The off-the-wall-song phenomenon hastens theological decline and illiteracy, leaving us vulnerable not only to doxological drivel but to blatant doctrinal error and apostasy.

GONE AWAY BIBLE

Another yet more pernicious loss when we abandoned our hymnals for the PowerPoint projection screen, is that in doing so we abandoned our Bibles. When we have the screen up there already, and the tech guys have the PowerPoint program at their fingertips, it's simple to project the biblical text up on the screen too. Consequently, few people bring their Bibles to church anymore. Why bother? I realize that this too is motivated by good intentions, even gospel intentions; we want visitors who are unfamiliar with a Bible to see the biblical text under consideration effortlessly, without the distraction of an actual Bible in hand.

Getting your Bible off the screen instead of from, well, the Bible, is the equivalent of taking a nutrition pill instead of pulling your chair up to the dining table and feasting on a slab of grass-fed beef steak with all the delectable accoutrements.

An unintended consequence of getting our Bible from a screen is that many do not know how to find their way around their Bibles. Many can't even find where they last laid their physical copy of the Bible (it's got to be here somewhere). I wonder how many millennials could even find Zephaniah 3:17, back there in the clean pages, in a physical Bible, with pages, margins, a concordance, maps—you know, a real book.

I began annotating the margins of my Bible(s) in college, cross referencing, adding hymn lyrics on similar themes and quotations from Puritans, Reformers, and other great preachers since. My Bible is precious to me. First and last, because it is the Word of God, but also because I own it. It is the same copy of it I read over and over. It has my marginalia in it. I can reread passages that I read and dated in times of celebration and thanksgiving, and in times of grief and sorrow.

Forfeiting our hymnals in favor of an ephemeral projection screen is one of the greatest contributors to biblical illiteracy. We are no longer a generation of Bible Christians. Oh, sure, we have the app on our phones, with all the notifications popping up to distract us, but we don't truly own our Bibles.

The loss of the Bible leaves us vulnerable to the theology of the new social revolutionaries, shouting their unflinching doctrinal priorities in our faces. One of the ways we can tell when we are being more shaped by our culture than being shapers of it is when the Bible's language and themes begin to sound odd to our ears, when we feel like we need to make apologies for the biblical authors—worse yet, for the Holy Spirit. They didn't really mean to put it that way. Couldn't they have been more sensitive to the priorities of our culture?

This is yet another important reason the Church must continue singing the psalms and the best hymns of our spiritual forebears. Then, after our minds, hearts, and imaginations have been thoroughly shaped by biblical and historical doxology, only then are we equipped to contribute new appropriate hymns for this generation of Christ's body to sing.

HYMNS AS POETRY

In the course of my research, writing, and teaching about hymns over the last decades I have learned many wonderful things about hymns, hymn writers, and hymnody—and every time I open the hymnal (usually the *Trinity*) I learn something new.

I love singing hymns. I love the very best of our hymn lyrics from the last 1,800 years or so, and I have come more and more to love them not only as heartfelt passionate expressions of praise to God, but as the best of English poetry.

It was American poet John Greenleaf Whittier who said, "The highest use of poetry is the hymn." In addition, I love many of the timeless musical settings of great classic hymn poetry, and I appreciate a growing number of the new hymns that are being written by thoughtful Christian poets and musicians.

Throughout decades of teaching, I have been incorporating the study and imitation of the best hymns as poetry worthy to be studied in its own right in my high school English classes and in my Oxford Creative Writing Master Classes. I have, however, discovered some significant obstacles to understanding and appreciating hymns for this generation of Christian young people.

Nowhere is this more obvious than when students attempt to write about hymns as poetry. I teach my students to explore the meaning of poetry by writing poetry explications, essays written specifically about poetry, wherein they observe and evaluate the effectiveness of the various poetic conventions used and the depth and richness of the meaning.

I've often had my students compare poets with the poetry of hymns written at the same time or in similar circumstances. For example, I include Lutheran pastor Martin Rinkhart's great lyric, "Now Thank We All Our God," written while the Thirty-Years War was raging through Germany, in my course on

World War I poets. Rinkhart's 17th century hymn was sung August 1, 1914 on the streets of Berlin when the Kaiser announced the mobilization of German troops to invade Belgium. It makes a dramatic counterpoint to the despair and anger of many of the WW I poets.

STUDENT WRITERS PANIC

Here is where I discovered the obstacle for my students. When I gave them a poem of Wordsworth or Cowper or Shakespeare to analyze and evaluate, they knew what to do. It looked like and read like poetry. It was there in front of them in the format in which the poet originally penned the words. They can observe the basic unit of poetry, the line, with its hard-left margins and capitalized first lines (center lining poetry is a Hallmark card reduction of meaning and content to visual form and is unlike the format the poet wrote the poetry in). They can find the parallel ideas, the progression of thought, the figures of speech, the allusions, the meter, the rhyme scheme, the poet's use of various sound devices, the use of inclusio, and other subtleties of the poetic art. But when I give them a hymn from the Trinity Hymnal (one of the best American hymnals; I use it daily), they are frustrated and confused. When I give them a hymn with the poetry embedded in and subordinated to the musical score, as it appears in almost every American hymnal since the mid-19th century, they panic.

At first, I didn't get this. I grew up singing hymns in church; I read music; I love music. At first, I concluded it was part of the decline of culture, the loss of the ability to read music and sing hymns. But as I traveled to various other countries around the world, I discovered the problem.

Maybe it's American exceptionalism again. But I'm not so sure. We Americans seem to be the only ones who hand hymnals to our congregations that have the poetry of the hymns in a subordinate role to the music so it does not look like or read like its genre—poetry. In every other country I have visited (UK, New Zealand, Australia, Tonga, Europe, Japan, Peru, Uganda, etc.), the hymnals have the lyric of the poetry visible as poetry, in lines and stanzas, the way the poet wrote it. I have talked to missionaries and Christians from other countries I have not visited. I discovered that we Americans are pretty much the only ones who do this.

REVIVALISM TORPEDOES CONTENT

So, I did some more research. As near as I can find, we began doing this as a direct result of the shift in priorities in 19th century Revivalism. We began replacing many of the psalm versifications from the Reformation, and many of the classic hymns with revival songs that in general were sentimental, repetitive, lacking in theological depth, and addressed largely to the sinner rather than as expressions of worship and adoration to God. This reduction of the content and the quality of lyric went hand in hand with the crafting of new music, designed to attract the lost into the camp meeting tent. The new popular musical sound (the worst of it somewhere between merry-go-round ditty, the frontier cowboy tune, and barbershop quartet sound) became more important because it was the hook to draw in the lost. Music was no longer accompaniment as an aid in taking the meaning of the poetry on the lips and in the heart and mind.

In Protestant Christian worship, music has always been in a subordinate role to aid the worshiper in taking to heart and mind the meaning and richness of the poetic lyric. Though Calvin knew and appreciated the incredible power of music to move hearts, he cautioned against getting music and the objective meaning of the words flipped around: "We must beware lest our ears be more intent on the music than our minds on the spiritual meaning of the words."

In Revivalism, that's precisely what happened. The words became less important. The new format of the hymnal reflects this shifting priority of Revivalism. Charles Finney's New Measures and Pelagian theology flipped things around. The new format of the American hymnal, reducing the central importance of the poetry, was born. Open any Revivalism-influenced hymnal and the first thing we see is the musical score, not the poetic lines. The format alone does exactly what Calvin cautioned us against, setting us up for our eye and ear to be "more intent on the music than our minds on the spiritual meaning of the words." Music first, the poetry chopped up to fit within the score.

When I gave my English students a timed essay to write under exam conditions about a hymn, I would give them the option of seeing the hymn formatted the way the poet wrote it—in lines and stanzas—or formatted with the poetry stripped and dissected to fit the musical format. They chose to have it in poetic form every time. But we might object and say that when we are singing in church we are not writing an essay; they are two entirely different activities.

Though that is true, both activities require the ones reading and singing the poetry to understand the meaning of what they are reading and singing. Christians rightly place a high premium on the engagement of the mind and of the imagination in worship. I would argue that singing hymns from a hymnal inadvertently formatted to make it more difficult to observe the subtleties of the poetry being sung is actually working against its own purpose.

RESCUE THE HYMNAL

Maybe it's time to take on a remaining reductionist influence of Revivalism on our hymnal (and thus on our worship). I propose a cross-page format, the poetry in lines and stanzas on the left, and facing the poetry the musical score. Let's rescue hymn poetry from the influence of Revivalism so that our hymnal format reflects biblical priorities, thereby confronting a significant obstacle to the engagement of mind and heart in our sung worship.

The majority of worshipers, especially our children, will sing from the poetry. Studies indicate that only about 27% of church goers read music anyway. Even those of us who do, when we use the hymnal in our private devotions, will likely meditate from the column that looks like poetry where the progression of thought and rich poetic conventions are uninterrupted by the musical notation.

Let's restore the hymnal to Christian worship. Let's return to a format that is consistent with how Christians have sung in worship since the Reformation itself—poetry and meaning first, music second. This will send a clear message to the worshiper that the meaning of the words, taken on the lips, in the heart, and understood in the mind, is of first importance in our worship.

This rich volume celebrating the great hymns is an enormous step in the right direction. Every family, every church, every homeschool coop, every Christian school, every community group, and every Bible study gathering should have multiple copies of Hidden in the Hymns to aid in the recovery of the worthiest of our hymns—and then pass them on to the next generation, adorned in such a way that our children will never want to let go of such richness.

....

Douglas Bond is author of numerous books of historical fiction, biography, and practical theology—including *God Sings (And Ways We Think He Ought To)*, the *Mr. Pipes* series on Christian hymnody, *Augustus Toplady: A Debtor to Mercy Alone*, and *The Poetic Wonder of Isaac Watts*. Learn more at **bondbooks.net**.

HYMNS

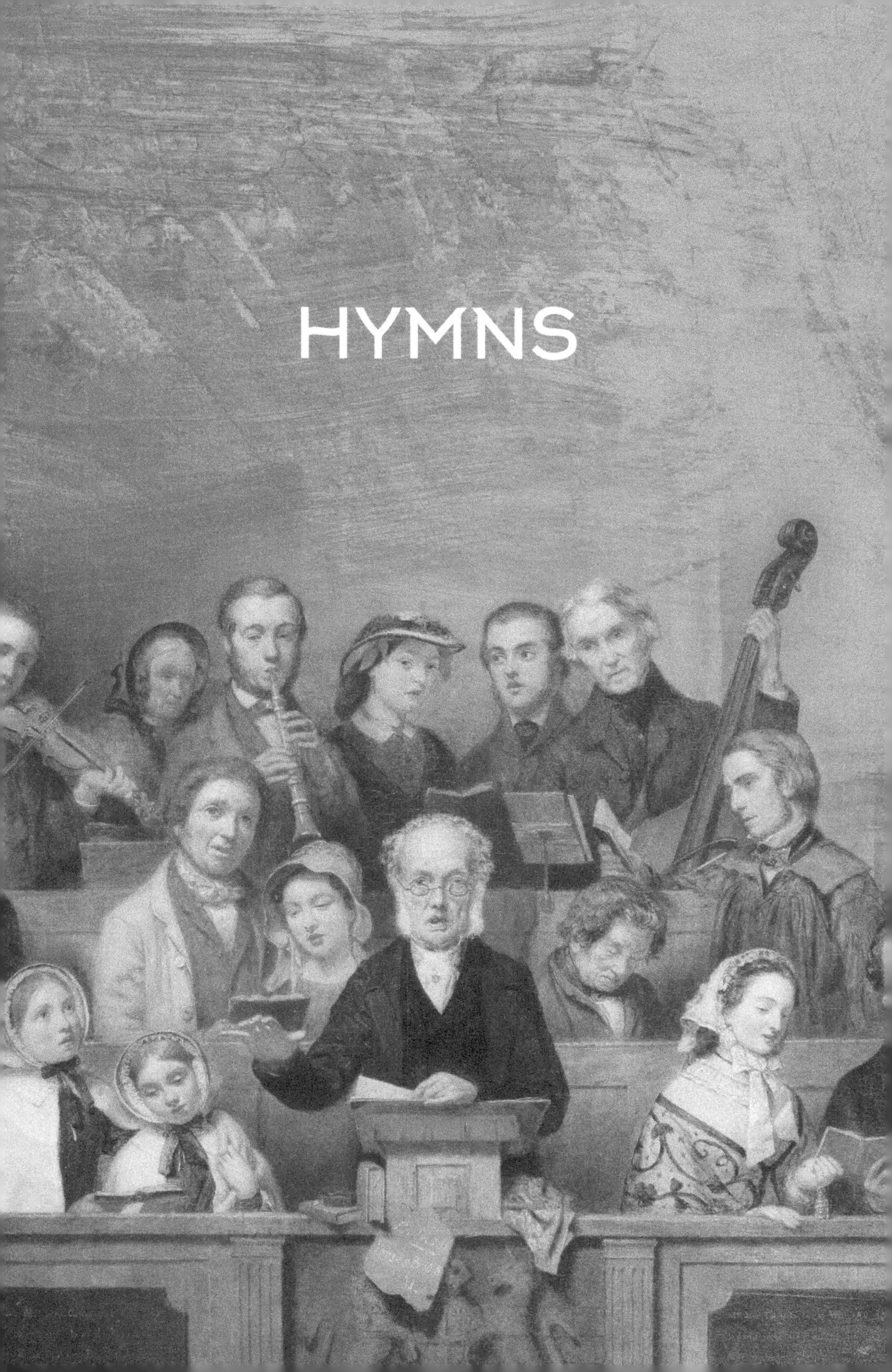

A DEBTOR TO MERCY ALONE

Lyrics by **Augustus Montague Toplady** (see page 329), mid-18th century

Set to the tunes *Trewen—Llangristiolus—De Fleury—Cleveland—Salome*

I am in debt to God's mercy, and nothing else. So my song is about the great mercy God shows His people, just as He promised He would! (Luke 1:67-75) Christ, because you have made me righteous like you, I do not have to be afraid to come to God. I no longer face God's anger or punishment for my sin—all because you, Christ my Savior, obeyed God perfectly and shed your blood to pay for my sins. Now my sins are done with! (Romans 10:4, Hebrews 9:12)

A debtor to mercy alone,
Of covenant mercy I sing;
Nor fear, with your righteousness on,
My person and off'ring to bring.
The terrors of law and of God
With me can have nothing to do;
My Savior's obedience and blood
Hide all my transgressions from view.

....

When Christ paid for my sins with his blood, that started the work of redeeming and changing my heart. And He is strong enough to *finish* that work! Every promise that God has made to His people is being fulfilled in Christ. (2 Corinthians 1:20) Not one of God's promises has failed yet, so I can trust that nothing will make God forget His promises to me—not anything that will happen, and not anything that is happening now. Nothing can keep my soul from my Father and His love for me.

The work which his goodness began,
The arm of his strength will complete;
His promise is yea and amen,
And never was forfeited yet.
Things future, nor things that are now,
Nor all things below or above,
Can make him his purpose forgo,
Or sever my soul from his love.

....

My name is written on the palm of God's hands (Isaiah 49:16), and not even an eternity of time can erase it. God will never forget me. My name remains on God's heart, and it is written in letters that cannot be removed, because God's own grace wrote them. I know I will be able endure until the end, because I trust God's promise to keep me in His hands. Those who are already in Heaven may be happier than I am, but I am just as safe in my Father's hands as they are!

My name from the palms of His hands
Eternity will not erase;
Impressed on His heart it remains,
In marks of indelible grace.
Yes, I to the end shall endure,
As sure as the earnest is giv'n;
More happy, but not more secure,
The glorified spirits in heav'n.

Sung to the tune of "All creatures of our God & King"

A HYMN OF GLORY LET US SING

Lyrics by **Bede the Venerable** (see page 280), late 7th or early 8th century

Originally written in Latin; translated by **Elizabeth Rundle Charles** (see page 343) and **Benjamin Webb**

Set to the tunes *Lasst Uns Erfreuen—Deo Gracias—Tugwood*

Let us sing a hymn together about God's glory! Let new songs of praise ring, all throughout the world. Praise the Lord! Praise the Lord, for Christ has gone back up to the throne of God, and He has gone by a way that no one ever has before. (Acts 1:9, Hebrews 4:14) Praise the Lord!

A hymn of glory let us sing;
New songs thro'out the world shall ring:
Alleluia! Alleluia!
Christ, by a road before untrod,
Ascendeth to the throne of God.
(Refrain)
Alleluia! Alleluia!
Alleluia! Alleluia! Alleluia!

....

The apostles stand on the Mount of Olives with Jesus' other followers, and they all see Jesus in His kingly majesty as He goes back up into Heaven.

The holy apostolic band
Upon the Mount of Olives stand;
Alleluia! Alleluia!
And with His followers they see
Jesus' resplendent majesty.

....

As the apostles stand there staring, angels come to them and ask, "Why are you watching the sky where Jesus went up?" They proclaim, "He is your Savior: He defeated sin and death, and this is His day of triumph and glory, when God will reward Him!" (Acts 1:10)

To whom the angels, drawing nigh,
"Why stand and gaze upon the sky?
Alleluia! Alleluia!
This is the Savior," thus they say;
"This is His noble triumph-day."

....

The angels promise, "You will see Jesus come again, and He will come back in the same way that you saw Him leave today. He will come in glory, through Heaven's palace gates in the sky." (Acts 1:11)

"Again shall ye behold Him so
As ye today have seen Him go.
Alleluia! Alleluia!
In glorious pomp ascending high
Up to the portals of the sky."

....

Oh Christ, let us travel toward Heaven, too! Let us come up to be with you. Keep our spirits strong and refreshed as we journey through life, up to your Kingdom and your throne. (Jude 1:24-25, Hebrews 12:1-2)

Oh, grant us thitherward to tend
And with unwearied hearts ascend,
Alleluia! Alleluia!
Unto Thy kingdom's throne, where Thou,
As is our faith, art seated now.

....

Christ, be our greatest joy, and be our defense and protection. When we come to you at last, you will repay each of us for what we have done in this life. (Matthew 16:27, Revelation 22:12) Then, the light that beams from your kingly face will be our light for all eternity. (Revelation 1:16)

Be thou our Joy and strong Defense,
Who art our future Recompense:
Alleluia! Alleluia!
So shall the light that springs from thee
Be ours through all eternity.

....

Oh Christ, who rose from the dead and went back to Heaven, let everyone who is on the earth give all their praises to you! (Philippians 2:9-11) For you are one with the Father and the Holy Spirit, and you will be for endless eternity. (John 14:9) Amen—it is true!

O risen Christ, ascended Lord,
All praise to thee let earth accord,
Alleluia! Alleluia!
Who art, while endless ages run,
With Father and with Spirit one.
Amen.

A LAMB GOES UNCOMPLAINING FORTH

Lyrics by **Paul Gerhardt** (see page 300), 1648

Originally written in German; translated by **Elizabeth Rundle Charles** (see page 343) and others

Set to the tunes *An Wasserflüssen Babylon—Dies Est Laetitiae—Vid Älfvarna I Babylon*

Look ... there goes a very special Lamb to be a sacrifice for sin. The Lamb knows He is going to be killed as a sacrifice, but He goes without a single complaint. (Isaiah 53:7) He is carrying all the sins of His people, by Himself—there is no one to help him carry that heavy load of guilt. He is weak and faint, but still this Lamb does not complain as He gives His life to pay for those sins. The Lamb is whipped, wounded, mocked, and then killed. Yet He says, "I am willing to suffer even this." (Matthew 26:39)

A Lamb goes uncomplaining forth,
The guilt of all men bearing;
'Tis laden with the sin of earth;
None else the burden sharing
It goes its way, grows weak and faint,
To slaughter led without complaint,
Its spotless life to offer;
Bears shame, and stripes, and wounds, and death,
Anguish and mockery, and saith,
"Willing all this I suffer."

....

Who is this Lamb? He is Christ, our souls' greatest friend, and our Savior! (John 1:29) God chose Him to end sin and bring us to God. "Go, my Son!" God said, "and save my children, who are doomed to go to Hell unless you,

Jesus, set them free. (Romans 5:12, Romans 6:23) The punishment for sin is heavy, and my anger at sin is dreadful. But your blood, Jesus, will save my children from being separated from me forever." (Romans 5:7-9, Hebrews 9:15)

This Lamb is Christ, the soul's great Friend
And everlasting Saviour;
Him, Him God chose, sin's reign to end
And bring us to His favor
"Go forth, my Son!" He said, "and bail
The children, who are doomed to Hell
Without thine intercession.
The punishment is great, and dread
The wrath, but thou thy blood shalt shed,
And save them from perdition."

....

"Yes, Father," Jesus said, "I will very willingly do what you command me. My desire is to do whatever you want me to do." Oh God, your love for us has made you do this! God the Father offers Jesus His Son to bear sin's punishment in our place, and Jesus is willing to come down to earth and do it! O God, how strong your love must be for us. You have laid Jesus in a grave—Jesus, who is so powerful that His words can break mountains!

"Yea, Father, yea, most willingly
I'll bear what thou commandest;
My will conforms to thy decree,
I do what thou demandest."
O wondrous Love! what hast thou done!
The Father offers up His Son,
The Son content descendeth!
O Love! O Love! how strong art thou!
In shroud and grave thou lay'st Him low
Whose word the mountains rendeth!

....

God, because you love us, you put Christ Jesus on the cross, and bruised Him with nails, spikes, and spears. You killed Him like a sacrificial lamb, to pay for *our* sins! (Leviticus 4) Jesus' blood flows from His body, and that crimson red flood is the price of our sin. (Hebrews 9:22) The suffering in Jesus' soul is strong, and it is for *my* sake that He is suffering. Oh Jesus, sweet Lamb of God, what could I ever do to repay you? Your love for me is the reason you are suffering. Because you love me, you chose to die in order to save me. (John 3:16, Ephesians 5:2, Romans 5:8)

Thou lay'st him, Love, upon the cross,
With nails and spikes Him bruising;
Thou slay'st Him as a lamb, His loss,
From soul and body oozing;
From body 'tis the crimson flood
Of precious sacrificial blood,
From soul, the strength of anguish:
My gain it is; sweet Lamb to thee
What can I give, whose love to me
For me doth make thee languish?

....

Lord Jesus, every day of my life I will cling to you, and forevermore I will know that you love me. I will hold tightly to you with loving arms, just as you always hold me. Yes, Christ, you will be my light to guide me, even through the darkness of death. You will cheer my soul when it is sorrowful and sad. From here on, I give myself and everything that is mine to you, my Savior—after all, everything I have, I have borrowed from you!

Lord, all my life I'll cleave to thee,
Thy love fore'er beholding,
Thee ever, as thou ever me,
With loving arms enfolding.
Yea, thou shalt be my beacon-light,
To guide me safe through death's dark night,
And cheer my heart in sorrow;
Henceforth myself and all that's mine
To thee, my Saviour, I consign,
From whom all things I borrow.

....

Both night and day, I will sing of your wonderful mercy. I give myself completely to you, Jesus, for you are what I want most. If my life is a stream of water, it will flow for you, and constant praise will be its current. I shall remember and treasure everything you've done for me, and I will adore *you* because you have such gracious love for *me.*

By morn and eve my theme shall be
Thy mercy's wondrous measure;
To sacrifice myself to thee,
My foremost aim and pleasure.
My stream of life shall flow for thee,
Its steadfast current ceaselessly
In praise to thee outpouring;
And all that thou hast done for me,

I'll treasure in my memory,
Thy gracious love adoring.

....

My heart is a shrine, a temple, the place where I worship the things I love most. And my heart must grow bigger, because a massive treasure is going to be put in it—a treasure that is worth more than all of earth and Heaven put together. Forget gold from Arabia, or any treasures from this earth. I have found a better jewel! Lord Jesus, my God, this priceless treasure is your holy, precious blood, which bled from the wounds they cruelly gave you when you sacrificed yourself to save me.

Dilate, shrine of my heart, and swell,
To thee shall now be given
A treasure that doth far excel
The worth of earth and Heaven.
Away with the Arabian gold,
With treasures of an earthly mold!
I found a better jewel.
My priceless treasure, Lord my God,
Is thy most holy, precious blood,
Which flowed from wounds so cruel.

....

Christ, forevermore I will use this gift that you have given me. It will never fail to help me, because this treasure—your blood, which made me free—means that *you love me.* When I am sorrowful and sad, remembering your love will give me joy. When I am battling sin and evil, knowing that you love me will be my shield. When I am joyful, your love will be like music. And when everything else on earth has lost its taste, and I am tired of it all, even then your love will be bread from Heaven to satisfy my heart. When I am thirsty, your love will be like a drink; when I am hungry, it will be like food. And when I am alone, your love will keep me company, to comfort me and show me where I should go.

This treasure ever I'll employ,
This ever aid shall yield me;
In sorrow it shall be my joy,
In conflict it shall shield me;
In joy, the music of my feast,
And when all else has lost its zest,
This manna still shall feed me;
In thirst my drink; in want my food;
My company in solitude,
To comfort and to lead me.

....

The poison of death and dying cannot hurt me now. Christ, your blood gives me new life. You are like shade to protect me from the heat when the sun glows hot at noon. When I am suffering from sadness in my heart, my weary, tired soul will rest on you like a sick man rests on his pillow. You are my anchor when my life is being tossed back and forth like a ship on waves of trouble.

Death's poison cannot harm me now,
Thy blood new life bestoweth;
My Shadow from the heat art thou,
When noonday's sunlight gloweth,
When I'm by inward grief opprest,
On thee my weary soul shall rest,
As sick man on his pillow.
Thou art my Anchor, when be woe
My bark is driven to fro
On trouble's restless billow.

....

And one day, when I have come to be with you, when I see your glory and feel the joy of being in your Heavenly Kingdom, then your blood will be a royal robe for me, and this treasure that was my comforted will become my glory!

(Isaiah 61:10) Your blood which set me free will be my glorious crown, and I will wear it when I come to God's throne. I will have no need to hide myself from God's anger at sin. God engaged the Church to be your bride, Christ, so on that day, I and all of your people will stand beside you as your beloved bride, dressed in the honor that you have given us by your blood. (Revelation 19:6-8)

And when thy glory I shall see
And taste thy kingdom's pleasure,
Thy blood shall then my purple be,
I'll clothe me in this treasure;
It then shall be my glorious crown.
Thus I'll appear before the throne
Of God, and need not hide me;
And shall, by Him to thee betrothed,
By thee in bridal garments clothed,
Stand as a bride beside thee.

A MIGHTY FORTRESS IS OUR GOD

By **Martin Luther** (see page 310), 1529; inspired by Psalm 46

Originally written in German; translated by **Frederick Henry Hedge**

Set to the tune *Ein Feste Burg*

God is a mighty fortress, a wall of defense that will never fail to protect us. (Psalm 46:1, Isaiah 25:1-5) *He* is our helper while we live in this world, feeling like we're drowning in a flood of sin and evil. (Jonah 4, Psalm 46:2-3) For it's very true that our ancient enemy, Satan, is still trying to hurt us, to ruin us—Satan's cleverness and his power are great, and he hates God's people far more than we can imagine. (1 Peter 5:8) There is no one on earth as powerful in evil as Satan.

A mighty fortress is our God,
A bulwark never failing;
Our helper He, amid the flood
Of mortal ills prevailing.
For still our ancient foe
Doth seek to work us woe;
His craft and power are great,
And armed with cruel hate,
On earth is not His equal.

....

If we had to depend on our own strength, we would be losing our battle against Satan. (Psalm 54:4) Yes, we would lose for certain ... that is, if we didn't have just the right man on our side, the man God chose to protect us. Do you ask who that "right man" is? It is Christ Jesus! (Ephesians 2:1-10) His name is *Lord*

Sabaoth, which means He is Lord of the Hosts of Heaven, Commander of the angel armies! Christ is the same forever, and *He will win* the battle against Satan.

Did we in our own strength confide,
Our striving would be losing;
Were not the right man on our side,
The man of God's own choosing.
Dost ask who that may be?
Christ Jesus, it is He,
Lord Sabaoth His name,
From age to age the same,
And He must win the battle.

....

This world is full of Satan's demons. But even though this world threatens to ruin us, we will not be afraid, because God has determined that He will use *us* to fight the war against Satan. So what about Satan, the grim Prince of Darkness? We are not afraid of him! We can endure Satan's anger and hatred, because his doom is certain: one little word from God will be the end of him. (Revelation 20:10, Matthew 25:41)

And though this world, with devils filled,
Should threaten to undo us,
We will not fear, for God hath willed
His truth to triumph through us.
The prince of darkness grim,
We tremble not for him;
His rage we can endure,
For lo, his doom is sure;
One little word shall fell him.

....

Christ is the living Word of God! He is far greater than any of the "powerful" people on earth. He is *alive,* without any help from mankind. (John 1:1-5) The Holy Spirit and the gifts of God have come to us because of Christ, who sided with us in the battle against Satan. (John 15:26) Hold on to this world loosely—don't cling too tightly to your things, or even your family, and don't even worry about your earthly life: people may kill your body, but your soul and God's truth will still live on. His kingdom will never end!

That Word above all earthly pow'rs,
No thanks to them, abideth;
The Spirit and the gifts are ours
Through Him who with us sideth.
Let goods and kindred go,
This mortal life also;
The body they may kill:
God's truth abideth still;
His kingdom is forever.

AH, HOLY JESUS, HOW HAST THOU OFFENDED?

Lyrics by **Johann Heermann** (see page 306), 1630

Originally written in German; translated by **Robert Seymour Bridges** (see page 342) in 1897

Set to the tunes *Herzliebster Jesu—Iste Confessor—Ecce Jam Noctis—Flemming—Nightfall*

Oh, holy Jesus, perfect Son of God, what have you done wrong that men have dragged you into court like a criminal? And they have not even judged you honestly—they have only pretended to, because they hate you. (Mark 14:55-56) Jesus, you are laughed at by your enemies (Matthew 27:27-31, Mark 15:32), and your own *friends* have left you and denied that they ever knew you. (Mark 14:71-72) What terrible pain and suffering you are enduring!

Ah, holy Jesus, how hast thou offended,
That man to judge thee hath in hate pretended?
By foes derided, by thine own rejected,
O most afflicted.

....

You are innocent, Jesus. So who was really guilty? Whose punishment are you taking, Christ? It was *my* treason against God, *my* disobedience, that has done this to you! It was me, Lord Jesus, who denied that I know you. It was really me who crucified you, because you died to pay the price for my sins.

Who was the guilty who brought this upon thee?
Alas, my treason, Jesus hath undone thee.
'Twas I, Lord Jesus, I it was denied thee:
I crucified thee.

....

People everywhere, see how Christ, our Good Shepherd, has been offered as a sacrifice to set His sheep free! (John 10:11) We were slaves to Satan, we were the ones who sinned, but the Son of God is the one who suffered the punishment for our sins to pay the price for our freedom. (Isaiah 53:5) Even when we didn't know that we needed to be rescued, God stepped in and saved His people through Christ. (Romans 5:6-8)

Lo, the Good Shepherd for the sheep is offered;
The slave hath sinned, and the Son hath suffered:
For man's atonement, while he nothing heedeth,
God intercedeth.

....

Kind Jesus, it was for *me* that you came down from Heaven and became a man. (Isaiah 7:14, Matthew 1:21) Your sorrow, your bitter pain, and your life being offered as a sacrifice for sin, all happened so that I could be free from my sins and come to God. (Isaiah 53:3-5, Galatians 3:13)

For me, kind Jesus, was thine incarnation,
Thy mortal sorrow, and thy life's oblation:
Thy death of anguish and thy bitter passion,
For my salvation.

....

So, kind Jesus, since I could never repay you for what you have done for me, I can and I *will* adore you forever. You will be the one I pray to, the one I trust. I will think on the pity you showed me when I was a filthy sinner, remembering your unchanging love for me, and I will never imagine that you saved me because I deserved it! (Romans 4:2-8, Mark 2:17, Ephesians 2:8-9)

Therefore kind Jesus, since I cannot pay thee,
I do adore thee, and will ever pray thee,
Think on thy pity and thy love unswerving,
Not my deserving.

ALAS! AND DID MY SAVIOR BLEED

Lyrics by **Isaac Watts** (see page 333), 1707

Sets to the tunes *Martyrdom—Hudson—Avon—Remember Me (Hull)—Remember Me (Jones)—Campmeeting—Communion—O, How I Love Jesus—Dundee—Suffering Savior—St. Agnes—Pisgah—Arlington—Manaoh—Walsall—Chelmsford—Serenity—Balerma—Salzburg—St. Mary (Prys)—Consolation—Burford—Marah—Faber—Sacramental Hymn—Submission—O Herre, Vi Församlas Här—Founders—Victoria—Weeping Savior—Love the Lord*—and many others. This hymn has been set to over 40 tunes in all… a testament to how beloved it is!

What a horrible thought—Christ, the perfect Son of God, shed His blood! How could it be that Christ, my King, would die? Would He really be willing to sacrifice Himself, to give over His kingly head to be wounded, all to save a worm like *me*?

Alas! and did my Saviour bleed!
And did my Sov'reign die?
Would He devote that sacred head,
For such a worm as I?

....

Yes, it is true! You gave up your body to be killed, sweet Jesus. You were bathed in your own blood when you, Christ, the glorious sufferer, stood and received God's anger at sin, so that I would not have to!

Thy body slain, sweet Jesus thine,
And bath'd in its own blood,
While all expos'd to wrath divine,
The glorious suff'rer stood!

....

Was it truly because of *my* sins that Jesus Christ groaned as he suffered on the cross? What amazing pity Christ had for me! And what grace He had for me—such grace has never been seen before, and never will be again! And what love He has for me—so much that it cannot be measured!

Was it for crimes that I had done
He groan'd upon the tree?
Amazing pity! grace unknown!
And love beyond degree!

....

It is good and right that the sun hid its happy shine behind the clouds, and covered the earth with darkness on the day that Christ died. (Matthew 27:45) For that dying man was *God Himself*, the mighty Maker of Earth, and he was dying to pay for the sins of the people He had made. (1 Corinthians 15:3)

Well might the sun in darkness hide
And shut his glories in,
When God the mighty Maker died
For Man the Creature's sin.

....

Just like the sun hid its face that day, I ought to hide my face and blush in shame when I think about Christ's cross. My heart should dissolve in thankfulness, and my eyes should melt into tears because of what Christ did for me.

Thus might I hide my blushing face,
While his dear cross appears,
Dissolve my heart in thankfulness,
And melt my eyes to tears.

....

But all the sorry tears in the world will not repay Christ for the love that He showed us on the cross. So, here I am, Lord; I give my whole self away to you. That is all I have to give, and all I can do for you. You died to set me free, and now I am yours!

But drops of grief can ne'er repay
The debt of love we owe;
Here, Lord, I give myself away,
'Tis all that I can do.

ALL HAIL THE POWER OF JESUS' NAME

Lyrics by **Edward Perronet**, 1779–80,
and **John Rippon** (see page 326), 1787

Set to the tunes *Coronation—Miles Lane—Diadem (Ellor)—Diadem (Proulx)—Diadem (Vail)—Let Us Crown Him—Laud—Diademata—Buckley—Ladywell—University—Baltzell—Elevation—Cleburne—Green Street—New Agatite*—and more

---

Let everyone on earth and in Heaven sing praises together about Jesus' powerful name! Let the angels in Heaven fall on their faces before His throne to honor Him. Bring out the royal crown, and crown Christ our "Lord of All!"

All hail the pow'r of Jesus' name!
Let angels prostrate fall:
Bring forth the royal diadem,
To crown Him Lord of All.

....

Let the noble seraphim angels tune up their harps (Isaiah 6:1-3) and get ready to sing Christ's praises. Let them fall down in honor before Him, for Christ is the Master Conductor of all Heaven's choirs. Let the angels crown Christ as our "Lord of All!"

Let high-born seraphs tune the lyre,
And, as they tune it, fall
Before His face who tunes their choir,
And crown Him Lord of All.

....

You bright stars that beautify the early morning sky, crown Him as your King! Christ is the one who secured the earth where it floats in space beside you. (Job 38:4, John 1:2-3) Praise Christ, for all His people's strength comes from Him only (Psalm 68:35), and crown Christ "Lord of All!"

Crown Him, ye morning stars of light,
He fix'd this floating ball;
Now hail the strength of Israel's might,
And crown Him Lord of All

....

Crown Christ, you martyrs, all you who have been killed for the sake of God's name, who wait at God's altar in Heaven. (Revelation 6:9-10) Praise Christ, who is the descendant of Jesse, the son of kings (Isaiah 11:1-3), and crown Him "Lord of All!"

Crown Him, ye martyrs of your God,
Who from His altar call,
Extol the stem of Jesse's rod,
And crown Him Lord of All.

....

You children of Israel, God's chosen people—you whom Christ bought back and saved from the punishment of the Fall (Genesis 3:15)—praise Christ who saved you with His grace, and crown Him "Lord of All!"

Ye seed of Israel's chosen race,
Ye ransom'd of the fall,
Hail Him who saves you by His grace,
And crown Him Lord of All.

....

You descendants of David, children of Israel, praise Christ! Yes, praise Him, for even the great King David called Him "my Lord." (Psalm 110:1, Matthew 22:41-45) Jesus Christ is God who came down from Heaven and became a man: the God-man. So crown Him "Lord of All!"

Hail Him, ye heirs of David's line,
Whom David Lord did call;
The God incarnate, Man divine,
And crown Him Lord of All.

....

All you sinners who love Jesus, who remember the bitter death that He suffered in order to save you, go and thank Him! Give all your treasures and honor to Him. Lay them down at His feet as gift to your King, to thank Him for dying to save you. (Revelation 4:9-11) And crown Him "Lord of All!"

Sinners! whose love can ne'er forget,
The wormwood and the gall,
Go—spread your trophies at His feet,
And crown Him Lord of All.

....

Whether you're a baby, a grown-up, or a grandfather, that does not matter—if you understand that you are a slave to sin unless Christ rescues you, then rejoice! Christ is your Savior, too! So join in with the joyful song in Heaven, and crown Him "Lord of All."

Babes, men, and sires who know His love,
Who feel your sin and thrall,
Now joy with all the hosts above
And crown Him Lord of All.

....

From every nation on earth, and in every language that is spoken, let everyone whom Jesus has called shout out in one song together. Let them crown Him "Lord of All!" (Philippians 2:8-11)

Let every tribe, and every tongue,
That hear the Saviour's call
Now shout in universal song,
And crown Him Lord of All.

....

Let every family and every tribe on earth give all their praises and honor to Christ, and let them crown Him "Lord of All." (Revelation 5:9-10)

Let ev'ry kindred, ev'ry tribe,
On this terrestrial ball,
To Him all majesty ascribe,
And crown Him Lord of All.

....

We look forward to the day when we will join the crowd of God's people in Heaven, and with them we will fall at Jesus' feet in worship. We will join them in singing the song of praise that never ends, and we will crown Him "Lord of All!"

Oh, that with yonder sacred throng
We at His feet may fall!
We'll join the everlasting song,
And crown Him Lord of All.

ALL PRAISE TO THEE, ETERNAL LORD

Lyrics by **Martin Luther** (see page 310), 1524; based on an 11th century Latin sequence

Originally written in German; translated in 1858 by an unknown translator

Set to the tunes *Canonbury—Gelobet Seist Du—Wimborne—Puer Nobis Nascitur—Schubert—Tallis' Canon—Breslau—Harmony Grove—Sweden—Festus—Samson—Hebron—Wareham*—and more

Let all our praises be for you alone, Christ Jesus, our eternal and everlasting Lord! You came down from Heaven, and now you wear a human body of muscles, skin, and blood, just like any other man. (John 1:14) You are King of All, yet you chose to come and be born in a barn. You chose to come and be laid in a manger, instead of sitting on your rightful throne—even though all of this world belongs to you! (Revelation 11:15)

All praise to thee, eternal Lord,
Clothed in a garb of flesh and blood;
Choosing a manger for thy throne,
While worlds on worlds were thine alone!

....

When you created the universe, the sky itself bowed down and worshiped you, Christ our King. But now you are a helpless infant lying in young Mary's arms. All the angels, who used to sing and rejoice over you in Heaven, now listen to hear you crying as a human baby.

Once did the skies before thee bow;
A virgin's arms contain thee now;
Angels, who did in thee rejoice,
Now listen for thine infant voice.

....

Christ, little child, you are our welcome guest on this earth! You came so that people who are tired from fighting the battle against Satan and sin can rest. (Matthew 1:21) Your birth as a human baby was humble and lonely, but we know that you came down from Heaven so that we can rise from earth and return to Heaven *with* you.

A little child, thou art our guest,
That weary ones in thee may rest;
Forlorn and lonely is thy birth,
That we may rise to Heaven from earth.

....

You were born as a baby in the dark of night, but you came to earth to make us children of the God of light. (1 John 3:1) You came to make us like the angels in Heaven, who stand shining around your Heavenly throne. (Luke 20:36)

Thou comest in the darksome night
To make us children of the light;
To make us, in the realms divine,
Like thine own angels 'round thee shine.

....

Even though it was a humiliation for you to come down to earth and become a man, you did it because you love us. (Philippians 2:8) Because we know this is true, our hearts are yours! For what you have done, we will sing our songs of praise and shout our joyful thanks to you forevermore. Amen—you have done this, Jesus, and we know it is true.

All this for us thy love hath done;
By this to thee our love is won;
For this we tune our cheerful lays,
And shout our thanks in ceaseless praise.
Amen.

ALLELUIA! ALLELUIA!

Lyrics by **Christopher Wordsworth** (see page 339), 1862

Set to the tunes *Ebenezer (or Ton-y-Botel)*—*Hyfrydol*—*Lux Eoi*—
Hymn to Joy—*Bethabara*—*Ecclesia*—*Weisse Flaggen*—*In Babilone*—
St. Casimer—*Adrian*—*Alleluia*—*Adoration*—*St. Andrew*—and more

Praise the Lord! Lift up your hearts to God, and send your voices up to Heaven with songs. (Psalm 30:4) Sing to God a hymn about your thankfulness and joy. Praise Him, because Jesus Christ, the King of Glory who bled on the cross so that His people would be saved from sin, is now risen from the dead and has come back to life! (Luke 24:6-7)

Alleluia! Alleluia!
Hearts and voices Heavenward raise:
Sing to God a hymn of gladness,
Sing to God a hymn of praise:
He, who on the cross a victim,
For the world's salvation bled,
Jesus Christ, the King of glory,
Now is risen from the dead.

....

Sin was our prison, keeping us separate from God. Now Christ has broken the iron bars and set us free! He is risen, born back to life from death. His life is glorious, and He will never die again (Romans 6:9) because He rose from the dead on this first Easter morning. Christ has won the battle against Satan and death, and now we will win the battle with Him because His blood has bought our freedom! We were dead while we were slaves to sin; now we will rise from the dead just like Christ. (Romans 6:11)

Now the iron bars are broken,
Christ from death to life is born,

Glorious life, and life immortal,
On this holy Easter morn:
Christ has triumphed, and we conquer
By His mighty enterprise,
We with Him to life eternal
By His resurrection rise.

....

Christ is risen! Jesus is the first one to rise from the dead (Colossians 1:18), but He is only the first—someday, His people will rise up too. All His people are like a field of wheat, and when Christ comes back again that field will be harvested. He will gather all of His people together, to bring them home. (Matthew 13:24-30,36-43) We will all bow before our King Jesus like so many wheat stalks bowing in the breeze. He will change us, and give us our immortal bodies, shining and glorious and ready for eternity. (1 Corinthians 15:51-53)

Christ is risen, Christ the first-fruits
Of the holy harvest-field,
Which will all its full abundance
At His second coming yield:
Then the golden ears of harvest
Will their heads before Him wave,
Ripened by His glorious sunshine
From the furrows of the grave.

....

Christ is risen from the dead, and we are risen too! (Romans 6:4, Revelation 20:6) Oh Christ, give us grace from Heaven. If we your people are a field of ripening wheat, then give us rain and dew so that we grow, and give us sunshine from the brightness of your Heavenly face. (Revelation 1:16) Our hearts are already in Heaven with you, Christ, but let us do good work for you while our bodies are still on earth. One day, when the angels come to gather the ripened wheat—your people—from your fields, let us come to stay with you forever. (1 Thessalonians 4:17)

Christ is risen, we are risen!
Shed upon us Heavenly grace,
Rain and dew and gleams of glory
From the brightness of thy face:
That, with hearts in Heaven dwelling,
We on earth may fruitful be,
And by angel-hands be gathered,
And be ever, Lord, with thee.

....

Praise the Lord! Give all glory to God, who lives in the high Heavens, and praise Christ our Savior, who won the battle against Satan and death. Praise the Holy Spirit, who is an overflowing fountain of love and perfection. Praise the Lord! Praise the majestic Trinity: God the Father, Jesus the Son, and the Holy Spirit. (Romans 8:2) Amen—it is true!

Alleluia! Alleluia!
Glory be to God on high;
Alleluia to the Saviour
Who has won the victory;
Alleluia to the Spirit,
Fount of love and sanctity;
Alleluia! Alleluia!
To the Triune Majesty.
Amen.

AMAZING GRACE

Lyrics by **John Newton** (see page 321), 1779

Set to the tunes *Amazing Grace—New Britain—Warwick—Arlington—Heber—State Street—Belmont—Azmon—Corinth—Martyrdom—Greenville—Lloyd*—and more

How amazing is God's grace! How sweet it is to think about that grace, which rescued a dirty sinner like me. (1 Timothy 1:15) I used to be lost in my sin, wandering away from God, but now God has found me. I was blinded by my sin so that I couldn't see the truth—but now, because of God's grace, I can see. (John 9:25)

Amazing grace (how sweet the sound!)
That sav'd a wretch like me!
I once was lost, but now am found,
Was blind, but now I see.

....

When God saved me and gave me His grace, that was when He first taught me to fear Him. His grace also helped me to not fear anything *else*. How precious, how special God's grace seemed in that hour that it first came to me and made me believe in Christ! (Ephesians 2:8-9)

Twas grace that taught my heart to fear,
And grace my fears reliev'd;
How precious did that grace appear,
The hour I first believ'd!

....

In my life, I have already been through danger, hard times, and temptations. It was God's grace that brought me through all of that safely, so that I am where I am today, and God's grace will lead me all the way home to Heaven. (Psalm 116:8-9)

Thro' many dangers, toils and snares,
I have already come;
'Tis grace has brought me safe thus far,
And grace will lead me home.

....

The Lord has promised good things to me. Because I trust His word, I have an unshakeable hope that He will do good things for me: He will be a shield to protect me (Deuteronomy 33:29, 2 Samuel 7:25), provide for my needs, and be everything that I need for as long as I live. (Nehemiah 9:21)

The Lord has promis'd good to me,
His word my hope secures;
He will my shield and portion be,
As long as life endures.

....

When my body stops working, my heart stops beating, and my life on earth is over, I will immediately go to be where God is (Psalm 73:26)—just as suddenly as if I stepped behind the veil in the tabernacle and entered the Holy of holies. (Exodus 26:33, Matthew 27:50-51, Hebrews 6:19) And even though my earthly life will be over, when I am there with God, I will have a joyful and peaceful life that will *never* end. (Revelation 14:13)

Yes, when this flesh and heart shall fail,
And mortal life shall cease;
I shall possess, within the veil,
A life of joy and peace.

....

One day, soon, this earth will dissolve, like snow melting away. The sun will no longer shine in the sky. (2 Peter 3:10) But even then, God, who called me to come to Him even while I lived on this earth, will be mine forever.

The earth shall soon dissolve like snow,
The sun forbear to shine;
But God, who call'd me here below,
Will be forever mine.

....

When all of God's people have been in Heaven for ten thousand years—all of us shining as bright as the sun, like the angels!—we *still* won't have any fewer days left to stay in Heaven and sing God's praise than we did when we first arrived. (1 Thessalonians 4:17)

When we've been there ten thousand years,
Bright shining as the sun,
We've no less days to sing God's praise
Than when we've first begun.*

* This last stanza was not in Newton's original hymn. Another author added it in 1790.

AMIDST US OUR BELOVED STANDS

Lyrics by **Charles Haddon Spurgeon** (see page 327), 1866

Set to the tunes *Hamburg—Rockingham—Angels' Song—Hampton—Austin*

People of God, we know that Christ—our dearly-loved Savior, and the Church's bridegroom—is standing here with us when we worship. (Matthew 18:20) He tells us to look at His hands, which were pierced through by the nails that held Him to the cross. He points to His feet, wounded by nails also, and to His side where the soldier speared Him. Jesus calls us to remember that these wounds are blessings for us—He received them because He loved us! He chose to be crucified so that He could pay the punishment for our sins. (John 20:27)

Amidst us our Beloved stands,
And bids us view His piercéd hands;
Points to the wounded feet and side,
Blest emblems of the Crucified.

....

What splendid food covers the Lord's communion table, where Christ Himself sits down to eat with us! The wine is so strong, and the bread is so sweet, whenever Jesus comes down from His throne to eat with us, His beloved guests. (1 Corinthians 10:16, Luke 22:19-20, Revelation 19:9, John 6:51)

What food luxurious loads the board,
When at His table sits the Lord!
The wine how rich, the bread how sweet,
When Jesus deigns the guests to meet!

....

While we are on earth, our eyes are blurred by sin, and we can't see God very well. (Isaiah 42:6-7) We may see *signs* that Christ is with us all the time, little hints that He is standing here beside us, but we find it hard to see *Him*. But Jesus' love for us is slowly taking away the blindness of sin, and one day—all because He loves us—we will see our Lord face-to-face! (1 Corinthians 13:12)

If now, with eyes defiled and dim,
We see the signs, but see not Him;
O may His love the scales displace,
And bid us see Him face to face!

....

Scripture says that Christ is a bridegroom, and the Church is His bride. (Revelation 21:9-10) Oh Christ, our glorious groom, knowing that you are smiling on us while we feast with you is like tasting Heaven. If there is a veil over our eyes that keeps us from seeing you completely, then lift our veil and let all of God's children behold your glory! (2 Corinthians 3:14)

O glorious Bridegroom of our hearts,
Your present smile a heav'n imparts!
O lift the veil, if veil there be,
Let every saint your glory see!

....

We each love to tell of how Christ has spoken with us before, when He called us and it felt as if we actually stood on the mountain of God with Him. Remembering those moments makes our souls long to see Christ's face again! It is scarred and wounded from His suffering on the cross, but it is lovely and wonderful to look at because those wounds are the proof that He loves us. (Isaiah 53:4-5)

Our former transports we recount,
When with Him in the holy mount:
These cause our souls to thirst anew
His marred but lovely face to view.

AND CAN IT BE, THAT I SHOULD GAIN?

Lyrics by **Charles Wesley** (see page 336), 1738

Set to the tunes *Sagina—Fillmore—Surrey (Carey)—Jena (Das Neugeborne Kindelein)—Holy Faith—St. Stephens—Lansdown—Didsbury*—and more

---

Can it be true? How is it that I get to be one of the ones saved by Christ's blood? Did He really die for *me*, when I am the one who caused His pain on that cross? Did He die for *me*, who forced Him to die because I kept running to sin? Yes, He did! What amazing love! How can it be, Lord Christ, that you would die for even *me*?

And can it be that I should gain
An int'rest in the Saviour's blood?
Died He for me, who caus'd His pain?
For me, who Him to death pursued?
Amazing love! how can it be,
That thou, my God, shouldst die for me?
(Refrain)
Amazing love! how can it be,
That thou, my God, shouldst die for me?

....

It's such a mystery: Christ, the Immortal Son of God, chose to die! Who could possibly understand His plan? Even the highest-ranking angel cannot measure how deep God's love is for us. It is all mercy! Let all the earth adore God, and let angels no longer wonder how much God loves us—Christ has shown us just how much. (Romans 5:8)

'Tis myst'ry all, th' Immortal dies!
Who can explore His strange design?

In vain the first-born seraph tries
To sound the depths of love divine;
'Tis mercy all! let earth adore:
Let angel minds inquire no more.

....

Christ left His home with God the Father in Heaven, and put away all of His glory and honor. He left behind everything except His love for us. His grace to us is free, and it never ends! (John 1:14) Christ bled on the cross to save us, His chosen people, sinful children of Adam. (1 Corinthians 15:22) It is all mercy, great and free, and oh, praise God! His grace even found me!

He left His Father's throne above;
(So free, so infinite His grace!)
Emptied Himself of all but love,
And bled for all His chosen race;
'Tis mercy all, immense and free,
For, O my God, it found out me!

....

For many years, my soul was in a prison as dark as night, chained up by sin. But then, Christ, you looked at me, and the light from your eyes made me come alive. I woke up, and my dungeon cell was filled with flaming light! My chains fell off, my heart was free, and I stood up and followed you. (Psalm 146:7)

Long my imprisoned spirit lay
Fast bound in sin and nature's night:
Thine eye diffused a quick'ning ray;
I woke: the dungeon flam'd with light;
My chains fell off, my heart was free—
I rose, went forth, and followed thee.

....

I don't have to fear God's judgment on my sins anymore. (John 5:24) Because perfect Jesus saved me and made me His own, He is mine and everything that He has is mine. (1 John 4:17) My soul is alive in Him, and He is my head, my leader. Jesus Christ has wrapped His righteousness and perfection around me like a robe. (Galatians 3:27) Now, I can boldly go stand before the throne of God, because God sees Christ's perfection on me instead of my sin. (Philippians 3:9) I will wear a winner's crown in Heaven because of Christ, who gave Himself to me! (James 1:12)

No condemnation now I dread;
Jesus, with all in Him, is mine;
Alive in Him my living Head,
And clothed in righteousness divine,
Bold I approach th' eternal throne
And claim the crown, thro' Christ my own.

ANGELS, FROM THE REALMS OF GLORY

Lyrics by **James Montgomery** (see page 317), 1825

Set to the tunes *Regent Square—Iris—Lewes—Cwm Rhondda—Feniton Court—Praise—Larkin—Happy Zion—Kensington New—Westborough—Angeli—Merlo—Osgood—Woodford Green—Wildersmouth*—and more

You angels from Heaven, come now and fly over all the earth. You sang the story when God created the world, so sing now that Christ the Messiah is born! Come and worship Christ, the newborn King.

Angels from the realms of glory,
Wing your flight o'er all the earth,
Ye who sang creation's story,
Now proclaim Messiah's birth;
(Refrain)
Come and worship,
Worship Christ the newborn King.

....

Listen, you shepherds who live in the fields, watching over your sheep all night: Christ, God's Son, has come down from Heaven and lives on earth with man. (John 1:14) Baby Jesus is over in Bethlehem, and His coming to us is a light shining on our dark world. (Isaiah 9:2)

Shepherds, in the field abiding,
Watching o'er your flocks by night,
God with man is now residing—
Yonder shines the infant-light.

....

You wisemen, stop all your thinking, wondering, and searching for visions—you'll find a brighter, better vision far away in Bethlehem. Go find Christ, the Son of God, the Savior that all the world has been been longing for. You have seen the star that announced His birth! (Matthew 2:1-2)

Sages, leave your contemplations,
Brighter visions beam afar,
Seek the great Desire of nations;
Ye have seen his natal star.

....

For so long, God's people have come to the temple and bowed down at the altar to worship God. They have hoped, and been afraid, and waited for God to keep His promise to send a Savior. (Jeremiah 31:33, Isaiah 9:6) Now, suddenly, Christ the Lord has come down from Heaven to stand in His own temple. (Acts 13:32-33)

Saints, before the altar bending,
Watching long in hope and fear,
Suddenly the Lord descending
In His temple shall appear.

....

All of us sinners would have been doomed to eternal punishment in Hell because of our sins. God is just, and He *must* punish sin. But now, if you truly repent and turn away from your sin, God cancels your punishment, because Christ took the punishment for you! (Titus 3:4-6, Acts 16:30-31) Your sins hold you down like chains, but God's mercy breaks those chains off of you. (Psalm 146:7)

Sinners, wrung with true repentance,
Doom'd for guilt to endless pains,

Justice now revokes the sentence,
Mercy calls you—break your chains.

....

Let everyone on this earth join together and sing praises to God the Father, Jesus the Son, and the Holy Spirit! All of you, raise your voices, and forevermore we will sing to the eternal Trinity.

All creation, join in praising
God the Father, Spirit, Son;
Evermore your voices raising
To th' eternal Three in One.

BE THOU MY VISION

Lyrics from the ancient Irish Gaelic poem "Rop tú mo baile,"
traditionally attributed to **Dallan Forgaill** (c. 530–598)

Mary Elizabeth Byrne made a literal English translation of the Irish poem in 1905, and **Eleanor Henrietta Hull** versified the English translation in 1912.

Set to the tune *Slane*

Oh God, you are the Lord and ruler of my heart. Be my vision—help me to see, and show me where to go. (Isaiah 42:16) Don't let anything in this world be more important to me than you. Let the only thing that I treasure be you, Lord, King of my heart. Of all the things I could think about, when I think about you, Lord, that is my best thought. (Psalm 63:6, Joshua 1:8) Whether it is night or day, whether I am awake or asleep, you are with me. (Psalm 4:8, Proverbs 3:24) Your presence is like a light shining on my path so that I can see where to go. (Psalm 119:105,

Be thou my vision, O Lord of my heart;
Naught be all else to me, save that thou art—
Thou my best thought, by day or by night,
Waking or sleeping, thy presence my light.

....

Oh Lord, give me wisdom, because all wisdom comes from you. (James 1:5) Teach me to speak about you—then my mouth will be full of true words, because you are truth. (2 Samuel 22:31) I am always with you, and you are always with me. You are my great Father, and you have made me your son. (John 1:12, Romans 8:16-17) You live in me, and you have given me your Spirit and made me a Child of God. (2 Timothy 1:14)

Be thou my wisdom, and thou my true word;
I ever with thee and thou with me, Lord;

Thou my great Father, I thy true son;
Thou in me dwelling, and I with thee one.

....

Oh Lord, cover me like a shield when I battle against sin, and be the sword with which I fight. (Psalm 35:1-3) If people respect me, let it be because they see that you are with me. Make my heart love you so much that nothing on earth will make my heart happy—only you! You are a safe place for my soul to hide. You guard me like a tall fortress tower. (Psalm 141:8) Raise me up to Heaven to be with you, Lord, for your Power is what gives me all of my power.

Be thou my battle shield, sword for my fight;
Be thou my dignity, thou my delight,
Thou my soul's shelter, thou my high tow'r;
Raise thou me heavenward, O Pow'r of my pow'r.

....

I care nothing about worldly riches, and I don't care whether or not the men and women on this earth praise me. Their praise means nothing. (Luke 6:26) You, Lord, are my riches and my honor, both while I'm on this earth and forever into eternity. You are the High King of Heaven, and you are my treasure. (Isaiah 33:6, Matthew 6:19-20)

Riches I heed not, nor man's empty praise,
Thou mine inheritance, now and always:
Thou and thou only, first in my heart,
High King of Heaven, my treasure thou art.

....

High King of Heaven, when I have finished fighting all the battles you give me to fight on this earth, let me come to Heaven with you! You are the bright sun in Heaven (Matthew 17:2, Ecclesiastes 11:7), and you have made my heart love the things that your heart loves. (Psalm 27:8) No matter what may happen, God, be my vision—help me to see what you see. Show me where to go, Ruler of All, and guide my way to you.

High King of Heaven, my victory won,
May I reach Heaven's joys, O bright heaven's Sun!
Heart of my own heart, whatever befall,
Still be my vision, O Ruler of all.

BY GRACE I'M SAVED, GRACE FREE AND BOUNDLESS

Lyrics by **Christian Ludwig Scheidt**, 1742

This hymn is *cento* poetry, meaning the author put together verses and bits of writing from various other authors to make a new poem.

Set to the tunes *Mentzer—O Dass Ich Tausend Zungen Hätte (Dretzel)—*
O Dass Ich Tausend Zungen Hätte (König)—
Salvation by Grace (Aus Gnaden Soll Ich Selig Werden)

It is God's grace that has saved me from sin's punishment! Oh my heart, do you believe that this is true? Heart, why do you tremble, when there is no more reason for you to be afraid? Has God ever told you a lie? The Bible, God's Word, is true (2 Timothy 3:16), and it tells me that grace has saved me. (Ephesians 2:8-9) I can know for certain that because of grace, I am a child of God, and there is a crown in Heaven that will someday be mine. (James 1:12, 1 Peter 5:4, Revelation 2:10)

By grace I'm saved, grace free and boundless!
My heart, believ'st thou this or not?
Why trembliest thou with terror groundless?
Has ever God a falsehood taught?
His Word is true—then this must be:
By grace there is a crown for thee.

....

I am saved by God's grace! Nothing I have ever done helped to save me. No matter how much I could boast of, my "good deeds" could never save me. (Romans 11:6, 2 Timothy 1:9) God's people waited so long for Jesus the mighty Savior to come, and now He has come and brought this lovely truth to us: His death took the punishment that should have fallen on us. (Romans 6:23, John 1:17) His grace for us is the *only* thing that saves us. (Philippians 3:4-9)

By grace! our works are all rejected,
All claims of merit pass for naught;
The mighty Savior, long-expected,
To us this blissful truth has brought,
That He by death redeems our race,
And we are saved alone by grace.

....

I am saved by God's grace! Heart, you must realize what that means, and remember it! Remember it when your heart is sad because you know you have sinned yet again. (Mark 2:17) Remember it when Satan comes to you and pridefully reminds you what a terrible person you are. (1 Timothy 1:15) Remember it when you are tired of sinning and wish that you could *feel* forgiven. God saved you and changed your heart because He loved you, even though you are a sinner. (Romans 3:23-25) Human minds can never understand why God would show us mercy while we do nothing to deserve it, but God sends us salvation through grace, anyway!

By grace! mark well this phrase's meaning,
When sin rolls sorrows o'er thy breast,
When Satan threats with pride o'erweening,
When troubled conscience sighs for rest;
What reason ne'er can comprehend
It pleases God by grace to send.

....

Because of God's grace and love for His people, Christ came to earth. Christ humbled Himself so that He could suffer the punishment for *your* sins. You were a sinner, and you had every reason to be afraid of God's anger—what did you ever do that would make Jesus want to be your friend, to save you? Did He not come because He wanted you to be safe in Heaven with Him? Because He loved you, He showed you grace and He Himself paid the price of your sin, so that you could come to God. (Romans 5:8)

By grace His Son, on earth appearing,
Vouchsafed beneath thy woe to bend;
Hadst thou, damnation justly fearing,
Done aught to render Him thy friend?
Was't not that He thy welfare sought,
And but by grace deliverance wrought?

....

"Saved by grace"—this one fact is the foundation on which we build our hope of Heaven. As long as God Himself is true, it will be true that we are saved by grace. God taught this to the men who wrote the Bible, and they wrote it down so that we would be comforted and know that we are saved by God's grace, through the work of Jesus—never by our own "good" actions.

By grace! this ground of our salvation
As long as God is true endures:
What saints have penned by inspiration,
What God to our poor souls secures,
What all our faith must rest upon,
Is grace, free grace through His dear Son.

....

I am saved by God's grace! Everyone who knows this must stop living in hypocrisy and lies, pretending that their good deeds deserve to be forgiven. (Romans 6:1-2) You won't understand why you need grace at all until you see that you are a sinner, and then walk away from your sins. (Luke 18:13) To a person who won't give up their sin, God's grace doesn't seem important. But to the person who hates their sin and trusts that God will save them, His grace is bright and glorious! (1 Corinthians 1:18)

By grace! They who have heard this sentence
Must bid hypocrisy farewell;
For only after deep repentance
The soul what grace imports can tell;

To sin while grace a trifle seems,
To faith it bright with glory beams.

....

I am saved by God's grace! When God gives His grace, people who are tired of sin can see God's heart full of love for them. (Matthew 11:28) With grace, they can remember that God loves them when fighting and sadness on earth make them forget their joy and their hopes. Where could I possibly find strength to carry on, if grace were not there to hold me steady like an anchor?

By grace! the timid hearts that languish,
Find access to the Father's heart,
When conflicts fierce and bitter anguish
Bid all their joy and hopes depart.
Where, ofttimes, should I strength obtain,
Did grace my anchor not remain!

....

I am saved by God's grace! I'll rest on that truth when it is time for me to die. (Romans 5:21) Even when I don't feel as if God can love me, I will rejoice—I won't trust my feelings; I will trust His *Word,* which assures me that I am safe in His grace. I know I am a sinner. Thinking about it used to weigh me down, and sadden me. But I also know Christ, who bought my soul back from sin! My heart will rejoice, and all sadness will run away, because my soul is saved by grace.

By grace! On this in death I'll rest me,
Rejoicing e'en though feeling naught;
I know my sin—it oft oppressed me—
But Him, too, who my soul hath bought:
My heart exults—grief flees apace—
Because my soul is saved by grace.

....

I am saved by God's grace! Hear this, sin! Hear this, Satan! I trust that God has grace for me, and I carry that with me like a battle flag. And even though I sometimes doubt and fear, I will pass through this world and arrive at Heaven, like walking through the Red Sea on my way to the promised land. (Exodus 14) Whether I *feel* forgiven or not, I *believe* what Christ my Savior taught: that grace has saved me.

By grace! O sin and Satan hear it!
I bear my flag of faith on hand,
And pass, in spite of doubts, nor fear it,
The Red Sea to the promised land;
I hold the Word my Savior taught
As certain, whether felt or not.

CHRIST IS MADE THE SURE FOUNDATION

Lyrics from a Latin monastic hymn, c. 7th century

Translated by **John Mason Neale** (see page 344), 1851-1861

Set to the tunes *Regent Square—Westminster Abbey—Oriel—Eden Church—St. Thomas—Christ Church—Unser Herrscher—Triumph—Neale—Bavaria—Urbs Beata—Tilleard—Corner-Stone—Grafton*—and more

God has decreed that Christ is our foundation—the steady, strong bedrock on which our salvation stands. (1 Corinthians 3:11) God's children working together are the body of Christ, and Christ Himself is our head. We are the Church, and He is the cornerstone that holds us up and gives us strength to stay together. (Ephesians 2:19-21, Isaiah 28:16) He was the one the Lord chose to be our precious Savior, and He holds the whole Church together in one Body. God's children are the city of God, set apart from the world (Psalm 125:1, Hebrews 11:16, Revelation 3:12), and Christ is our helper forever, the only one we trust.

Christ is made the sure foundation,
Christ the head and cornerstone,
Chosen of the Lord and precious,
Binding all the Church in one;
Holy Zion's help forever
And her confidence alone.

....

When Christ comes back to bring His people home, God will create a new city for them to live in. Imagine that day: all over that special city that God dearly loves, never-ending joyful songs are ringing out! All through the city, forevermore, God's children will praise and sing about their love for God the Father, Jesus the Son, and the Holy Spirit.

All that dedicated city,
Dearly loved of God on high,
In exultant jubilation
Pours perpetual melody;
God the One in Three adoring
In glad hymns eternally.

....

Oh Lord of hosts, Lord of angel armies, come meet us in this temple, in this church where we call for you! Come bring your love and kindness which you never fail to give to us, and hear your people as we pray to you. (2 Chronicles 6:21,40, 7:13-16) Here, in this place, give us your blessing always. (Deuteronomy 28:1-10)

To this temple, where we call thee,
Come, O Lord of hosts today:
With thy wonted loving-kindness
Hear thy people as they pray;
And thy fullest benediction
Shed within its walls alway.

....

Here in this church, grant to us your servants everything we ask in your name. (John 14:13-14, John 16:23) You have already given us life that will last forever (Romans 6:23), just like our brothers and sisters in Christ who have now gone to be with you. (Hebrews 12:1-2) So, after our lives on earth are over, let us come to you in your glorious Heaven, and let us reign there with you forever. (Revelation 20:6)

Here vouchsafe to all thy servants
What they ask of thee to gain,
What they gain from thee forever
With the blesséd to retain,

And hereafter in thy glory
Evermore with thee to reign.

....

Let us all give praise and honor to God the Father! Let us praise and honor Jesus the Son! And let us praise and honor the Holy Spirit! Forevermore, they are the Trinity—they are always three, yet always one. They will be strong together as one, and glorified together as one, for all of eternity.

Laud and honor to the Father,
Laud and honor to the Son,
Laud and honor to the Spirit,
Ever Three and ever One,
One in might, and One in glory,
While unending ages run.

CHRIST, OF ALL MY HOPES THE GROUND

Lyrics by **Ralph Wardlaw** (see page 331), 1817

Set to the tunes *Hendon—Gott Sei Dank—Lübeck—Gibbons—Pleyel—Messiah—Jewel—Mozart—Vienna (Knecht)—Essex*—and more

Christ is the ground in which all my hopes are planted (1 Corinthians 3:11), and the spring of water from which all my joys flow. Christ, let me be with you forever, and let me use all my gifts and talents for you! (Romans 12:6)

Christ, of all my hopes the ground,
Christ the spring of all my joy,
Still in thee may I be found,
Still for thee my powers employ.

....

Christ, let your love light my heart on fire so that it burns with love like yours. Don't let me forget my fear of God. Help me always remember how *you* fear God, as an example for me. (Deuteronomy 6:13, Philippians 2:8) Let praising you be the best thing I can dream of doing, and let your smile be the thing that gives me the most delight.

Let your love my heart inflame;
Keep your fear before my sight;
Be your praise my highest aim;
Be your smile my chief delight.

....

Christ, you are like a fountain that overflows with grace from God, so give me plenty of that grace! (John 1:16) Until I finish running my race, my life on this earth, let me show the world what it means when your Word says "to live is Christ"—let me show them what it means to live my life only for you. (Hebrews 12:1, Philippians 1:21)

Fountain of o'erflowing grace,
Freely from Thy fulness give;
Till I close my earthly race,
May I prove it "Christ to live."

....

Christ, I firmly trust that your blood has saved me from my sins, so nothing else will confuse or worry my heart in this life. I will safely walk through the flood of evil in this world, and I will safely arrive in your land: Heaven. (Romans 8:35)

Firmly trusting in thy blood,
Nothing shall my heart confound;
Safely I shall pass the flood,
Safely reach Emmanuel's ground.

....

When I reach the blessed shore of Heaven, the waves of evil of this world that have tried to drown me will roll back. Then the darkness of death will never separate my delighted soul from you!

When I touch the blessèd shore,
Back the closing waves shall roll;
Death's dark stream shall nevermore
Part from thee my ravished soul.

....

So, Christ, show me the way to Heaven, that land where the sky has no clouds! Since I will have found out what your Word means when it says "to live is Christ," show what it means when it says "to die is gain." (Philippians 1:21)

Thus, O thus, an entrance give
To the land of cloudless sky;
Having known it "Christ to live,"
Let me know it "gain to die."

CHRIST THE LORD IS RISEN TODAY

Lyrics by **Charles Wesley** (see page 336), 1739

Set to the tunes *Easter Hymn—Llanfair—Nuremburg—St. George's, Windsor—Mozart—Orientus Partibus—Clarion—Telemann—Hendon—Christus Ist Erstanden—University College—Württemberg—Pleyel's Hymn—Posen (Strattner)—Savannah (Herrnhut)—Gud Vår Gud, För Världen—Gwalchmai—Monkland—Mercy—Wakeman—Wilmot—Southampton—Essex—Andover—Alleluia—Resurrection—Barnby—Lebanon*—and more

Christ the Lord is risen today! Praise the Lord! Angels and all mankind sing together, "Praise the Lord!" Sing, lift up your joy to Heaven, and raise your victory-cry, too—Christ has won the battle against sin for you. Praise the Lord! Oh sing, you Heavens; and earth, you sing the reply: "Praise the Lord!" (Isaiah 44:23)

Christ the Lord is ris'n today, Alleluia!
Sons of men and angels say, "Alleluia!"
Raise your joys and triumphs high; Alleluia!
Sing, ye heav'ns, and earth, reply. Alleluia!

....

Christ came down to earth to save you from sin, because He loves you, and now that saving work is done. (1 John 4:10) Praise the Lord! Christ fought the fight against Satan and sin, and He won the battle. Praise the Lord! Satan tried to keep Christ in death, but it was no use—he could not stop Christ. Praise the Lord! Christ has paid the punishment for sin, and opened up the way to Heaven. Praise the Lord!

Love's redeeming work is done; Alleluia!
Fought the fight, the battle won; Alleluia!

Death in vain forbids Him rise; Alleluia!
Christ hath opened paradise. Alleluia!

....

The stone that sealed up the door of Christ's tomb was useless. The soldiers that guarded His body could not keep Him in the tomb. Praise the Lord! Christ has burst open the gates of Hell itself, and let out the prisoners. Praise the Lord! Death tried to hold onto Christ, but it could not stop Him from coming to life again. Praise the Lord! Christ has paid the punishment for sin, and opened up the way to Heaven. Praise the Lord!

Vain the stone, the watch, the seal; Alleluia!
Christ hath burst the gates of Hell; Alleluia!
Death in vain forbids him rise; Alleluia!
Christ hath opened paradise. Alleluia!

....

Christ, our glorious King, lives again. Praise the Lord! Christ has taken the pain out of even death—so why should we be afraid of you, Death? Christ saves our souls from being separated from God, so now death only means that we go to be with our Father. (John 5:24, 8:51) Praise the Lord! Christ died *one* time, to pay for our sins' punishment, so that we will be alive forever with Him. Praise the Lord! You cold grave, you empty tomb, did you think you had won the battle when Christ died? Christ has conquered you! Praise the Lord!

Lives again our glorious King; Alleluia!
Where, O death, is now thy sting? Alleluia!
Once He died, our souls to save; Alleluia!
Where thy victory, O grave? Alleluia!

....

Now we fly upward, to Heaven, where Christ has led the way. Praise the Lord! We are the body of Christ, and we follow Christ, our King and Commander. (Ephesians 2:4-6) Praise the Lord! (Ephesians 2:4-6) Christ died for our sakes, and if we have been baptized, we have died to sin, too. (Romans 5:15) Just like He rose from the dead, we will rise up after our bodies die. Praise the Lord! We share the victory that Christ won on the cross and the tomb, and we share in Heaven, too! Praise the Lord!

Soar we now where Christ hath led, Alleluia!
Foll'wing our exalted Head; Alleluia!
Made like Him, like Him we rise; Alleluia!
Ours the cross, the grave, the skies. Alleluia!

....

Praise be to Christ, the ruler of earth and Heaven! Praise the Lord! Let both earth and Heaven praise you, Christ. Praise the Lord! When we each meet you in Heaven, we are victors in the war—we have won the battle against sin, because *you* won it for us. (1 Corinthians 15:57) Praise the Lord! We can rise up after our deaths and live forever in Heaven because *you* rose from the dead first. We praise you, Christ—*you* are the Resurrection! Praise the Lord!

Hail, the Lord of earth and heav'n! Alleluia!
Praise to thee by both be giv'n; Alleluia!
Thee we greet triumphant now; Alleluia!
Hail, the Resurrection, thou! Alleluia!

CHRISTIAN, DOST THOU SEE THEM?

Lyrics traditionally attributed to **Andrew of Crete**, c. late 7th to early 8th century

Originally written in Greek; translated by **John Mason Neale** (see page 344) in 1862

Set to the tunes *St. Andrew of Crete—Holy War—Gute Bäume Bringen—Kiel—King's Weston—Sohren—Greek Hymn—Quebec*—and more

Christian, do you see them? The powers of darkness lurk on the ground around you—demons, the servants of Satan, your spiritual enemies. (Ephesians 6:12) As you walk through life the way God has told you to, they follow you in hatred. Christian, get up and strike them! Fight them back! They are sneaky as they work against you. They love to distract you, so beware: if you find something that keeps you from following Christ, it is not good for you—it is a *loss*. (2 Corinthians 11:13-15, Philippians 3:4-9) Christ has given you His strength with which to fight, and that is the only strength you can depend on to fight these dark enemies. (1 Timothy 1:12, Ephesians 6:10)

Christian, dost thou see them
On the holy ground,
How the pow'rs of darkness
Rage thy steps around?
Christian, up and smite them,
Counting gain but loss,
In the strength that cometh
By the holy cross.

....

Christian, do you feel those dark enemies? Do you feel how they work inside your heart? They work hard to make you want sin. (Luke 17:1) But Christian, don't ever tremble in fear because of what they do, and don't get discouraged (Psalm 37:1)—just put on the weapons God gives you, and you will be protected. (Ephesians 6:11-17) Keep a wary eye out to see where your enemies might be attacking... they hate the good ways of God, so watch what you choose, think, and do. Always be praying and talking with God, so that you know what *He* would want you to choose, think, and do. (Psalm 25:4, 2 Timothy 2:15, 2 Timothy 2:15)

Christian, dost thou feel them,
How they work within,
Striving, tempting, luring,
Goading into sin?
Christian, never tremble;
Never be downcast;
Gird thee for the battle,
Watch and pray and fast.

....

Christian, do you hear those dark enemies? Do you hear how they speak to you in soft, nice voices? They whisper to you, "Aren't you so tired? Does God really expect you to always be praying and watching yourself closely?" (Genesis 3:1) Christian, answer them boldly: "Yes! As long as I am breathing, I will be praying to my God!" Take heart—remember that even though you are battling spiritual enemies right now, every war ends eventually. Don't get tired of fighting—*peace will come,* and then you will be able to rest. Night lasts for a long time, but day always comes afterward. (1 Peter 5:10)

Christian, dost thou hear them,
How they speak thee fair?
"Always fast and vigil?
Always watch and prayer?"
Christian, answer boldly,
"While I breathe, I pray!"
Peace shall follow battle,
Night shall end in day.

....

Hear what Jesus says to you: "Oh Christian, you are my faithful servant. You are tired of fighting, I know. I was tired, too, when I lived on the earth and fought against Satan for you. But the work you are doing now is making you more like me. And at the end of your life, when all your fighting and sadness are ended, you will come to be with me beside my throne in Heaven." (Hebrews 4:15, Matthew 17:17, Isaiah 53:3)

Hear the words of Jesus:
"O my servant true:
Thou art very weary—
I was weary too;
But that toil shall make thee
Some day all mine own,
And the end of sorrow
Shall be near my throne."

COME, THOU FOUNT OF EVERY BLESSING

Lyrics by **Robert Robinson**, 1758

Altered by **Martin Madan**, 1760

Set to the tunes *Nettleton—Greenville—Trust—Warrenton—Mariners—Hyfrydol—Olney—Restoration—Normandy (Bost)—Cecile—Brocklesbury—Stuttgart—Har Du Mod Att Följa Jesus—Lord, Revive Us (Holy Manna)—Our Journey Home—Albro—Halladale—Guide—The Gospel Ship—Shipston—Camp of the Hebrews—Autumn—Incarnation—Rathbun—Sardis—All for Jesus—Arwelfa—Bavaria—Glorious News—Hallelujah Third—Batty—Arundel—Palms of Victory—Corinth—Harpswell—Crystal Fountain—Mount of Olives—Ebenezer—Jewin Street—Hallelujah—Family Circle—Rest for the Weary—Keokuck*—and more. This hymn has been set to over 50 tunes in all... a testament to how beloved it is!

Christ, you are the fountain from which all of God's blessings flow. (Psalm 36:9) Come to me, Christ, and tune up my heart like a musical instrument so that I can sing songs about your grace! I know that streams full of God's mercy flow from you, never running dry—and *that* calls for songs of the very loudest, most joyful praise. Christ, teach me how to sing the songs the angels in Heaven sing when they praise you. (Revelation 5:9-10) Lord, your love for us stands like a massive mountain, and it will never change. (Psalm 117:2) I praise you for that mountain of your love! It is the steady ground on which I stand.

Come, thou fount of ev'ry blessing,
Tune my heart to sing thy grace;
Streams of mercy, never ceasing,
Call for songs of loudest praise.
Teach me some melodious sonnet,
Sung by flaming tongues above;
Praise the mount! I'm fixed upon it,
Mount of God's unchanging love.

Just like the prophet Samuel, I recognize that you, Lord, are my "Ebenezer"—my trustworthy "stone of help." (1 Samuel 7:12, Deuteronomy 32:4) This song is my monument to you, my declaration to the world that I have only come this far because you helped me all the way. And I hope you will lead me safely home—to Heaven! Jesus went searching for me, when I still didn't know who He was, when I was like a lost sheep wandering far away from God's flock. (Romans 5:8) Jesus, my great Shepherd, came to rescue me from danger. (Matthew 2:6) I was wandering away toward sin, and I could not come back to God on my own. That is why Jesus died on the cross for me: now He stands between God's perfection and my dirty sinfulness, and God sees Jesus' perfection when He looks at me. (John 10:11)

Here I raise my Ebenezer;
Hither by thy help I'm come;
And I hope, by thy good pleasure,
Safely to arrive at home.
Jesus sought me when a stranger,
Wand'ring from the fold of God:
He, to rescue me from danger,
Interposed His precious blood.

....

Oh, how much I am forced to rely on God's grace, every day! I sin, yet again, and I have to receive new grace, over and over. (John 1:16-17, Romans 3:24) Lord, let your grace tie me to you like shackles! I always seem to wander away, Lord. (Psalm 119:10, Isaiah 63:17) I always seem to leave the God I love. Here is my heart, Lord: please, seal it up so that I remain pure for Heaven. (2 Corinthians 1:21-22)

O to grace how great a debtor
Daily I'm constrained to be;
Let that grace now, like a fetter,
Bind my wand'ring heart to thee.
Prone to wander—Lord, I feel it—

Prone to leave the God I love:
Here's my heart, O take and seal it,
Seal it for thy courts above.

COME, MY SOUL, THOU MUST BE WAKING

Lyrics by **Friedrich Rudolf Ludwig Freiherr von Canitz**, 1700

Originally written in German; translated by **Henry James Buckoll**

Set to the tunes *Haydn—Matins—Richter—Carman—Columbia College—Birkdale—Veni, Anima Mea—Franc—Courtland—Moring*—and more

My soul, it's time for you to wake—another day is dawning on the earth. Come to God, who made all the splendor and beauty of mornings. (Job 38:12) Be sure that you give all your work, all your efforts, to God today. Even though your power is weak, everything you have should be offered to God.

Come, my soul, thou must be waking;
Now is breaking o'er the earth another day:
Come to Him who made this splendor;
See thou render all thy feeble pow'rs can pay.

....

My soul, when the sunlight returns for another day, greet it by being ready! (Psalm 5:3, 59:16, 88:13) Whatever strength you have today, be ready to offer it to God like the sweet-smelling incense the priests used to burn for Him in the mornings. (Exodus 30:7) The night is safely over, and God has watched over you and cared for you while you were asleep and helpless. (Psalm 121:4)

Thou too hail the light returning;
Ready burning be the incense of thy pow'rs;
For the night is safely ended,
God hath tended with His care thy helpless hours.

....

Pray, my soul, and ask that God would bless the work you have to do today when you are aiming to accomplish good things (Psalm 143:8, Deuteronomy 28:12)… but pray that He will *stop* you when you are working toward something evil, that He would help you see where you were wrong. (Psalm 19:13, Proverbs 22:12)

Pray that He may prosper ever
Each endeavor, when thine aim is good and true;
But that He may ever thwart thee,
And convert thee, when thou evil wouldst pursue.

……………

Remember that God sees everything you think and do! He uncovers every secret sin that hides inside you. He reveals every little sin that you tried to forget and cover up, and He knows about every sinful act. You cannot hide anything from Him. (1 Chronicles 28:9, Proverbs 21:2)

Think that He thy ways beholdeth;
He unfoldeth ev'ry fault that lurks within;
Every stain of shame glossed over
Can discover, and discern each deed of sin.

……………

My soul, God gives you forgiveness and grace when you sin, and He gives those gifts freely—over and over again, every morning! (Lamentations 3:22-23) But don't abuse His gifts. Don't ever choose to sin simply because He will forgive you. (Romans 6:1-2) Remember, He also gives you *wisdom*, like a light to show you where to go. Do not refuse that gift! (Proverbs 4:11) The Holy Spirit will whisper to your heart throughout the day, so listen and obey. If you do these things, you will dwell with God. And even on a cloudy day, you will see His light shining on everything that you see.

Only God's free gifts abuse not,
Light refuse not, but His Spirit's voice obey;
Thou with Him shalt dwell, beholding
Light enfolding all things in unclouded day.

COME, MY SOUL, THY SUIT PREPARE

Lyrics by **John Newton** (see page 321), 1779

Set to the tunes *Hendon—Seymour—Horton—Savannah—Vienna—Theodora—Brasted—Aletta—New* Calabar*—Solitude—St. Lucy—Redhead no. 47—Nuremburg—Minster—Purity—Come Thou Saviour of Our Race—Litany—Pleyel's Hymn—Great High Priest—Newington (Maclagan)—Tossing Like a Troubled Ocean—Dallas—Innocents—Morris—Eve—St. Edmund—Fulton—Preparation—Song 13 (Gibbons)—East Peckham—Christ Chapel—Angelic Praise—Messiah—* and more

---

Come, my soul, my heart—prepare yourself to talk to the Lord Jesus. Plan what you will say to Him. Jesus loves to answer prayer! Christ Himself is the one who told you to pray (Matthew 6:9, Luke 18:1), so He will not say "No" to the things you ask Him when you pray. (Matthew 21:22, John 14:13-14, John 16:23-24)

Come, my soul, thy suit prepare:
Jesus loves to answer prayer;
He himself has bid thee pray,
Therefore will not say thee nay.

....

When you pray to the Lord Jesus Christ, you are standing before the King of kings. (Revelation 1:5, 19:16, John 18:36, Hebrews 4:16) So never be afraid to ask big things when you pray! He has so much grace and power to give that you could never ask for too much of it, even if you wanted. (Ephesians 3:20)

Thou art coming to a King,
Large petitions with thee bring;
For his grace and pow'r are such,
None can ever ask too much.

....

When I go to pray, I start by dealing with the heavy load that weighs down my spirit: my sins. (Hebrews 12:1) I start by praying, "Lord Jesus, take this load of sin off of me. Christ, you shed your blood on the cross to save sinners, so let your blood wash away the guilt and sin from my heart. (Hebrews 9:13-14,22, 1 Peter 1:18-19)

With my burden I begin:
"Lord, remove this load of sin;
Let thy blood, for sinners spilt,
Set my conscience free from guilt.

....

"Lord Jesus, I am tired from fighting against sin. I come to you, asking for rest. (Galatians 6:9) Take over my heart, so that I cannot love anything in this world more than I love you. You bought my heart when you shed your blood to save me, so take what is yours! May you alone rule in my heart, without any rival. (1 Peter 3:15, 2 Thessalonians 3:5)

"Lord, I come to thee for rest,
Take possession of my breast;
There thy blood-bought right maintain,
And without a rival reign.

....

"Just like a mirror reflects the face of the person who looks into it, make my heart reflect your face, Christ. Print your face's reflection on my heart, and make *my* life look like your *righteous* life. (Galatians 3:27, James 1:23-24)

"As the image in the glass
Answers the beholder's face;
Thus unto my heart appear,
Print thine own resemblance there.

....

"This world is not my home. (Hebrews 11:13) So while I am a traveler and a stranger on this earth, Christ, let my spirit be cheered up whenever I remember your love for me. You are my Guide, my Guard, and my Friend, so lead me to the end of my travels—lead me home to Heaven! (2 Corinthians 5:1)

"While I am a pilgrim here,
Let thy love my spirit cheer;
As my Guide, my Guard, my Friend,
Lead me to my journey's end.

....

"Christ, show me what you want me to do. In every hour of every day, give me new strength to keep going. Give me faith in you, and let the way I live show others that I trust in you. (Philippians 1:27, 1 Timothy 6:12) And when I die, let me die the way your people should. Let me not be sad; instead, let me remember that I am coming home to you!" (Revelation 14:13)

"Show me what I have to do,
Ev'ry hour my strength renew:
Let me live a life of faith,
Let me die thy people's death."

COME, WE THAT LOVE THE LORD

Lyrics by **Isaac Watts** (see page 333), 1707

Set to the tunes *Come, We That Love the Lord (Lowry)—Marching to Zion—St. Thomas—Dunbar—Albion—Silver Street—Webster—Waugh—Ain (Correlli/Mason)—Ain (Lowry)—Vineyard Haven—Ascension—Festal Song—Shirland—Kane—Laban—Greenwood—Mount Ephraim—Olmutz—Sirioldeb—The Angels Sing—St. Michael—Elmswood—Alice—Concord—Nearer Home—Allenza—Barber—Thatcher—Silchester—Lockport—Iowa—Marshfield—Diademata—Spurgeon—Ridge—Wynnewood—Narenza—Pilgrim's Song—Novakoski—Idumea—Whitefield*—and more

Come with me, all of you who love the Lord. Tell all the world about your joy in Christ. Let all of God's children on earth join together in a song (Psalm 47), and as we sing that sweet harmony together, our spirits surround the throne of God! (Revelation 7:9-11)

Come we that love the Lord,
And let our joys be known,
Join in a song with sweet accord,
And thus surround the throne.

....

If anyone does not know God, they should not sing praises to Him. (John 9:31) But the ones who *do* know Him, who live to serve and glorify our Heavenly King, should sing and tell the whole world about the joy they have in Christ. (Psalm 107:21-22)

Let those refuse to sing
That never knew our God;
But servants of the Heavenly King
May speak their joys abroad.

....

God rules in the high Heavens, and sees everything that happens on earth. (Psalm 47:8) God rides on the storm clouds in the sky, and calms the high waves of the angry seas. (Psalm 104:3)

The God that rules on high,
That all the Earth surveys
That rides upon the stormy sky,
And calms the roaring seas.

....

All of earth and Heaven are in awe of God ... and that powerful God is *our* God! (Exodus 15:11, Deuteronomy 7:21, Nehemiah 1:5, Isaiah 64:3) He is our Heavenly Father (Matthew 6:14,26,32)—He loves us, and we love Him. Christ came down from Heaven and brought God's power down to earth, so that He could save us from our sins and carry us back to Heaven with Him.

This awful God is ours,
Our Father and our Love:
Thou shalt send down His Heavenly powers
To carry us above.

....

Once we are in Heaven, God, we will see your face! In Heaven, we will finally never sin again! (Revelation 22:3-4) There, your grace will flow by like rivers, and from those rivers we will drink in Heavenly pleasures forever. (Revelation 22:1)

There we shall see thy face,
And never, never Sin;
There from the rivers of thy grace,
Drink endless pleasures in.

....

Even now, before we rise up into Heaven and never die again, just thinking about such amazing bliss, wonder, and pleasure should give us constant joy while wait here on earth.

Yes, and before we rise
To that immortal state,
The thoughts of such amazing bliss
Should constant joys create.

....

God's children, the ones who have received His grace and forgiveness, have already seen glimpses of His glory. (Isaiah 6:3) When we have faith and hope, we are able to see little tastes of the Heaven that is coming to us, even while we are still on earth.

The Men of Grace have found
Glory begun below;
Celestial fruits on earthly ground
From faith and hope may grow.

....

So let God's children sing songs of joy—one song after another! (Psalm 95:1) Let every one of our tears on earth be dried up, because we look forward to everlasting joy. (Revelation 21:4) We are only on earth for a little while, marching through this place where Christ came to be with God's people. We are headed for a far better world on high—Heaven!

Then let our songs abound,
And every tear be dry;
We're marching thro' Immanuel's ground
To fairer worlds on high.

CROWN HIM WITH MANY CROWNS

Lyrics by **Matthew Bridges**, 1851, and **Godfrey Thring**, c. 1882

Set to the tunes *Diademata—Nevin's Processional—Alfred—Tibberton—Coronae—Corona*—and more

Let us crown Christ as King! He is worthy of *many* crowns, and all the crowns of earth are His by right. Christ is the Lamb of God, the sacrifice that paid for our sins (Leviticus 23:19, Genesis 22:8, John 1:29), and now He sits on His throne in Heaven beside His Father. (Hebrews 10:12, Revelation 22:1) Listen! The song being sung in Heaven to praise Christ is so loud that it drowns out every other music! (Revelation 5:9, 15:3) Wake up, my soul, and sing a song of praise to Christ, who died to save you! Bow down to Him, and worship Him as your King. No one is His equal, and He will reign as King without any rival forever.

Crown Him with many crowns,
The Lamb upon His throne;
Hark! how the heav'nly anthem drowns
All music but its own:
Awake, my soul, and sing
Of Him who died for thee,
And hail Him as thy matchless King
Through all eternity.

....

Crown Him again, because He is the Son of God! Christ was with God before the world was ever created. (John 1:1-2) All of you who walk on this earth, where Christ once did, you must crown Him as the Son of *Man* also, because He came down from Heaven and became one of us. (Matthew 9:6, 16:27) Whatever sadnesses we feel, whatever sorrow makes our hearts ache, we can know that Christ felt them too while He was here on earth. (Isaiah 53:3, Hebrews 4:15) He knows what it is to be sad. He takes those pains and sorrows from us and bears them Himself, so that we can rest in Him. (Matthew 11:28-29, 2 Corinthians 12:9)

Crown Him the Son of God
Before the worlds began,
And ye, who tread where He hath trod,
Crown Him the Son of Man;
Who every grief hath known
That wrings the human breast,
And takes and bears them for His own,
That all in Him may rest.

....

Crown Him yet again, because He is the Lord of life! Christ died once, but death could not hold Him down—He triumphed over death and the grave. (Romans 6:9-11) Christ rose up from the dead after He won the battle against Satan for the sake of His people, whom He came to save. And now we, the ones He saved, sing about His triumphant glory! Christ died one time, but now He reigns as King in Heaven. He *died* so that He could give us eternal *life*, and now He lives again in order to defeat death once and for all. (1 Corinthians 15:25-26,54)

Crown Him the Lord of life,
Triumphant o'er the grave,
Who rose victorious from the strife
For those He came to save.
His glories now we sing,
Who died and reigns on high;
He died, eternal life to bring,
And lives that death may die.

....

Crown Him yet again, because He is the Lord of love! Look at the marks in His hands and His side, where He was nailed to the cross and pierced by the soldier's spear. They are awful to see, but they mean much to His people, because those wounds have saved our souls. (John 20:20, 27) In Heaven Christ's scars can still be seen, glorified and beautiful because of all that they mean for God's children. No angel in Heaven can look directly at Him, He shines so brightly! (Isaiah 6:1-3) His eyes shine like flames, and those eyes see and understand all the mysteries of Heaven. (Revelation 1:12-16)

Crown Him the Lord of love;
Behold His hands and side,
Rich wounds, yet visible above,
In beauty glorified:
No angel in the sky
Can fully bear that sight,
But downward bends His burning eye
At mysteries so bright.

....

Crown Him yet again, because He is the Lord of peace! Christ controls the kings and presidents and rulers of the earth. (Proverbs 21:1) He arranges everything that happens, from the North Pole to the South Pole. Christ is directing history and leading us through time so that one day, every war will be over, His peace will rule over the whole earth, and all the people of the world will be absorbed in worshipping their Maker and Lord. (Romans 8:28) His reign will never end! And when Christ sits on His throne, the ground around His feet, which were once pierced on the cross, will be covered with the sweet-smelling flowers of Heaven.

Crown Him the Lord of peace;
Whose pow'r a scepter sways
From pole to pole, that wars may cease,
Absorbed in pray'r and praise:
His reign shall know no end;

And 'round His pierced feet
Fair flow'rs of paradise extend
Their fragrance ever sweet.

....

Crown Him yet again, because He is the Lord of years! Christ is the commander of time. He is the one who created the planets that spin and orbit to give us hours, days, and years. (Genesis 1:14, John 1:2-3) His power and beauty are too excellent to describe! Praise Christ who redeems us, and buys us back from sin! Praise Him! Christ, you have died to save me, so my songs of praise to you will never stop, even through all eternity. (Job 19:25)

Crown Him the Lord of years,
The Potentate of time;
Creator of the rolling spheres,
Ineffably sublime:
All hail, Redeemer, hail!
For thou hast died for me:
Thy praise shall never, never fail
Throughout eternity.

....

Crown Him yet again, because He is the Lord of lords! He rules over all the rulers of this earth. (1 Timothy 6:15, Revelation 17:14, 19:16) Christ was once on earth—God's Son, who became a Son of Man—and He was killed once so that He could buy sinners back from their sin. Now, Christ lives in Heaven, a land of light! In Heaven, all the angels and all God's children who have already died sing to Christ all day and all night, praising Him as their God, their King, and their Savior who bought them back from sin. (Isaiah 6:3, Revelation 15:3)

Crown Him of the Lord of lords,
Who over all doth reign,
Who once on earth, th' Incarnate Word,
For ransomed sinners slain,

Now lives in realms of light,
Where saints with angels sing
Their songs before Him day and night,
Their God, Redeemer, King.

....

Give Christ even one more crown, because He sits on a throne as Lord of Heaven above. Crown Christ as your King—He has been named "Love" because of what He did for you! Crown Him with *many* crowns, while all thrones and kingdoms of this earth are given to Him. (Revelation 4:10) Crown Him, you earthly kings, with many crowns, for He is King of all! (Revelation 1:5)

Crown Him the Lord of Heaven,
Enthroned in worlds above;
Crown Him the King, to Whom is given,
The wondrous name of Love.
Crown Him with many crowns,
As thrones before Him fall,
Crown Him, ye kings, with many crowns,
For He is King of all.

FOUNTAIN OF NEVER-CEASING GRACE

Lyrics by **Augustus Montague Toplady** (see page 329), mid-18th century

Set to the tune *St. Matthew (Croft)*

Christ, you are a fountain of God's never-ending grace. (Psalm 36:9, John 1:17) God's children on earth never get tired of singing your praise! (2 Chronicles 30:21, Nehemiah 12:46, Psalm 7:17, 61:8, 66:4, 84:4, Romans 15:9) Even the angels and God's children in Heaven sing their praises to you. (Revelation 14:13, 15:3) Because you are the Son of God, you are honored far above everything else in Heaven and earth. Christ, we bless you for the marvelous spiritual gifts, the fruits of the Spirit—we only have them because you came down from Heaven and became a man so that you could save us. (Philippians 1:11) We bless you, Christ, because you have given us *your* righteousness, *your* perfection, which we wear like a robe so that when God sees us, He sees your perfection on us. (Isaiah 61:10) By His grace God offers this gift to us, and we may only receive it if we have faith that your righteousness, Christ, is enough to save us. (Philippians 3:9)

Fountain of never ceasing grace,
Thy saints' exhaustless theme,
Great object of immortal praise,
Essentially supreme;
We bless thee for the glorious fruits
Thine incarnation gives;
The righteousness which grace imputes,
And faith alone receives.

....

Christ—the one that all the angels of Heaven adore!—was killed so that He could pay the punishment for *our* sins. All of the guilt, all the sin, was ours, Lord Christ, not yours. But you took the punishment for us! Christ is God, yet He was willing to become a man, with a human body like ours. The reason Christ appeared on earth was to set us free from the sin that held us prisoners. He quietly and humbly died on the cross and bore the punishment for our sins. (Philippians 3:9) Christ was the perfect lamb of God, the sacrifice for sin, and He died so that we could put on His perfect righteousness like a robe. (John 1:29, Isaiah 61:10)

Whom Heaven's angelic host adores,
Was slaughtered for our sin;
The guilt, O Lord, was wholly ours,
The punishment was thine:
Our God in the flesh, to set us free,
Was manifested here;
And meekly bare our sins, that we
His righteousness might wear.

....

Because *we* are guilty, and He came to take in our place (Philippians 3:9), He had to take our sins and die as if *He* were a guilty sinner. (2 Corinthians 5:21) Blood and death is the price for sin (Hebrews 9:22), so Christ shed His blood so that we could be forgiven of our sins. (Romans 6:23) He offered Himself as the bloody sacrifice in order to take away the sadness of sin. Every pain, every wound, everything He suffered while He was on the cross was *for our sake.* (1 Peter 2:24) Everything Christ did, He did because He loves us. (Romans 5:8, Ephesians 5:2,25)

Imputatively guilty then
Our substitute was made,
That we the blessings might obtain
For which His blood was shed:
Himself He offered on the cross,

Our sorrows to remove;
And all He suffered was for us,
And all He did was love.

....

If we trust in Christ, we wear His perfection and righteousness on us like new clothes. We can be certain that God approves of that righteousness, because He approves of Christ! (Romans 3:5,18) That one truth is the rock, the firm foundation on which we build our lives, and it will be never be moved. By shedding His blood, Christ paid the price of sin, and bought freedom for all His people. (2 Corinthians 5:14-15) Unlike us, Christ obeyed God's laws perfectly while He lived on earth, so He was able to die as a perfect sacrifice—and that paid the price that allows us to enter Heaven. (Romans 10:14, Hebrews 7:27)

In Him we have a righteousness
By God Himself approved;
Our rock, our sure foundation this,
Which never can be moved.
Our ransom by His death He paid,
For all His people giv'n,
The law He perfectly obeyed,
That they might enter heav'n.

....

When one man—Adam—sinned in the Garden of Eden, all of his children—that's us—became sinners, too. In that same way, when one man—Jesus—lived a perfect, righteous, sinless life, all His people's sins were forgiven, and they were made righteous, too. (Romans 5:15) Oh gracious Lord Christ, we humbly recognize that it is only *your* goodness that saves us, and not our own goodness. How thankful we are for it! We are brought back home to Heaven, to be with God again as we were always supposed to be. (Hebrews 11:6, James 4:8) If we trust in you, Christ, whenever we come short of perfection, your perfection makes us complete. (Romans 3:23-24)

As all, when Adam sinned alone,
In his transgression died,
So by the righteousness of one,
Are sinners justified,
We to thy merit, gracious Lord,
With humblest joy submit,
Again to paradise restored,
In thee alone complete.

....

Even when we trust Christ Jesus, our hearts will sometimes wander away from Him. (Psalm 119:176, Jeremiah 50:6) Yet Christ loves us and watches over us, bringing us back to Him and keeping us from wandering into sin again. (Matthew 15:24, Luke 15:6-7) He gives us His righteousness, His perfection, to put on, and He takes our sins from us and puts them on Himself so that He can take the punishment for us. We can only say we are saved because of Christ's perfection. We are God's adopted sons and daughters, forgiven of all our sins! (1 John 3:1) We wear Christ's goodness like a robe of shining light (Isaiah 61:10), and we look at His death on the cross and say, "That sacrifice opened the gate into Heaven!" (Romans 7:13-14)

Our souls His watchful love retrieves,
Nor lets them go astray,
His righteousness to us He gives,
And takes our sins away:
We claim salvation in His right,
Adopted and forgiv'n,
His merit is our robe of light,
His death the gate of Heav'n.

GLORIOUS THINGS OF THEE ARE SPOKEN

Lyrics by **John Newton** (see page 321), 1779

Set to the tunes *Austrian Hymn—Harwell—Abbot's Leigh—Jefferson—Rustington—Stoughton—Worthing—Ripley—Sion's Security*—and more

Oh Zion, city of God, we have been told glorious and wonderful things about you! God cannot break His word, and no one else can cause His word to be broken. And He is the God who built *you,* City of Zion, to be His own home. (Psalm 48:1-2, 132:13) The foundation the city is built on is Christ Himself, because Christ's sacrifice made the way for God's people to live in His city with Him. (Isaiah 28:16, 1 Peter 2:6) Oh City of Zion, since you are held up by Christ, the steady Rock of Ages Himself, what could possibly disturb your peace and rest? (Psalm 2:6) You are the city built for God's people, and you represent their safety. (Psalm 84:5) Because you know that Christ Himself protects you, you can hear Satan's and his demons' threats against you and just smile ... for you know they cannot harm you! (Hebrews 12:28)

Glorious things of thee are spoken,
Zion, city of our God;
He whose word cannot be broken
Formed thee for his own abode:
On the Rock of Ages founded,
What can shake thy sure repose?
With salvation's walls surrounded,
Thou may'st smile at all thy foes.

....

See the rivers of life-giving water that flow through the City of Zion, coming from God's throne. (Revelation 22:1) Because God has everlasting love for His people, He has made this water that will supply everything his sons and daughters need for all eternity. Who can get hot, thirsty, or faint when there is a river like this one, flowing forever and quenching their thirst? (Revelation 7:16-17) And what is this river's water? Grace! Just as the Lord never fails, neither does His grace—it lasts forever, and it takes care of every generation of His people. (John 1:16, Romans 4:16, 2 Corinthians 9:8)

See, the streams of living waters,
Springing from eternal love,
Well supply thy sons and daughters,
And all fear of want remove;
Who can faint, while such a river
Ever flows their thirst t'assuage?
Grace which, like the Lord, the giver,
Never fails from age to age.

....

Look and see: God Himself is there, in cloud and fire, hovering around each of His children's houses in Zion. That cloud and fire is a covering for the glory of God's holy city, showing that He Himself is there. (Exodus 40:34) His presence gives His children light at night, and shades them during the day. (Isaiah 4:5-6) He will give them manna when they pray to Him, to satisfy their hunger throughout all eternity. (Revelation 2:17)

Round each habitation hov'ring,
See the cloud and fire appear
For a glory and a cov'ring,
Showing that the Lord is near:
Thus deriving from their banner
Light by night and shade by day,
Safe they feed upon the manna
Which He gives them when they pray.

....

Savior Jesus Christ, if by God's grace I am a child of God, who will come to live in the Heavenly city of Zion with you, then it does not matter anymore what the world says to me. Let the world laugh at me or pity me for following you (John 15:19)—my only glory is that I am called by your name, Lord. (Jeremiah 9:24) Any person who only loves this world has a kind of pleasure that won't last long, no matter how much he boasts about his "happiness" and worldly wealth. (Psalm 37:10,16, 1 John 2:15) But there is a true joy and treasure that lasts forever—and no one has it except God's children, the people of Zion. (James 2:5, Psalm 37:18, Romans 8:17, Titus 3:7)

Savior, if of Zion's city
I, through grace, a member am,
Let the world deride or pity,
I will glory in thy name:
Fading is the worldling's pleasure,
All his boasted pomp and show;
Solid joys and lasting treasure
None but Zion's children know.

GOD THE ALL-TERRIBLE!

Lyrics by **Henry Fothergill Chorley**, 1842,
and **John Ellerton** (see page 295), 1870

Set to the tunes *Russian Hymn—Consolator—Liebster Immanuel*

You are God, the terrible, awe-inspiring one! (Nehemiah 1:5, Exodus 15:11, Deuteronomy 7:21) You are King, and you make fierce winds to serve as trumpets to announce that you are coming. (Exodus 19:16-19) The lightning you make is your sword. (Zechariah 9:14) Oh God, from your throne in high Heaven where you reign as King, show us your pity. In your power, give us peace during our days on this earth, oh Lord. (John 14:27, Leviticus 26:6)

God the all-terrible! King, who ordainest
Great winds thy clarions, lightnings thy sword,
Show forth thy pity on high where thou reignest;
Give to us peace in our time, O Lord.

....

You are God the All-Powerful! You are the mighty avenger who defends the weak. (Psalm 99:8, 1 Thessalonians 4:6) You watch us on earth, though we don't notice it, and you judge what we do, though we don't hear you. (Psalm 7:11, 58:11) Show us mercy, Lord! Keep us safe from all danger. (2 Samuel 24:14) Please, let us have peace during our days on this earth, oh Lord.

God the omnipotent! Mighty avenger,
Watching invisible, judging unheard,
Save us in mercy, O save us from danger;
Give to us peace in our time, O Lord.

....

You are God, the merciful one! (Psalm 145:9) This wicked earth has thrown away your law, the righteous way you told us to live. (Daniel 9:11, Romans 3:23) This world has turned away from your Word. Please, do not wake up your wrath and terrible anger against us for these sins against you! (Deuteronomy 13:17, 1 Kings 8:49-51) Let us have peace during our days on this earth, oh Lord.

God the all-merciful! Earth hath forsaken
Thy ways of blessedness, slighted thy Word;
Bid not thy wrath in its terrors awaken;
Give to us peace in our time, O Lord.

....

You are God, the only righteous One! Mankind has defied you, and ignored your commands. But that doesn't change that fact that your Word, the Bible, stands true, and it will for all eternity. (Psalm 119:160, 2 Timothy 3:16) Lies and wrongdoing and sin may not come near you, Lord. You will not allow evil to stay where you are. (Psalm 1:5, 5:4) Oh, let us have peace during our days on this earth, oh Lord.

God the all-righteous One! Man hath defied thee;
Yet to eternity standeth thy Word;
Falsehood and wrong shall not tarry beside thee;
Give to us peace in our time, O Lord.

....

You are God of all wisdom! (Romans 11:33, 1 Corinthians 1:25) Your discipline in this sinful world is like purifying fire, and that discipline is what will bring this earth back to freedom and truth. (Deuteronomy 8:5, Revelation 3:19, Hebrews 12:11) We see thick darkness and chaos all around us, but through this darkness, your Heavenly Kingdom is hurrying to come to us! (Revelation 22:20) We know you will give us peace in your perfect time, Lord; not when we demand it.

God the all-wise! By the fire of thy chastening,
Earth shall to freedom and truth be restored;
Through the thick darkness thy kingdom is hast'ning;
Thou wilt give peace in thy time, O Lord.

....

For this reason, let your people be thankful for your mercy and peace, and let them be faithful to you alone. (Psalm 50:23) Let them praise God, for you have saved them from danger, from all who want to hurt them. (Psalm 18:3, Luke 1:68-71) Let your people be singing, from one ocean to the next (2 Corinthians 4:15), "Let all the nations of this world live in peace, and all praise be to the Lord our God!"

So shall thy people, with thankful devotion,
Praise Him who saved them from peril and sword,
Singing in chorus from ocean to ocean,
Peace to the nations and praise to the Lord.

HAIL, THOU ONCE-DESPISED JESUS!

Lyrics by **John Bakewell**, 1757

Altered by **Martin Madan**, 1760; altered again by **Augustus Montague Toplady** (see page 329), 1776

Set to the tunes *Autumn—In Babilone—St. Hilda—Conqueror—Hyfrydol—Supplication—Cassel—Beecher—Ebenezer—Lux Eoi—Austria—Everton—St. Hilary—Pleading Saviour—Lammets Folk Och Sions Fränder—Arfon (Major)—Noble—Eifionydd—Gorton—Folkstone—St. Mabyn—Faben—Rathbun—St. Andrew's—Middleton—Hope—Tanycastle—Smart—Salvator—Alla Trinita Beata—Greenville—Messiah—Rustington—Vesper Hymn—Penobscot*

Be glorified, Jesus, you who were despised and hated while you lived on this earth! (Isaiah 53:3, Psalm 118:22, John 11:53:54) Praise to you, King Jesus from Galilee! (Matthew 21:11) The reason you endured torture and suffering on the cross was to set us free from our sin. By your suffering you bought salvation from sin, then freely gave it to us—we did nothing to earn it from you. (1 Peter 2:24) Be glorified, Jesus our Savior, who suffered in pain and agony for us and took on our sin and shame! It is because of *your* merits, *your* perfection, that God shows *us* favor. (Philippians 3:9) We receive true life, eternal life, only because you bought us with your blood and we are named with your name. (John 20:31)

Hail, thou once despiséd Jesus!
Hail, thou Galilean King!
Thou didst suffer to release us:
Thou didst free salvation bring.
Hail, thou agonizing Savior,
Bearer of our sin and shame!
By thy merits we find favor;
Life is given through thy name.

....

Christ Jesus, God appointed you to be the sacrifice, like a Passover lamb to pay for our sins. (Exodus 12, 2 Chronicles 30:17, John 13:1, John 1:29) When you died in our place, all of our sins were taken off of us and laid on you. (Isaiah 53:6) Because of His almighty love for us, God sent you to earth for this purpose. (Matthew 1:21) Christ, Your sacrificial death has paid for every one of our sins—there is nothing left to be paid! (Hebrews 10:10) All your chosen people are completely forgiven of their sins because it was *your* blood that was shed—because you never sinned, your perfect blood was able to pay the debt. (Hebrews 7:27) Now, the gate of Heaven has been opened up for your people to go in. Though our filthy sins once kept us apart from our righteous God (Psalm 5:4), your sacrifice made peace between God and His people, and we can be with Him. (Ephesians 2:13)

Paschal Lamb, by God appointed,
All our sins were on thee laid;
By almighty love anointed,
Thou hast full atonement made.
All thy people are forgiven
Through the virtue of thy blood;
Opened is the gate of Heaven,
Peace is made 'twixt man and God.

....

Jesus, we praise you! You are now in Heaven, sitting on a throne in glory, and you will be there forever. (Hebrews 10:12) All the angels and all God's children who have gone to Heaven adore you as you sit on a throne beside God the Father. (Acts 2:33, 1 Peter 3:22) From your place at God's side, you constantly plead with Him to show us mercy for our sins, for the sake of your blood. (Hebrews 7:25) You are busy preparing a home to be ready for us when we come to you. (John 14:2-3) Ever and always, you are constantly praying to God for us until we come to Heaven and appear in glory with you.

Jesus, hail! Enthroned in glory,
There forever to abide;
All the heav'nly hosts adore thee,
Seated at thy Father's side.
There for sinners thou art pleading;
There thou dost our place prepare;
Ever for us interceding
Till in glory we appear.

....

Christ, you are the one who deserves all the worship, honor, power, and blessing this world can give! (Jude 1:25) You deserve the very loudest, most joyful, never-ending praises, and it is good and right for us to give them to you. Help us to praise Him, all you bright angels, and bring your sweetest, noblest songs. Help us to sing about all our Savior's perfections! Help us to chant praises to Immanuel—God who came to be with us on earth! (Revelation 5:11-13)

Worship, honor, pow'r, and blessing
Thou art worthy to receive:
Loudest praises, without ceasing,
Meet it is for us to give.
Help, ye bright angelic spirits,
Bring your sweetest, noblest lays;
Help to sing our Savior's merits,
Help to chant Immanuel's praise!

HARK! THE HERALD ANGELS SING

Lyrics by **Charles Wesley** (see page 336), 1739-1753

Altered by **George Whitefield**, mid-18th century

Set to the tunes *Mendelssohn—Monkland—Herald Angels—Judas Maccabeus—Aletta—Cookham—Berlin—Hendon—Sabbath—Morning—Mozart—Herald—Eli—Nativity—Sabbatsdag, Hur Skön Du Är—Piankashaw*—and more

Listen! Angels have come to tell us that a King has come. They're singing, "Glory to Jesus, the newborn King! God has sent peace to the earth, and He offers you His kind mercy. Because of what this baby Jesus will do, lost sinners will come home to God." (Luke 2:13-14) Be joyful, all people and nations of this earth! Stand up and join in the angels' song that tells the world, "Your King is here! Jesus Christ was born in Bethlehem!" Listen: the angels are singing, "Glory to Jesus, the newborn King!"

Hark! the herald angels sing,
"Glory to the newborn King;
Peace on earth, and mercy mild,
God and sinners reconciled!"
Joyful, all ye nations, rise,
Join the triumph of the skies;
With th' angelic host proclaim,
"Christ is born in Bethlehem!"
(Refrain)
Hark! the herald angels sing,
"Glory to the newborn King."

....

Christ is adored in Heaven—by God the Father, all the angels, and all of God's children in Heaven. Christ is Lord, and He will rule forever! (Isaiah 9:6) God's people have been waiting for a long time, but at last Christ has come to us, as the son of young Mary. But even though He wears a human body now, that body is only a veil: look and see that Christ is still God! Praise Christ, our God who came down to earth to be with us. (John 1:14, Colossians 1:19) It pleased Christ to become a human and live with humans, so we call Him "Jesus, our Immanuel"—God with us. (Isaiah 7:14)

Christ, by highest heav'n adored,
Christ, the everlasting Lord!
Late in time behold him come,
Offspring of the Virgin's womb.
Veiled in flesh the Godhead see;
Hail th' incarnate Deity,
Pleased as man with men to dwell,
Jesus, our Emmanuel.

....

Praise Christ, the Prince of Peace, who was first born in Heaven as the Son of God. Praise Christ, the glorious Sun of perfect righteousness! He came to us like the sun rising in the morning, bringing light to this dark world of sin, giving eternal life to God's people and healing them from the sickness of sin. (Malachi 4:2) In his kindness, Christ put away all the glory He had in Heaven and came to earth. He was born on earth as the God-man so that His people would not die in their sins. (Philippians 2:8) He was born as a man so that he could bring us to God, born-again and free from our sins. (Hebrews 4:15-16)

Hail, the heav'n-born Prince of Peace!
Hail the Sun of Righteousness!
Light and life to all He brings,
Ris'n with healing in His wings.
Mild He lays his glory by,
Born that man no more may die,
Born to raise the sons of earth,
Born to give them second birth.

HE WHO WOULD VALIANT BE

Lyrics by **John Bunyan** (see page 286) in *The Pilgrim's Progress,* 1678

Set to the tunes *Monk's Gate—St. Dunstan's—Egbert*

Do you want to be valiant, courageous, and brave? If anyone would like to be truly valiant, he should come here—to Christ! (Psalms 60:12) The one who lives for Christ will be steadfast and trustworthy. No matter how much Satan huffs and puffs hard winds and bad weather at that man's spirit, he will stay valiant and strong, because he gets his strength from Christ. (Matthew 7:25) No amount of discouragement and hard times in this life will make that valiant man even once regret his first decision to follow Christ. Like a pilgrim on a journey, that man follows Christ's example in traveling through this world, on his way home to Heaven. (1 Peter 2:9-11)

Who would true valour see,
Let him come hither;
One here will constant be,
Come wind, come weather
There's no discouragement
Shall make him once relent
His first avowed intent
To be a pilgrim.

....

Worldly people will try to tell that valiant man frightening stories and lies, to discourage him from following Christ. (Nehemiah 6, 2 Corinthians 11:3, 1 John 2:26, 3:7) Those liars only confuse themselves, and cause themselves to trip! (Isaiah 41:11, Proverbs 24:16) The valiant man will be stronger than ever, because his strength is in Christ. (2 Corinthians 12:9, Isaiah 40:29,

Romans 16:25) Not even a lion can scare the man who trusts in Christ! He will be brave enough to fight with giants. (1 Samuel 17:36-37, Daniel 6) If he follows Christ, then he is a child of God (John 1:12), and that means this earth is not his home anymore. He is only a traveler, a stranger in this world, because his true home is Heaven. (John 15:19)

Whoso beset him 'round
With dismal stories
Do but themselves confound;
His strength the more is.
No lion can him fright,
He'll with a giant fight,
He will have a right
To be a pilgrim.

....

Satan's demons and goblins cannot frighten that valiant man's spirit. They cannot scare him away from doing the work Christ has told him to do. (Nehemiah 6:9) Because he trusts Christ, that man knows that when his earthly life is over, he will have an eternal life with Christ! (John 17:3, 5:24) And when the valiant man remembers this, all his fears fly away and leave him. (Luke 12:7, 1 John 4:18) No more will that he be afraid of what men say about him. (Hebrews 13:6) Night and day, he will simply keep doing the work that Christ gave him to do, and learning how to be a better pilgrim, traveling through this world for Christ's glory. (Ephesians 5:15-17)

Hobgoblin nor foul fiend
Can daunt his spirit,
He knows he at the end
Shall life inherit.
Then fancies fly away,
He'll fear not what men say,
He'll labor night and day
To be a pilgrim.

HOLY, HOLY, HOLY

Lyrics by **Reginald Heber** (see page 304), 1827

Set to the tunes *Nicaea (Dykes)—Trinity—Tersanctus*—and more

Lord, you are holy! You are utterly separate from sin and darkness. No sin may come near you. (Psalm 1:5, 5:4, 99) You are God the All-Powerful! (Job 11:7) Every morning, as soon as our eyes open, we your children will begin singing our praise to you. God, you are holy, perfect, set apart! You are full of strength (Luke 1:49) and mercy—instead of punishing us for our sins as we deserved, you sent Jesus to wash us clean from sin. (1 Peter 1:3, Romans 6:23) We bless you, Holy Trinity: God the Father, Jesus the Son, and the Holy Spirit. (2 Corinthians 13:14)

Holy, holy, holy! Lord God Almighty!
Early in the morning our song shall rise to thee.
Holy, holy, holy! Merciful and mighty!
God in three Persons, blessed Trinity!

....

Lord, you are holy and perfect! All of your children adore you as they stand around your throne in Heaven. The holiness that you gave us is like gold crowns on our heads, and we give those crowns back to you. (Revelation 4:4,10) Cherubim and seraphim angels fall down and worship you, too (Revelation 7:11), for you are the God who reigned in the beginning, you are the God who reigns now, and you are the God who will reign forevermore! (Revelation 4:8)

Holy, holy, holy! All the saints adore thee,
Casting down their golden crowns around the glassy sea;
Cherubim and seraphim falling down before thee,
Who wert, and art, and evermore shalt be.

....

Lord, you are holy and perfect! Even though the darkness in this world hides you from us now, and though our eyes can't see or understand your glory, we still know that you are the only holy, perfect one. (1 Corinthians 13:12) No one is like you, whose power, love, and purity are perfect. (Revelation 15:4) There is no fault in you.

Holy, holy, holy! Though the darkness hide thee,
Though the eye of sinful man thy glory may not see,
Only thou art holy; there is none beside thee
Perfect in pow'r, in love, and purity.

....

Lord, you are holy and perfect! All-powerful God, you are holy! On earth, in the sky, and in the sea, all of your creations stand up like monuments to honor you. (Psalm 19:1, Revelation 4:11) Lord, you are holy! You are full of mercy for us, and you are powerful. (Isaiah 30:18) We bless you, Holy Trinity: Father, Son, and Holy Spirit!

Holy, holy, holy! Lord God Almighty!
All thy works shall praise thy name in earth and sky and sea.
Holy, holy, holy! Merciful and mighty!
God in three Persons, blessed Trinity!

HOW FIRM A FOUNDATION

Lyrics attributed to "K—" (possibly **Robert Keen**, but not definitely); originally found in *Rippon's Selection of Hymns*, 1787

Set to the tunes *Foundation (trad. American melody)—Adeste Fidelis—St. Denio—Montgomery—Foundation (Parker)—Lyons—Firm Foundation—Sincerity—Solicitude—Kirby—Judea—St. Cyprian (Redhead)—Datchet—The Promises—Missionary*—and more

Children of God, what a steady foundation you've been given to stand on! That foundation is God's excellent Word. (Deuteronomy 12:28, Joshua 23:14, 2 Samuel 22:31, Matthew 4:4) To all of you who have run to Jesus to be saved: what more could you want God to say to you than what He has *already* said in Scripture? What promises could you ask Him for that would be better than the ones He *already* gave you? (1 Corinthians 3:11, 2 Corinthians 1:20)

How firm a foundation, ye saints of the Lord,
Is laid for your faith in His excellent Word!
What more can He say than to you He has said,
Who unto the Saviour for refuge have fled?

....

Just see what a firm foundation God has given you: He has said, "No matter what kind of circumstances you are in, whether you are sick or healthy (James 5:14-15), poor or rich (Proverbs 30:8-9), at home or far away (2 Corinthians 5:1), on the land or on the sea (Psalm 95:5), no matter what is happening to you—whatever you need to keep going, I will give to you." (Isaiah 35:3-4)

"In every condition—in sickness, in health,
In poverty's vale, or abounding in wealth,
At home and abroad, on the land, on the sea,
As thy days may demand, so thy succor shall be."

....

In His Word, God has also said to you, "Don't be afraid! I am here with you. (Deuteronomy 20:1, Jeremiah 1:8, John 14:27) Do not be discouraged or concerned about *anything,* because *I am your God*—no matter what happens to you, I will come to help you! (Leviticus 26:12) I will strengthen you, and stand you back up when you have fallen down. You will be held up by my perfect, all-powerful hand." (Isaiah 41:10)

"Fear not, I am with thee; oh, be not dismayed;
For I am thy God, and will still give thee aid;
I'll strengthen thee, help thee, and cause thee to stand,
Upheld by my righteous, omnipotent hand."

....

God has even told you, "When your life is so hard that it feels as if you're walking through fire, my grace will be there to supply everything you need. (2 Corinthians 12:9, Psalm 66:12) Those flames will not hurt you! They are for your good—I am only leading you through that fire so that all the dirty sin that still clings to you will be burned up. (Proverbs 25:4, Isaiah 1:24-16) Then the golden, pure, new heart that I put inside you when I saved you will shine even more beautifully." (Hebrews 10:22)

"When through fiery trials thy pathway shall lie,
My grace, all-sufficient, shall be thy supply;
The flame shall not hurt thee; I only design
Thy dross to consume, and thy gold to refine."

....

God has promised, "When I call you to walk through a hard part of life, so that you feel as if you're drowning in deep waters, those rivers of sadness will not get too deep. (Isaiah 43:2) That trouble in your life will not be harder than I allow it to be! (Psalm 77:15-16) I will be there in the deep water with you (Psalm 23:4), using those hard times as a blessing for you. I do not send you trouble for no reason—I am using it to make you more like me." (James 1:2-3, 1 Thessalonians 5:23)

"When through the deep waters I call you to go,
The rivers of sorrow shall not overflow;
For I will be with you, your troubles to bless,
And sanctify to you your deepest distress."

....

Christian, the firm foundation in God's Word will last all of your life. You will never outgrow it. God has said, "Even when they reach old age, each of my people will see the proof that my love for them is powerful (Romans 8:38-39), never-ending (Psalm 103:17), and never-changing. (Psalm 136) And even when grey hairs cover their heads, I will still be carrying them close to me, for I am their Shepherd, and they are my lambs." (Psalm 71:18, Isaiah 40:11)

"E'en down to old age, all my people shall prove
My sovereign, eternal, unchangeable love;
And then, when gray hairs shall their temples adorn
Like lambs they shall still in My bosom be borne."

....

Child of God, that firm foundation will never betray you! God has said, "Every soul, every person that has trusted in my Son, Jesus, is my child. And I will not, I will not let any child of mine be hurt by Satan. (Psalm 44:4-5) No, I will hold on tight to that soul, that dear child of mine. (John 10:28-29) Even if all Hell tries to shake that child and take him from me, I will never, no never, no *never* leave him." (Hebrews 13:5)

"The soul that on Jesus hath leaned for repose,
I will not, I will not desert to its foes;
That soul, though all Hell should endeavor to shake,
I will never, no never, no never forsake!"

IF THOU BUT SUFFER GOD TO GUIDE THEE

Lyrics by **Georg Neumark** (see page 319), 1641

Originally written in German; translated by **Catherine Winkworth** (see page 346) in 1855–1863

Set to the tunes *Wer Nur Den Lieben Gott (or Neumark)—Elton—Nicht Das Ich's Schon Ergriffen—Celebration*

If you will allow God to guide you through life, and if you hope in Him in everything you do, then God will give you the strength you need no matter what happens. (Psalm 42:5, Romans 15:13) He will carry you through the hard days of trouble. Anyone who trusts in God's never-changing love is building their faith on a steady Rock, which nothing can move! (Isaiah 26:4)

If thou but suffer God to guide thee
And hope in Him through all thy ways,
He'll give thee strength, whate'er betide thee,
And bear thee through the evil days.
Who trust in God's unchanging love
Builds on the Rock that naught can move.

....

How is worrying helping you? What good is it doing to moan and sigh and complain about what is happening? How does it help to cry about every little trouble that comes? (Matthew 6:25-34) Jesus told us we would have to carry crosses of our own if we wanted to follow Him. (Luke 9:23) These troubles that come to us in life are our "crosses"—and those crosses only grow heavier and harder to carry if we are bitter about having to live through trouble.

What can these anxious cares avail thee
These never ceasing moans and sighs?

What can it help if thou bewail thee
O'er each dark moment as it flies?
Our cross and trials do but press
The heavier for our bitterness.

....

Be patient, and wait for God to take away that trouble when *He* decides the time is right. (Psalm 69:13, 37:7, James 5:7-8) While you are waiting, keep a cheerful hope that God will save you, and let your heart be content with whatever your Heavenly Father sends you. (Romans 12:12) Remember that it is God's wise *love* that sends you these troubles, to purify your heart and pull you closer to Him. (2 Corinthians 1:5) God chose to make you His own, so never doubt that He knows what you want in your secret heart. (Psalm 44:21, 37:4)

Be patient and await His leisure
In cheerful hope, with heart content
To take whatever thy Father's pleasure
And His discerning love hath sent,
Nor doubt our inmost want are known
To Him who chose us for His own.

....

God knows perfectly well when a glad, lighter time is what your heart truly needs. After He has tested your heart by making you walk through some sad troubles, when He has seen that your heart is pure, He will suddenly come and show you His loving care, instead of sadness. (1 Kings 5:4, 8:56, Isaiah 14:3)

God knows full well when time of gladness
Shall be the needful thing for thee.
When He has tried thy soul with sadness
And from all guile has found thee free,
He comes to thee all unaware
And makes thee own His loving care.

....

When you're living through a time so hard that it feels as if you're walking through fire, do not think that God has cast you away and doesn't hear you calling to Him. (2 Samuel 22:7, Psalm 34;17) If you know someone who seems to have all their hopes fulfilled, whom God never seems to tell "No," don't think this person is somehow God's favorite. (Psalm 73) God controls time, and as time passes, much will change. God will decide how long something will last, whether it is a time of blessing or a time of trouble. (Ecclesiastes 3:1-8)

Nor think amid the fiery trial
That God hath cast thee off unheard,
That he whose hopes meet no denial
Must surely be of God preferred.
Time passes and much change doth bring
And set a bound to everything.

....

All of God's children are alike in His eyes. He does not have "favorites." (Romans 2:11) We know that it is easy for God to raise you up when you are low, and it is just as easy for Him to bring down a high and mighty man! (Isaiah 45:7) God is still working, and His acts are true, real wonders. He honors this person, and humbles that one—however He wants to. (Daniel 2:21)

All are alike before the Highest:
'Tis easy for our God, we know,
To raise thee up, though low thou liest,
To make the rich man poor and low.
True wonders still by Him are wrought
Who setteth up and brings to naught.

....

So even if you are in a time of trouble, keep singing! Keep praying! (James 5:13, Romans 12:12) Whatever God has given you to do in your life, do it well. (Ecclesiastes 3:22, 9:10) And trust in God's Word. Even though you don't deserve it—even though none of us deserve it!—you will see that God's word is true for you. (Psalm 56:4, Revelation 22:6) Do you trust in God completely? God has never yet turned away from anyone who trusted Him, when they needed Him. (Isaiah 41:17)

Sing, pray, and keep His ways unswerving,
Perform thy duties faithfully,
And trust His Word: though undeserving,
Thou yet shalt find it true for thee.
God never yet forsook in need
The soul that trusted Him indeed.

IMMORTAL, INVISIBLE, GOD ONLY WISE

Lyrics by **Walter Chalmers Smith**, 1867

Set to the tunes *St. Denio (or Joanna)—St. Basil—Trinity Church—Montgomery*

God, you are immortal—you will live forever, and never grow old or die. (Genesis 21:33, Isaiah 26:4,) You are invisible—you are not part of this created world, so our human eyes cannot see you. And you are wise! (Isaiah 40:28) You are hidden from our eyes because you live in the bright and glorious light of Heaven, where we cannot go yet. (John 6:46) God, you are the most blessed, the most glorious! You are called the Ancient of Days, because you were God before this earth ever existed, and you will be God when this earth is gone. (Daniel 7:9) Mighty, victorious God, we your children praise your great name! (1 Timothy 1:17)

Immortal, invisible, God only wise,
In light inaccessible hid from our eyes,
Most blessèd, most glorious, the Ancient of Days,
Almighty, victorious, thy great name we praise.

....

God, you watch over your creation at all times, because you never sleep. (Psalm 121:3) You are the Master of Time; time does not control you, so you have no need to "hurry" when you work out your plans. (2 Peter 3:8, Psalm 69:13, Joshua 10:12-13) When you direct our lives, you're as quiet as a beam of light—we don't see or hear you working out your plans, but you are working! Your love and goodness are overflowing fountains, reaching up to the clouds, and your holy *justice* is like a grand mountain that reaches even higher. (Psalm 36:5-6)

Unresting, unhasting, and silent as light,
Nor wanting, nor wasting, thou rulest in might;
Thy justice, like mountains, high soaring above
Thy clouds, which are fountains of goodness and love.

....

You give life to every living thing, to big and small creatures alike (Acts 17:25, 1 Timothy 6:13), and you are present in every bit of that life, for *you* are the true life of us all. (John 17:3) All we your creatures bloom and grow strong like healthy leaves on a tree, but in the end, we shrivel up and die ... but you, God, are the *true* life, and nothing will ever change you. (Isaiah 40:7-8)

To all, life thou givest, to both great and small;
In all life, thou livest, the true life of all;
We blossom and flourish as leaves on the tree,
And wither and perish—but naught changeth thee.

....

God our glorious Father, you are the Father of Light. (James 1:17) You are pure, unstained by any sin. Your angels love you (Revelation 7:11), and even they cover their faces before you because you are too bright for them to look at! (Isaiah 6:2-3) You offer us so many rich and wonderful graces and mercies, Lord, but we ask you for this one grace in particular: please take the veil off of our faces that keeps us from seeing you, and take the filth of sin out of our hearts. (2 Corinthians 3:15-16)

Great Father of glory, pure Father of light,
Thine angels adore thee, all veiling their sight;
Of all thy rich graces this grace, Lord, impart:
Take the veil from our faces, the vile from our heart.

....

All praise and glory belong to you, God! (Psalm 45:17) When we are sad because we cannot see you face-to-face (Psalm 13:1), help us to understand that it is only marvelous *light* that hides you from our eyes right now! We cannot see you because you are too magnificent and glorious for our earthly eyes to see. (Exodus 33:17-23) So for now, mighty God, help us remember that you sent Christ to us so that we could come to you someday, and let us keep Christ in our hearts until then. (John 1:17-18, Luke 10:22)

All laud we would render; O help us to see
'Tis only the splendor of light hideth thee,
And so let thy glory, Almighty, impart,
Through Christ in His story, thy Christ to the heart.

IN THE HOUR OF TRIAL

Lyrics by **James Montgomery** (see page 317), 1834

Set to the tunes *Penitence (Lane)—St. Mary Magdalene—Warum Sind Der Thränen—Urswicke—Entreaty—St. Fabian—Bohemia—Intercessor*—and more

Jesus, when I am suffering in this life, plead with God and ask that He would have mercy on me! (Hebrews 7:25) Oh Jesus, do not let me forget that you are with me, or else my sinful heart will despair, and I might wickedly deny you and turn away from you. (Matthew 10:33, Luke 12:9) Jesus, when you see me weakening, look at me and call me back to you. (Luke 15:4-7, 1 Peter 2:25) For if I fear what the world will do to me, that fear might make me stumble. If I am too proud of my blessings and I forget that God is the one who blessed me, that pride might trip me. Jesus, do not let me fall because of either one! (Proverbs 30:7-9)

In the hour of trial,
Jesus, plead for me;
Lest by base denial
I depart from thee;
When thou seest me waver,
With a look recall,
Nor for fear or favor
Suffer me to fall.

....

This world wants to charm and bewitch my heart with its empty "happiness." The world spreads out all of its filthy sin before me, and tells me those dirty things are treasure—but those sins would do me harm! (Hebrews 11:25, Matthew 6:19-10) When I am tempted to sin, Jesus, remind me what you went through to free me from my sin. (Romans 6:6-7, Hebrews 6:4-6) Remind me of how you suffered in the Garden of Gethsemane in terrible agony, and of the even darker pain you went through on the cross at Calvary.

With its witching pleasures
Would this vain world charm,
Or its sordid treasures
Spread to work me harm,
Bring to my remembrance
Sad Gethsemane,
Or, in darker semblance,
Cross-crowned Calvary.

....

Because you love me, you will not let me keep my sins. (Ephesians 2:1-7, Romans 5:8) Jesus, if you decide that I need to go through a hard time to make me pure, then please bless that suffering and let it do its good work on me. (Romans 5:3-5) That time of trouble will be a test, offering me up to you like a sacrifice on an altar. (Romans 12:1-2) Jesus, if you bless me in that testing-time, then even if my earthly body is weak, my faith will be able to accept whatever you send me. (Luke 22:31-32, John 17:15-17, Mark 14:38)

If with sore affliction
Thou in love chastise,
Pour thy benediction
On the sacrifice;
Then, upon thine altar
Freely offered up,
Though the flesh may falter,
Faith shall drink the cup.

....

When I am sick and dying and getting ready to return to the dust from which I was made (Genesis 3:19), when I am at the brink of my grave, I will see flashes of the Heaven glorious shores, waiting for me! (Acts 7:54-60) At the end of my life, I will still rely on the truth that *you have saved me,* Jesus. After my struggle on earth is over, and I have died, Lord Jesus, take me to live forever with you! (1 Thessalonians 5:9-10, 2 Timothy 2:11)

When in dust and ashes
To the grave I sink,
While heav'n's glory flashes
O'er the shelving brink,
On thy truth relying
Through that mortal strife,
Lord, receive me, dying,
To eternal life.

IT IS WELL WITH MY SOUL

Lyrics by **Horatio Gates Spafford**, 1873

Set to the tune *Ville Du Havre*

Sometimes, my life is easy, when peace and comfort flow like a river all around me. But other times, my life is full of sorrows as big as ocean waves. But either way, no matter what you have sent into my life, my God, you have taught me that I should *always* be ready to say, "I am content, Lord! My soul trusts in you no matter what comes." (Philippians 4:11-13)

When peace like a river attendeth my way,
When sorrows like sea billows roll;
Whatever my lot, thou has taught me to say,
"It is well, it is well with my soul."

....

Even though Satan will try to tempt and trip me, even though hard times and trouble will come, this one truth will have control over my heart: Christ saw that I was a sinner and that I could never save myself, so He shed His *own* blood to set me free from sin. (Romans 5:8, 1 John 4:9) So no matter what happens to my body, my soul is safe, because I belong to Christ! (Matthew 10:28)

Though Satan should buffet, though trials should come,
Let this blest assurance control,
That Christ has regarded my helpless estate,
And hath shed his own blood for my soul.

....

Oh, what a beautiful thought this is. My sin—not just some of it, *all of it*—was nailed to the cross with Jesus. He took *all* of my sin and *all* of my punishment, and I do not carry my sins and guilt anymore! (Isaiah 53:6, 1 Peter 2:24) Oh, praise the Lord, my soul! Praise the Lord, I'm free!

My sin—oh, the bliss of this glorious thought!—
My sin, not in part, but the whole
Is nailed to the cross, and I bear it no more!
Praise the Lord, praise the Lord, O my soul!

....

Because He has bought me with His blood, let the rest of my life be dedicated to Christ. (Acts 21:13) Even if that means troubles as big as the Jordan river will try to drown my soul, I won't feel the pain of it, because both throughout my life *and* after my death, Jesus, you will whisper comfort and peace to my soul. (2 Corinthians 1:3-5, Psalm 119:50)

For me, be it Christ, be it Christ hence to live:
If Jordan above me shall roll,
No pang shall be mine, for in death as in life
Thou wilt whisper thy peace to my soul.

....

Ultimately, the thing your people are waiting for is your return, Lord Jesus. (Titus 2:11-14) We know that death and the grave won't be the end of us (Romans 6:3-5)—our lives will go on forever in Heaven with you. (Romans 5:10) Oh, how ready I am to hear that angel's trumpet which will mean our Lord is coming back to bring us home! (1 Corinthians 15:51-52) How excited I am to hear King Jesus' voice with my own ears! What a comforting thought it is for my soul, to remember that *He will come*, someday soon. (Revelation 22:20, Hebrews 10:36-38)

But, Lord, 'tis for thee, for thy coming we wait,
The sky, not the grave, is our goal;
Oh trump of the angel! Oh voice of the Lord!
Blessèd hope, blessèd rest of my soul!

....

My God, please let that day come quickly, the day when I won't have to rely on faith anymore to know that you're there: I'll see you with my own eyes! Bring the day when the sky will roll up like a scroll to make way for Jesus to return from Heaven. (Isaiah 34:4) On that day, the angels will blow their trumpets (Revelation 11:15), and my Lord will come down from Heaven the same way He went up. (Acts 1:9-11) But that day will come when *you* decide it's time, God, and not when I do. (Matthew 24:36) So until then, I am content, and my soul is at peace.

And Lord, haste the day when my faith shall be sight,
The clouds be rolled back as a scroll;
The trump shall resound, and the Lord shall descend.
Even so—it is well with my soul.

JESUS, AND SHALL IT EVER BE

Lyrics by **Joseph Grigg**, 1765

Altered by **Benjamin Francis**, 1787

Set to the tunes *Federal Street—Hamburg—Brookfield—Woodworth—Mainzer—Cornith—Rest (Bradbury)—Blendon—Duane Street—Stonefield—Angelus—Uxbridge—Crichlow—Meroe—Russia—Llef—St. Agnes—Not Ashamed of Jesus—Breslau—St. Stephen's Church—Winscott—Florence—Staincliffe—St. Crispin—Wells—Retreat—Melcombe—Sacrament—Totland—Whitburn—Hebron—Ashamed*—and more

Oh, Jesus! Is it possible that any man, woman, or child might ever be ashamed of you? (Mark 8:38) What a thought! Ashamed of you, Jesus—you who are worshiped by all the angels in Heaven (Hebrews 1:6), you whose glory will shine forever! (Revelation 11:15) How could anyone be ashamed to belong to *you*, Jesus? (Matthew 11:6)

Jesus, and shall it ever be,
A mortal man ashamed of thee?
Ashamed of thee whom angels praise,
Whose glories shine through endless days!

....

Ashamed of Jesus?! If it were possible for the night sky to be ashamed of its stars, then it would be possible for me to be ashamed of Jesus, for Jesus shines His bright and glorious light all over my dark and sinful soul. (2 Corinthians 4:6, John 12:46, 1 Peter 2:9)

Ashamed of Jesus! sooner far
Let evening blush to own a star:
He sheds the beams of light divine
O'er this benighted soul of mine.

....

Ashamed of Jesus?! I could be ashamed of Jesus, if dark midnight could be ashamed of the bright light of noonday! For you see, in my sinful soul it used to be as dark as midnight... until Jesus, the Bright Morning Star, came to me and told the darkness to flee away from me. (Isaiah 9:2, Luke 1:79, Ephesians 5:8)

Ashamed of Jesus! just as soon
Let midnight be ashamed of noon;
'Tis midnight with my soul till He,
Bright Morning Star, bid darkness flee.

....

Ashamed of Jesus?! How could I be ashamed of my dearest Friend? He is the only one who makes it possible for me to go to Heaven and live forever with God. (John 14:6, Matthew 25:34) No—it would be shameful if I was embarrassed for people to know that I belong to Jesus. (Matthew 10:33, Luke 9:26) Yes, that would be my shame, because it would mean I did not respect and worship Christ's wonderful, saving name. (John 20:31)

Ashamed of Jesus, that dear Friend
On whom my hopes of heav'n depend!
No, when I blush, be this my shame,
That I no more revere His name.

....

Ashamed of Jesus?! I can afford to be ashamed of Jesus just as soon as I have no more sins that need to be washed away, and no more reason to want to be a better person. (1 John 1:8-10, Ephesians 4:20-24) I can be ashamed of Jesus when I have no more tears or sadness that need comforting. (Isaiah 25:8, Revelation 7:17, 1 Peter 4:16) I can be ashamed of Jesus when I have no more needs to be provided for. (John 14:13, Philippians 4:19) I can be ashamed of Jesus when I have no more fears that scare me (Philippians 1:20), or when I have no soul that needs to be saved from eternal death! (Matthew 10:28)

Ashamed of Jesus! yes, I may
When I've no guilt to wash away,
No tear to wipe, no good to crave,
No fears to quell, no soul to save.

....

So, until then, I have only one boast (and my boasting is not prideful or meaningless!): I boast that I have been saved by Jesus Christ, my Savior, who died to pay the punishment for my sins, so that I would not have to be separated from God forever. (Jeremiah 9:24) Let my only reason for glory, my only boast, be in *this one thing*: that Jesus Christ is not ashamed of *me*! (Hebrews 2:11)

Till then (nor is my boasting vain)
Till then I boast a Savior slain;
And O may this my glory be,
That Christ is not ashamed of me.

JESUS, I MY CROSS HAVE TAKEN

Lyrics by **Henry Francis Lyte** (see page 313), 1824–1833

Set to the tunes *Ellesdie—Autumn—Crucifer—St. Polycarp—Nettleton—Mariners—Welt Ade, Ich Ben Dein Müde—Falfield—Zundel—Greenville—Hyfrydol—Aberporth—Freetown—Bayley—Gloaming—Bohemia—St. Sebastian—Ripley—Tanymarian—Mendelssohn—Deerhurst—Theodoret—Seraphim—Armstrong—Austria—Divine Compassion—Lugano—St. Asaph—Epworth—Benediction—St. Ignatius—Jag Behöfver Dig, O Jesus—St. Hilary—Monroe*—and more

Jesus, you told me that if I wanted to follow you, I would have to pick up my cross and suffer like you did when you were on earth. (Luke 9:23) I have picked up my cross, Jesus! I am ready to leave everything I have in order to follow you. You were poor, laughed at, and left alone in this world, and I may be too—so from now on, Jesus, you will be everything I need. (Philippians 1:21, 2 Corinthians 1:5, Hebrews 13:20-22) Let me get rid of every earthly desire, no matter how much I want it. (1 John 2:16, Galatians 5:16) Let me forget everything I've ever searched for, or hoped for, or thought I knew—everything except you, Jesus. (Philippians 3:3-8) And then, even though I have lost everything in this world, how rich I am! I am rich indeed, because I still have God and Heaven! (Romans 11:33, Mark 12:41-44)

Jesus, I my cross have taken,
All to leave, and follow thee;
Destitute, despised, forsaken,
Thou from hence my all shalt be.
Perish ev'ry fond ambition,
All I've sought or hoped or known;
Yet how rich is my condition,
God and heav'n are still my own.

....

Let this sinful world hate me, and let me be left without any friends if I must. (John 15:18, 17:14, 1 John 3:13) What will that really matter? They did the same thing to you, Jesus! (Isaiah 53:3) Because we are sinful people, human friendship can be a lie—a person I thought was my true friend might betray me. But you, Jesus, are not a sinful man, and you will never betray me. (Hebrews 13:5, John 15:13) You are the God of wisdom (1 Corinthians 1:30), the God of love (2 Thessalonians 2:16), and the God of strength, Jesus. (Isaiah 9:6) So if you will keep smiling on me, then even if enemies hate me, and even if friends turn away from me, I will still have *your* friendship. If you will only show me your face, then all my world will be bright and hopeful! (1 Peter 1:13)

Let the world despise and leave me,
They have left my Savior too;
Human hearts and looks deceive me;
Thou art not, like man, untrue;
And, while thou shalt smile upon me,
God of wisdom, love, and might,
Foes may hate and friends may shun me;
Show thy face, and all is bright.

....

Sinful people may hurt me or make me afraid, but that will only make me run to you, Jesus. (Romans 8:31) A life of trouble and hard times may weigh me down now, but I can know that I will have sweet, never-ending rest with you when I come to Heaven. (Zephaniah 3:15) Grief and sadness have no power to hurt me, as long as I have your love. (Psalm 91:14) And I would not be able to feel joy at all, Jesus, if I did not have you with it!

Man may trouble and distress me,
'Twill but drive me to thy breast;
Life with trials hard may press me,
Heav'n will bring me sweeter rest.
O 'tis not in grief to harm me
While thy love is left to me;

O 'twere not in joy to charm me,
Were that joy unmixed with thee.

....

My soul, grab hold of all the salvation that Jesus has offered you! Rise up over sin, and fear, and worries. (Matthew 31:36-34) I will rejoice, because I know that no matter where I am, there will be some work for me to do, or something hard to go through which will make me more like Christ. (1 Peter 1:6-7) Oh my soul, remember that the Holy Spirit Himself lives in your heart! Remember what a loving Father your God is, who smiles on you because He loves you and is pleased with you. (Matthew 7:11, Zephaniah 3:17, Romans 5:8) Remember what a gracious Savior died to save you from sin—Jesus Christ Himself, the Son of God! (Romans 8:35, Ephesians 5:25) Oh child of God, when all these things are true, why should you fret? (2 Corinthians 2:14)

Take, my soul, thy full salvation,
Rise o'er sin and fear and care;
Joy to find in ev'ry station
Something still to do or bear;
Think what Spirit dwells within thee,
What a Father's smile is thine,
What a Savior died to win thee:
Child of heav'n, shouldst thou repine?

....

In this life, God gives you grace, and when you reach heaven He will give you glory, because you are His child—so keep marching onward, from grace to glory! (1 Peter 5:10, Romans 5:2) In this world, faith will be your weapon, and prayer will carry you along like wings. (Ephesians 6:16-18) Everlasting life in Heaven is waiting for you (2 Peter 3:13), and God's own hand is what guides you safely there. (Philippians 1:6) It may seem long now, but your time on earth will be over soon. Your days traveling as a stranger in this world won't last long. Right now, you have to *hope* for Heaven—soon enough, you will *have* Heaven. (Hebrews 10:36, James 1:12) Now, you have faith that God is there, but then, you will see Him face-to-face (1 Corinthians 13:12) Someday soon, you won't need to pray anymore—instead, you will spend all of eternity praising God! (Revelation 21:1-7)

Hasten on from grace to glory,
Armed by faith, and winged by prayer;
Heav'n's eternal day's before thee,
God's own hand shall guide thee there.
Soon shall close thy earthly mission,
Swift shall pass thy pilgrim days;
Hope soon change to glad fruition,
Faith to sight, and prayer to praise.

JESUS, LOVER OF MY SOUL

Lyrics by **Charles Wesley** (see page 336), 1740

Set to the tunes *Abersystwyth—Martyn—Refuge (Holbrook)—New St. Andrew—Refuge (Pugh)—Refuge (Minshall)—Refuge (Beethoven)—Refuge (Smart)—Hollingside—St. Fabian—Merdin—Charles Wesley—Hotham—Blumenthal—Elijah—Little Heath—Bowring—Philip—Frankfort—Ruth—Wickham—Allen—Spanish Hymn—Yarbrough—St. Edmund—Belgrave—Invocation—School St. Choir—Ages—Haven—Jesu Refugiem Meum—Worcester—Judd Street—Slio—Beecher—Benning*—and many more

Jesus, you who love my soul so much, let me run to you for safety when the trouble in my life feels like angry waters rolling in to drown me. (Psalm 69:14-15) When storms of this life are raging over my head, hide me, Jesus my Savior! Hide me safe with you until this life is over. (Psalm 57:1) Lead me safely home to Heaven, and so that I may be with you! (Psalm 107:29-30)

Jesus, lover of my soul,
Let me to thy bosom fly,
While the nearer waters roll,
While the tempest still is high:
Hide me, O my Savior, hide,
Till the storm of life is past;
Safe into the haven guide,
O receive my soul at last!

....

I have not one single safe place to run, except to *you*, Jesus. (Psalm 4:8) My helpless soul clings to you, and I depend on you, because you are my *only* safety. (Psalm 9:10) Oh Jesus, please, do not leave me! No matter what happens to me, stay here with me to hold me up and comfort me. (Psalm 71) I trust you to keep me safe, and I trust in absolutely nothing besides you, Jesus. (Psalm 118:8-9, Proverbs 3:5) If I need help to keep going when I am falling under the heavy evil of this world, I go to *you* to ask for that help. (Jeremiah 17:5-8)

I can't protect myself, so Jesus, cover me and protect me from the evil that attacks me here! (Deuteronomy 32:10-12, Psalm 17:8-9, 36:7, 91:1, 140:7)

Other refuge have I none,
Hangs my helpless soul on thee;
Leave, ah! leave me not alone,
Still support and comfort me!
All my trust on thee is stayed,
All my help from thee I bring;
Cover my defenseless head
With the shadow of thy wing.

....

Jesus Christ, you are everything I want. I don't just receive everything I need from you—I receive far *more* than I could ever need! (Ephesians 2:7, Philippians 4:19) Jesus, if any of your people fall down under the heaviness of sin, pick them back up. (Romans 14:4) If any of your people are sad, weak, or discouraged, cheer them up. (Psalm 35:5) If any of your people are sick, please heal them. (James 5:14-15, Psalm 34:18) And if any of your people are blind—for even if they can see with their eyes, they may be blind in their hearts—then show them where to walk. (Isaiah 42:16) Jesus, your name is just and holy! You will judge this world without partiality (Acts 17:31, Romans 2:11), and you yourself are completely separate from all sin. (1 John 2:1) But I am *only* sinful! (Isaiah 64:6) There is nothing good in me. I say I will be true, but I always sin again. (Romans 7:18-20) I am full of sin, but *you* are full of truth and grace. (John 1:14)

Thou, O Christ, art all I want;
More than all in thee I find:
Raise the fallen, cheer the faint,
Heal the sick, and lead the blind.
Just and holy is thy name;
I am all unrighteousness;

False and full of sin I am,
Thou art full of truth and grace.

....

Jesus, you have plenty of grace to give! You have enough grace to cover even *my* horrible sins. (1 Timothy 1:15, Romans 5:15, 2 Corinthians 9:8) Your grace is like a stream of healing water, so let the stream flow! (John 1:16) Give me a new, clean heart, and then *keep* my heart pure. (Ezekiel 36:26) True life flows from you like water from a fountain, so let me come and take all the new life I need. (Revelation 21:6) Let your life bubble up in my heart like fresh water from a spring, and let that life keep flowing for all eternity.

Plenteous grace with thee is found,
Grace to cover all my sin;
Let the healing streams abound;
Make and keep me pure within:
Thou of life the fountain art,
Freely let me take of thee;
Spring thou up within my heart,
Rise to all eternity.

JESUS, PRICELESS TREASURE

Lyrics by **Johann Franck** (see page 297), 1655

Originally written in German; translated by **Catherine Winkworth** (see page 346) in 1863

Set to the tunes *Jesu, Meine Freude—Gud Skal Alting Mage—Freyberg*

Jesus, you are a treasure that is worth more than all the money in this world could buy. (Matthew 13:44) My truest happiness comes from you, Jesus, my faithful friend. (Psalm 16:11, 68:3, John 16:20-22) Oh Jesus, I long to see you face-to-face! How long will my spirit have to wait and suffer here before I can come to you? You are the perfect sacrificial lamb that was killed to pay for my sins, and I belong to you. (1 Corinthians 6:19-20) This world will know that I am yours, for I will not allow anything to hide my love for you. You are everything my heart needs, so I do not ask for anything except *you,* Jesus. (Philippians 4:19)

Jesus, priceless treasure,
Source of purest pleasure,
Truest Friend to me:
Ah, how long in anguish
Shall my spirit languish,
Yearning, Lord, for thee?
Thine I am, O spotless Lamb!
I will suffer naught to hide thee,
Naught I ask beside thee.

....

When I am tired of this world, I go to your arms to rest. When I am safe in your arms, my enemies who would hurt me cannot get to me! (John 10:28-29) Even if there is so much trouble that the earth seems to shake under my feet, and even if everyone else's hearts are trembling in fear, Jesus will calm my heart so that I am not afraid. (Psalm 46:1-3) Let the lightning flash, and the thunder crash! Even if all of my sins taunt me and Hell itself attacks me, Jesus will not leave me. (Matthew 28:20)

In thine arms I rest me;
Foes who would molest me
Cannot reach me here.
Though the earth be shaking,
Ev'ry heart be quaking,
Jesus calms my fear.
Lightnings flash and thunders crash;
Yet, though sin and Hell assail me,
Jesus will not fail me.

....

Satan, you have no power over me! (1 John 5:19) Death, you will not be the end of me! (Hosea 13:14, Romans 6:3-11) Fear, leave me alone. Evil world, you cannot hurt me, and your threats will not scare me. Jesus has paid for my sins and made peace between me and God my Father, so I sing for joy! (Colossians 1:19-23) God's strong power guards me every hour of my life. All of Creation belongs to God, even the earth and its oceans adore God, and bow down to worship Him. (Luke 8:24-25) So why should I be afraid?

Satan, I defy thee;
Death, I now decry thee;
Fear, I bid thee cease.
World, thou shalt not harm me
Nor thy threats alarm me
While I sing of peace.
God's great pow'r guards ev'ry hour;
Earth and all its depths adore Him,
Silent bow before Him.

....

Forget worldly treasure and wealth! (1 Timothy 6:17-19) Jesus, *you* are my only true happiness, and you are the only thing I want. (Mark 10:21) Forget worldly glory, and praises from people; it is all empty! (Hebrews 11:24-26, Matthew 23:2-8) Wicked world, that story that you tell me—tempting me, saying that you can give me everything I want—it means *nothing*. (John 12:25, 1 John 2:15) I know that because I love Jesus, I will have pain, loss, shame, and suffering in this life, just as Jesus did. (John 15:20) But not even suffering can make me leave Jesus. I will stand with Him, because He chose to love me first! (1 Peter 5:10, Romans 8:38-39)

Hence with earthly treasure!
Thou art all my pleasure,
Jesus, all my choice.
Hence, thou empty glory!
Naught to me thy story,
Told with tempting voice.
Pain or loss or shame or cross
Shall not from my Savior move me,
Since He deigns to love me.

....

Goodbye, you people who love this sinful world and refuse Heaven. (John 3:19, Matthew 16:26) You will try to tempt me to love this world too, but your tempting will not work. (1 Corinthians 10:13) Goodbye, sins! You cannot blind my heart anymore. (John 9:39) Sin, I say to you what Jesus said to Satan: "Get behind me!" and don't show your face to me again. (Matthew 16:23) Pride, your reign is over. I cut myself free from the ways of this sinful earth. Goodbye, sin and Satan, forever!

Farewell, thou who choosest
Earth, and Heaven refusest,
Thou wilt tempt in vain;
Farewell, sins, nor blind me,
Get ye all behind me,

Come not forth again:
Past your hour, O pride and power;
Worldly life, thy bonds I sever,
Farewell now forever!

....

Be gone from me, fear and sadness! Jesus, the Lord of *gladness*, takes up all the room in my heart. Those who love God our Father will always have peace in their hearts, even when their life on this earth feels like a terrible storm. (Philippians 4:7) Yes, no matter what I have to go through in this life, Jesus, you will always be the one who brings me all my joy—Jesus, my priceless treasure!

Hence, all fear and sadness!
For the Lord of gladness,
Jesus, enters in.
Those who love the Father,
Though the storms may gather,
Still have peace within.
Yea, whate'er I here must bear,
Thou art still my purest pleasure,
Jesus, priceless treasure.

JESUS, THOU JOY OF LOVING HEARTS

Lyrics by **Bernard of Clairvaux** (see page 282), c. 1150

Originally written in Latin; translated by **Ray Palmer** (see page 324) in 1858

Set to the tunes *Quebec—Maryton—Walton (Germany)—Wareham—Christe Redemptor—Canonbury—Communion—Westcott—Baca—Migdol—Jesu Dulcis Memoria—Zephyr—Federal Street—St. Sepulchre—Eisenach—Abends—Ealing—Welton—Winscott—Holley—Hereford—Creation—St. Bernard—Nurnberg—Dickinson College—Crispinian—Hamburg—Eden—Leigh—Emmaus—Ontario—Thirsk—Hebron—Jesus, the Thought of Thee—Brookfield—Joy—Mt. Airy—Seasons—Florence—St. Alkmund—Dwight—Broadway—Ward—Jesu Dulcedo Cordium—Gonfalon Royal—Invitation (Devonshire)—Exultet Caelum Laudibus—Mendon—Crasselius—Melcombe—Heirapolis—Cromer—Hampstead*—and more

---

Jesus, we can only truly have loving hearts if *you* live in our hearts. (1 John 4:7) So you, Jesus, are the pride and joy of every heart that loves! (Psalm 84:2) All true life—eternal life—comes through you, overflowing like a fountain. (Psalm 36:9) You are the light in our hearts that shows us where to go. (John 1:5) This sinful world can offer us its best happiness, but even its very best will never fill up our hearts. (Hebrews 11:24-25) This world is not able to satisfy us, so we go to the only one who can: Jesus. (Psalm 37:4)

Jesus, thou joy of loving hearts,
Thou fount of life, thou light of men,
From the best bliss that earth imparts
We turn unfilled to thee again.

....

Jesus, *you* are the only truth. You have been true since the world was made, and you are true now. (John 1:1-3,17) You save the ones who call for you to save them, instead of trying to save themselves. (Joel 2:32, Romans 10:12-13) When anyone goes searching for you, you go to them and show them that you are good, that you are everything they could ever need. (Philippians 4:12-13,19)

Thy truth unchanged hath ever stood;
Thou savest those that on thee call;
To them that seek thee thou art good,
To them that find thee all in all.

....

You gave us your body as a sacrifice to pay for our sins, and like sweet bread, you give us all the nourishment we need to live. (Luke 22:19) That bread means that we belong to you—we taste it, and we long to feast on it forever. (Psalm 34:8) You gave your blood for us, and it is like water alive inside of us, making us alive too. (1 Corinthians 11:25) Jesus, you are a fountain of true life, so satisfy our thirsty souls with that life. (John 4:13-14, 7:38)

We taste thee, O thou living bread,
And long to feast upon thee still;
We drink of thee, the fountain-head,
And thirst our souls from thee to fill.

....

Wherever we go, whatever we do, our spirits are tired in this hard world full of sin. (Hebrews 12:1-3) We long to be with you, Jesus, in Heaven! But this is where you want us to be right now. Just to see you smiling on us makes our spirits glad again! (Numbers 6:24-26) You bless us by giving us the faith to keep going, to keep holding on tightly to you. (Hebrews 11)

Our restless spirits yearn for thee,
Where'er our changeful lot is cast;
Glad when thy gracious smile we see,
Blest when our faith can hold thee fast.

....

Oh Jesus, stay with us here. Walk beside us through our life on earth. (Jeremiah 31:33, Hebrews 8:10) Even in times of trouble, help us always to be calm and hopeful—after all, even in trouble, we still have *you* right beside us. (1 Peter

4:12-13) Come Jesus, chase away our sin that tries to keep us in a dark night. Come and shine your light over all this world! (2 Corinthians 4:6, John 1:4-5)

O Jesus, ever with us stay,
Make all our moments calm and bright;
Chase the dark night of sin away,
Shed o'er the world thy holy light.

JESUS! WHAT A FRIEND FOR SINNERS!

Lyrics by **John Wilbur Chapman**, 1910

Set to the tunes *Hyfrydol—Holy Manna*

Jesus, you are such a perfect Friend for us sinners! (John 15:13-15) Jesus is the one who loves me, who truly cares about my soul. Even my friends on this earth might betray me, and my enemies here will fight against me ... just like Jesus' friends and enemies betrayed Him. (Psalm 41:9, John 13:18) But Jesus, who saved me from my sins, will be there to heal my broken heart. (Isaiah 42:3, Matthew 12:20)

Refrain: Praise be to God, for He gave us Jesus! (John 8:42) What a wonderful savior Jesus is. Praise God, what a wonderful friend! Jesus saved me from sin once and for all (Matthew 1:21), and every day He helps me go on when my heart is tired (Matthew 11:28-29), keeps me safe (Psalm 54:4), stops me from sinning (John 16:1, Jude 1:24-25), and He loves me better than anyone else could. (Romans 8:35) This Jesus will walk with me all the way to the end of my life! (Matthew 28:19-20)

Jesus! what a friend for sinners!
Jesus! lover of my soul;
Friends may fail me, foes assail me,
He, my Savior, makes me whole.
(Refrain)
Hallelujah! what a Savior!
Hallelujah, what a Friend!
Saving, helping, keeping, loving,
He is with me to the end.

Jesus! He is strong for me, when I am weak. When I am worn out in this world, let me hide in Him and rest. Satan still tempts me, and I have to walk through hard troubles in this life, and sometimes I fall back into my sin. (James 3:2, Romans 7:18-20) But when I am so weak, Jesus becomes my strength. (2 Corinthians 12:9) He has already won the battle against sin for me. (Hebrews 10:10)

Jesus! what a strength in weakness!
Let me hide myself in Him;
Tempted, tried, and sometimes failing,
He, my strength, my vict'ry wins.

....

Oh, Jesus! He is the best comforter I could have when I am sad. When life is so hard that it feels as if ocean waves are crashing down on me, and even when my sad heart feels like it's being torn in two, Jesus comforts my soul and helps me go on. (2 Corinthians 1:3-5, 4:8-10)

Jesus! what a help in sorrow!
While the billows o'er me roll,
Even when my heart is breaking,
He, my comfort, helps my soul.

....

Jesus—what a perfect guide He is! How well He keeps me safe from danger and sin. (Psalm 73:24, John 16:13-14) Sometimes this life seems like there are angry storms above me and dark night around me, and I cannot see my way forward. Then Jesus hears me call for help, and guides me safely through the storm. (Psalm 34:17, 2 Corinthians 1:9-10)

Jesus! what a guide and keeper!
While the tempest still is high,
Storms about me, night o'ertakes me,
He, my pilot, hears my cry.

....

Jesus! Oh yes, He is mine! In Jesus, I don't simply find everything I need—I find more than I could ever dream of needing. (Philippians 4:19) He will never run out of comfort for my soul, and He will never leave me. (Hebrews 13:5) I belong to Him, and He is my dear Lord. (Song of Solomon 2:16)

Jesus! I do now receive Him,
More than all in Him I find;
He hath granted me forgiveness,
I am His, and He is mine.

LET OUR CHOIR NEW ANTHEMS RAISE

Lyrics by **Joseph the Hymnographer**, 9th century

Originally written in Latin; translated by **John Mason Neale** (see page 344) in 1862

Set to the tunes *St. Kevin—St. Joseph of the Studium—*
Gaudeamus Pariter—Chestnut Hill—Weimar

Let us sing new songs to God! Christians, wake up the sun, and start the morning with a song about your joy and gladness, for God Himself works in our lives. (Psalm 30:11-12) We live in an evil world, and sometimes the children of God will be killed because they love Christ. (Matthew 10:16-24) But God brings them out of the pain of death, and into joy and praise in Heaven! (Psalm 116:15, 1 Thessalonians 4:13-14) Remembering when a Christian was killed, we may think that day was dark and terrible. But really, how bright is was, for that was the day that child of God walked through the gates of Heaven, and went to be home with God forever. (John 14:1-3) On that day, they laid down their short, sad earthly life and put on the perfect, joyful, never-ending life that God had prepared for them. (1 Corinthians 15:51-57, Philippians 1:21)

Let our choir new anthems raise,
Wake the morn with gladness;
God Himself to joy and praise
Turns the martyrs' sadness:
Bright the day that won their crown,
Opened heav'ns bright portal,
As they laid the mortal down
And put on th' immortal.

....

Even when they were being threatened with torture and death, those Christian martyrs did not give in. (Luke 12:4-5) They never denied that they belonged to

Christ. (Matthew 10:32-33) Their enemies—Christ's enemies—hunted them down and tortured them with all their evil might, but it did not matter. Satan tried as hard as he could to make them betray Christ, but it did not work. The children of God were faithful, even if it meant they were killed. (Revelation 2:10) They were able to stand strong against Satan's attacks because their faith reminded them what was waiting for them: *Heaven!* It was as if they could see Heaven waiting for them. (2 Corinthians 5:1-9) And now, that bright, eternal city is where those Christians are standing! The story of their lives is a story of victory, because Christ helped them to stay strong, and they never gave up. (1 John 5:4-5, James 1:12)

Never flinched they from the flame,
From the torture never;
Vain the foeman's sharpest aim,
Satan's best endeavor;
For by faith they saw the land
Decked in all its glory,
Where triumphant now they stand
With the victor's story.

....

Those Christians had faith so strong that they could not even *imagine* being ashamed of Christ's name. What did they care if the world knew they belonged to Him? Christ was their King! They knew Christ's love for them would last forever, so their love for Him never failed either. While they suffered here for a little while, they looked forward to being with God forever. (Hebrews 10:23) You Christians of today, get up and follow their example! (Hebrews 12:1-6) Stay faithful to King Jesus even in times of trouble, just as they did. Keep going, even when your work here is hard and your sadness is heavy. (Matthew 11:28-29) This life is like a dark night, full of fear, but don't stop to worry about it. (Psalm 139:11-12) Just keep on following Christ, step by step... and when this dark life is over, there will be Heaven—and how glorious that never-ending day will be! (Isaiah 60:19-21)

Faith they had that knew not shame,
Love that could not languish;
And eternal hope o'ercame
Momentary anguish.
Up and follow, Christian men!
Press through toil and sorrow;
Spurn the night of fear and then,
O the glorious morrow!

LET US LOVE AND SING AND WONDER

Lyrics by **John Newton** (see page 321), 1774

Set to the tunes *All Saints Old—Palms*

Children of God, let us gather together to love our God and sing His praises! Be amazed with me at how wonderful His works are. (Numbers 14:19) And let us sing praise to Christ our Savior! May His name be honored in this world. (Philippians 2:9-11) Before Christ came, God's people lived under God's law, which was meant to show us how perfect God is, and how hopelessly sinful we are. The law reminded us that we could never be good enough to save ourselves. But then Christ came and silenced the law's reminders! (Hebrews 7:11-23, John 1:17) We still can never live a perfect life, but Christ lived perfectly *for* us. We can never perfectly obey the Ten Commandments that God gave to Moses on Mount Sinai, but Christ obeyed them *for* us. (Romans 5:12-16) Jesus' blood has washed away our sins from us. We could never have come near God when we were dirty in our sins, but Jesus has brought us to be with God forever. (Philippians 3:8-11)

Let us love and sing and wonder,
Let us praise the Savior's name!
He has hushed the law's loud thunder,
He has quenched Mount Sinai's flame;
He has washed us with His blood,
He has brought us nigh to God.

....

Christians, let us love Jesus, our Lord who bought us back from sin with His own blood. (1 Corinthians 7:23) He is perfect, so when we lived in sin, we were His enemies. But He pitied us even then, and came to make us holy.

(Romans 5:8-11) Christ showed us grace, called us by name to come to Him, and taught us about God His Father—our Father! (Matthew 4:23) When we lived in our sins, we didn't have the ears to hear God speaking, nor the eyes to see what God had done for us. (Deuteronomy 29:4, Isaiah 44:18) Jesus gave us open ears, and open eyes! (Acts 26:15-18) Jesus' blood has washed us clean from the sin that made us dirty, and now He leads us to God's throne. (Revelation 7:13-15)

Let us love the Lord who bought us,
Pitied us when enemies,
Called us by His grace, and taught us,
Gave us ears and gave us eyes:
He has washed us with His blood,
He presents our souls to God.

....

Christians, let us sing for joy because of these things! (Revelation 4:11, 5:9) Let us sing even when Satan is trying to drag us down and tempt us to sin again. Yes, let us sing even then, for our Lord Jesus has already defeated Satan. He wears the winner's crown (Romans 6:8-11, Revelation 1:17-18), and He offers a crown to each of us who remain faithful till the end. (James 1:12, Revelation 2:10-11) And Jesus, who washed us clean and saved us from our sins in the first place, will also make sure we arrive safely home to God—very soon! (Philippians 1:6, Colossians 1:19-23)

Let us sing, though fierce temptation
Threaten hard to bear us down!
For the Lord, our strong salvation,
Holds in view the conqu'ror's crown;
He who washed us with His blood,
Soon will bring us home to God.

....

Christians, be amazed with me! We cannot imagine how great God's love is for us! (Psalm 118:21-23) God is perfectly holy—sin cannot come near Him, and He *must* punish it. That is God's justice. (Deuteronomy 32:4, Psalm 5:4, Lamentations 3:38-40) But He has joined His justice with His grace by sending a substitute to be punished *instead* of us: Jesus. (John 1:14-16, Romans 3:23-26, 1 John 4:10) This shows us God's mercy: He doesn't give us the punishment we deserve. When we trust that Christ's blood is enough to save us, God's justice is satisfied—nothing else is needed. The price has been paid, and we are free! (Romans 6:3-8,23) Jesus, who washed us clean with His blood, has made the way for us to be with God. (Hebrews 4:14-16)

Let us wonder; grace and justice
Join, and point to mercy's store;
When through grace in Christ our trust is,
Justice smiles, and asks no more:
He who washed us with His blood,
Has secured our way to God.

....

Listen! Hear how loudly the angels in Heaven are singing praise to Jesus' name! (Isaiah 6:1-4) Lord Jesus, we are ashamed, because our praises for you are not loud and strong like the angels', and our love for you has gone cold. (Revelation 3:14-16) But how can that be?! How could we not praise you with all of our strength, Lord, when you have done so much for us? (Hebrews 13:12-15) Jesus, you have washed our souls clean with your blood, so wash our songs of praise clean, too. Teach us to praise you the way we ought to, Christ, for you are the reason we can come to God. (John 14:6)

Hark! the name of Jesus sounded
Loud, from golden harps above;
Lord we blush, and are confounded,
Faint our praise, and cold our love;

Wash our souls and songs with blood,
For by thee we come to God.

....

Christians, let us sing our praises! The Christians of the past are singing Christ's praises in Heaven, so let us join in with their songs! (Revelation 7:9-12) Those Christians trusted Christ, just like we do, and now their praises fill all of Heaven. Just like us, they sing, "You have washed away our sins with your blood, Christ! You are worthy of all worship, Jesus, Lamb of God!" (Revelation 5:11-13)

Let us praise, and join the chorus
Of the saints enthroned on high;
Here they trusted Him before us,
Now their praises fill the sky:
"You have washed us with your blood;
You are worthy, Lamb of God!"

....

Yes, we praise you, Jesus our glorious Savior. We are amazed that your love for us is so strong! We love you, Lord, and we bless your name, the name that has saved us. (Acts 4:12) We are not capable of praising you the way you deserve—please forgive our weak attempts! Have compassion on us, Lord, for you know how weak we are. (Psalm 103:13-14) But with all the strength we do have, we must sing, because Jesus Christ has washed us clean in His blood, and He has brought us near to God! (Ephesians 2:13)

Yes we praise thee, glorious Saviour;
Wonder, love and bless thy name;
Pardon, Lord, our poor endeavour,
Pity, for thou know'st our frame.
He has wash'd us with His blood,
He has brought us nigh to God.

LO! HE COMES, WITH CLOUDS DESCENDING

Lyrics by **John Cennick** (stanzas 3 and 4; see page 288), 1750,
and **Charles Wesley** (stanzas 1, 2, and 5; see page 336), 1758

Altered by **Martin Madan**, 1760

Set to the tunes *Holywood—Epiphany*

Imagine the day Jesus comes back to earth ... We will say to each other, "Look and see!" Christ the King is coming down from Heaven, riding the clouds like a chariot of war. (Mark 14:62, Matthew 24:30, Isaiah 66:15-16) When He came to earth the first time, He was killed in order to set His chosen people free from sin. But now Christ is coming back to earth to claim what He bought with His blood the first time (Revelation 19:7)—and this time, He has a thousand times a thousand Christians following Him! (Revelation 19:14, 1 Thessalonians 3:12-13) That number grows as all the Christians from the past and the present join together to sing of how Christ has won the war against Satan and sin. (Revelation 19:11-16) "Praise the Lord! Praise the Lord!" we sing. "God has come back to His world, to rule forever." (Revelation 11:15)

Lo! He comes with clouds descending,
Once for favored sinners slain;
Thousand thousand saints attending
Swell the triumph of His train.
Alleluia! Alleluia!
God appears on earth to reign.

....

Now every person on earth will see God Himself with their own eyes. (1 John 3:2) Jesus sits on His throne as the rightful King of this world, wearing His glory and majesty like a robe around Him. All those who ignored Him when He came to earth the first time will have no choice but to see Him now, and they will understand who He is. All the enemies who handed Him over to be killed, who put *Jesus* in prison and let a *murderer* go free, will have to look at Him now and see what happened to all their plans! (Mark 15:6-15) The cruel men who tortured Him, who pierced Him with thorns and whips and spears, who nailed Him to a cross, will have to look at Christ on His throne and know who they killed. (Zechariah 12:10, Revelation 1:7) They will all wail and moan, because they will finally see who He is: *the Messiah, God's own Son!* (Revelation 1:17-18)

Ev'ry eye shall now behold Him,
Robed in dreadful majesty;
Those who set at naught and sold Him,
Pierced, and nailed Him to the tree,
Deeply wailing, deeply wailing,
Shall the true Messiah see.

....

Every bit of this rotten world will be swept away. Every island, every sea, every mountain, everything in the sky and on the earth, will be burned up to nothing... and then God will make them all again, new and perfect. (2 Peter 3:10-13, Isaiah 65:17-25, 66:22-23) Everyone who hates Christ will now be confused and silenced. It will be terrible for them, but they will hear the Heavenly trumpets that mean, "This is the day that Jesus Christ will judge the earth! Come and be judged for what you have done." (Matthew 16:27, Romans 2:1-11, Revelation 8) Everyone on the earth, and everyone who has ever lived on the earth, will come and stand before the throne of God. (Isaiah 66:18) Each one of us will have to tell God, the Judge of all, how we lived the life He gave us, and He will judge our actions, our words, and our secret thoughts. (Matthew 12:36, Revelation 20:11-15)

Ev'ry island, sea, and mountain,
heav'n and earth, shall flee away;
All who hate Him must, confounded,
Hear the trump proclaim the day:

Come to judgement! Come to judgement!
Come to judgement, come away!

....

Ever since Christ rose from the dead and went back up to Heaven, we His people have been waiting for our Lord to come back and take us home to Heaven with Him. (Acts 1:6-11) Now that long-waited-for redemption is here at last! (Isaiah 25:8-9) That day has come, with all the glory and celebration that Christ's victory over Satan deserves! Christ's people have suffered and been hated by the world, just as Christ was. (John 17:12-16) But now Christ's people will go to meet Him in the sky! (1 Thessalonians 4:16-18) Praise the Lord! Praise the Lord! See, it is here: the day of redemption that God promised has come.

Now Redemption, long expected,
See in solemn pomp appear!
All His saints, by man rejected,
Now shall meet Him in the air.
Alleluia! Alleluia!
See the day of God appear!

....

Yes Lord, let everything be just as you command, forever! (Revelation 1:5-6) Let every knee on earth bow down to honor Christ our King. He will sit in glory on His rightful throne for eternity. (Isaiah 45:23, Romans 14:11, Philippians 2:10) Jesus our Savior, take all the power and glory—claim this world that you bought with your blood, and be its only King! (1 Timothy 6:13-16) That day hasn't come just yet... we are still waiting for Jesus to return. (Revelation 14:12) But He *will come,* because He promised us He would. (Hebrews 10:36-38) Bring that day quickly, Jesus! Come soon! Praise the Lord, for we know you will. (Revelation 22:20)

Yea, amen! let all adore thee,
High on thine eternal throne;
Savior, take the pow'r and glory,

Claim the kingdom for thine own:
O come quickly, O come quickly;
Alleluia! come, Lord, come.

LORD, MY WEAK THOUGHT IN VAIN WOULD CLIMB

Lyrics by **Ray Palmer** (see page 324), 1858

Set to the tunes *Canonbury—Hamburg—Germany—Hebron—Rockingham—Louvan*

Oh God, my mind is weak. *Your* mind invented this universe and every detail in it.(Isaiah 55:8-9, Hebrews 11:3) But even though I can never completely understand you, I want my weak mind to understand as much as it can. God, I want to study the night sky, to seek out as many stars as I can find, and I want to be amazed at how incredible it all is. (Psalm 8:3-4, Psalm 19:1-2, 1 Chronicles 16:26, Job 38:33) Though I can never really understand, I want my thoughts to fly high up into thoughts about you and your Creation. (Proverbs 3:19-20, Job 38) God, let me study your world as if I was looking for the edges of the sky itself—even though I will never, ever find them!

Lord, my weak thought in vain would climb
To search the starry vault profound;
In vain would wing her flight sublime
To find Creation's utmost bound.

....

Yes, my mind is weak ... but really, that is the only way I can hope to understand anything at all. If I believed I could understand your plan, Lord, then that pride would keep me from seeing anything but myself! (Ephesians 4:18, Psalm 10:4, 138:6, 1 Corinthians 1:20) But if I understand that you are the Great Creator and I am the small, created thing, if I understand that you are God and I am not, then you will teach me about yourself. (Psalm 25:9) I must be very humble indeed if I ever want to understand your plan, God—the way you decide how things will happen on earth, and no one can change what you command. Your plan for this world is built on your love for us. (Psalm 40:5)

You formed that loving plan long before you ever made this world, and it still stands! (1 Corinthians 2:7)

But weaker yet that thought must prove
To search thy great eternal plan,
Thy sovereign counsels, born of love
Long ages ere the world began.

....

Sometimes my weak mind wants to demand that you explain to me why you, God, chose for something to happen the way it did. (Romans 9:20) When I do that, it's as if I'm standing beside an ocean filled with knowledge about you and asking to swallow it all. I'm not capable of understanding your plan, so why am I asking? I will never understand those secrets that only *you* can understand. (1 Corinthians 2:11, Deuteronomy 29:29)

When my dim reason would demand
Why that, or this, thou dost ordain,
By some vast deep I seem to stand,
Whose secrets I must ask in vain.

....

When there is so much trouble around me that my heart feels sick and I am tempted to doubt that you really love me, when life feels so dark that I can't see where I am, then I still have this truth like a hard rock to stand on: it is your will for me to be here right now. (1 Peter 2:19, 4:19) You did not leave me or forget about me or make a mistake. (Job 34:10) Even *this* is part of the complex plan that your love has for me, Lord, and it makes no difference if I understand or not. (Psalm 22)

When doubts disturb my troubled breast,
And all is dark as night to me,
Here, as on solid rock, I rest—
That so it seemeth good to thee.

....

No matter what happens, it will be true forever that you rule this world, God Almighty. (Psalm 45:6, Hebrews 1:8) So let that fact give me joy! (Romans 5:3-5) Everything happens because it was your will for it to happen. Lord God, how I love your perfect wisdom, because it is built on your love for me! No one can interfere with your plan. (1 John 4:16, Psalm 2:1-6) Because I know this is true, my God, I will be calm, and joyfully trust that you are directing my life. (Proverbs 16:9)

Be this my joy, that evermore
Thou rulest all things at thy will;
Thy sovereign wisdom I adore,
And calmly, sweetly, trust thee still.

LORD, WITH GLOWING HEART I'D PRAISE THEE

Lyrics by **Francis Scott Key**, 1817

Set to the tunes *Faben—St. Chad—Ripley—Autumn—Sanctuary—Key—Vesper Hymn—Cross—Vesper—Womit Soll Ich Dich Woll Loben—Preston—Pleading Savior—Crucifer—Adoration—Nettleton—Sorrento—Rathbun—Hyfrydol—Lord, with Glowing Heart*—and more

Lord, I want to praise you with my heart full of gratitude and love. I have so much joy because I know that you love me, and I glorify you for that! (Ecclesiastes 9:7) I thank you for your grace that forgives me of my sins. (1 Corinthians 1:4, Ephesians 1:3-6) Because I know that your grace will hold me up, I have peace in my heart—and I honor you for that, too! (2 Corinthians 12:9, John 14:27) God, I am not capable of worshipping you the way you deserve, so help me when I try. I can't force my dull, sleepy heart to feel the joy I *should* have when I sing to you. My soul should be on Heavenly fire when I worship you, but I can't light that fire on my own. You, God, must light that fire, or my love for you will never grow hot enough to turn into worship!

Lord, with glowing heart I'd praise thee
For the bliss thy love bestows,
For the pard'ning grace that saves me,
And the peace that from it flows.
Help, O God, my weak endeavor;
This dull soul to rapture raise;
Thou must light the flame, or never
Can my love be warmed to praise.

....

Oh my soul, praise God who ran after you when you were running away from Him, chasing your sin! (1 Peter 2:25) When you were lost, far away from Him, He came to find you. (Jeremiah 31:10) He kindly led you back home, far away from the roads that would have taken you to Hell and kept you prisoner forever. Oh my soul, praise Him by loving Him with all your heart! My soul, God knew you were afraid because, deep down, you knew that you were sinful and could not come back to God on your own. (Ecclesiastes 3:11, John 14:6) That's when God shined hope on you like a light to show you the way home. He pointed to the cross, and showed you that you were safe—Jesus had paid for your sins. (Hebrews 12:1-2)

Praise, my soul, the God that sought thee,
Wretched wand'rer far astray;
Found thee lost, and kindly brought thee
From the paths of death away.
Praise, with love's devoutest feeling,
Him who saw thy guilt-born fear,
And, the light of hope revealing,
Bade the blood-stained cross appear.

....

My soul, praise God, your Savior who gave you Jesus' cross! God took away your old, sinful life and gave you a new one. (2 Corinthians 5:17, Romans 6:10-11) Sin must be paid for with blood (Hebrews 9:22), and Jesus' perfect blood, shed on that cross, was enough to pay for all of your sins. (Hebrews 9:13-14) God showed you that cross, and told you that if you trusted that Jesus' blood could save you, you would be forgiven of *all* your sins. (John 11:25-26) Oh my soul, praise God for His grace! At first you were scared when that grace showed you how sinful you were. But how good it really was, because it woke you up before it was too late! God's grace showed you that you needed to be saved, and then it showed you *how* to be saved. My soul, praise God for His grace, which brought your sin-dead heart back to life. (Ephesians 2:1-7, Isaiah 57:15) Praise God for His grace, which gave you peace with your Heavenly Father again! (Romans 5:1)

Praise thy Savior God that drew thee
To that cross, new life to give,
Held a blood-sealed pardon to thee,
Bade thee look to Him and live.
Praise the grace whose threats alarmed thee,
Roused thee from thy fatal ease;
Praise the grace whose promise warmed thee,
Praise the grace that whispered peace.

....

Lord God, I can feel it—my heart is warm with love for you because of all you have done for me. But I'm not able to put that love into words of praise such as you deserve! So I humbly kneel down at your feet, my God, and I ask you to have compassion on me and bless my prayer. (Romans 8:26) Lord, your love is my most valuable treasure. Let *your* perfect love come into my heart and light *my* weak love on fire, so that I will be able to praise you as I ought to. Since no mere words could ever say enough about you, let the way I live be praise for you!

Lord, this bosom's ardent feeling
Vainly would my lips express;
Low before thy footstool kneeling,
Deign thy suppliant's pray'r to bless.
Let thy love, my soul's chief treasure,
Love's pure flame within me raise;
And, since words can never measure,
Let my life show forth thy praise.

LOVED WITH EVERLASTING LOVE

Lyrics by **George Wade Robinson**, 1890
Revised by **Edmund Prosper Clowney**, 1986
Set to the tune *Everlasting Love*

I am greatly loved, and it is a love that will last forever, because it is *God's* love. (Jeremiah 31:3) God pulled me close to Him with His grace (Galatians 1:15), and then He wrapped me in His love. Holy Spirit who lives in my heart, you remind me every day that this is true! (John 15:26) Oh, what a precious, complete peace I have in my heart, because God has brought me near to Him. (Colossians 3:15) God holds me close with a love that is not even *able* to fade away, because it is the love of God Himself. (Ezra 3:11, Psalm 118) I belong to God, and God has given Himself to me. (Romans 8:15-17, Ephesians 1:13-14)

Loved with everlasting love,
Drawn by grace that love to know,
Spirit sent from Christ above,
Thou dost witness it is so.
O this full and precious peace
From His presence all divine;
In a love that cannot cease,
I am His and He is mine.

....

Ever since God opened my eyes and showed me His love, to my eyes the sky seems to be even more blue, and the earth is a more lovely green than it used to be! God is teaching me to see His Creation the way it was always meant to be seen. (John 9:25, Isaiah 42:6-7) Someone who lives in sin, separate from God, is blinded by their sin. If they do not have Christ in their heart, they cannot see

God and His ways. Yet God has let me see the *true* beauty of His Creation! When I hear the birds' songs, I can hear that they are really songs about God's glory. (Luke 19:37-41) The flowers I see are even more breathtaking ever since I first knew what I know now: that I belong to God, and God has given Himself to me.

Heav'n above is deeper blue,
Earth around is sweeter green;
That which glows in every hue
Christless eyes have never seen.
Birds in song His glories show,
Flowers with richer beauties shine
Since I know, as now I know,
I am His and He is mine.

....

My friend, if you get even a small taste of God's goodness, you will understand! (Psalm 34:8) Come and be welcomed home to God. He showed us how much love He has for us by pouring it out in Jesus' blood on the cross, when God took the punishment for our sins so that we would not have to. (Ephesians 5:2, Hebrews 2:9) How could I possibly doubt whether He loves me, when I think of that cross and remember what awful suffering God chose to take on *because* He loves me? (Romans 5:8-10) Because God Himself died on the cross at Calvary to buy my freedom from sin, I belong to Him, and He has given Himself to me. (Ephesians 2:13)

Taste the goodness of the Lord:
Welcomed home to His embrace,
All His love as blood outpoured
Seals the pardon of His grace.
Can I doubt His love for me,
When I trace that love's design?
By the cross of Calvary,
I am His and He is mine.

....

I am God's forever, and *only* His. Who could pull me out of the arms of God? No one! (John 10:28-29, Romans 8:31-39) Oh, my friends, Christ fills the hearts of those who love Him with perfect calm and joy. (Romans 15:13) The skies and this earth will fade away and disappear someday. All sunrises eventually become sunsets. But as long as God and I both exist (and that will be for eternity!), I will belong to God, and He will be mine. (Matthew 24:35)

His forever, only His—
Who the Lord and me shall part?
Ah, with what a rest of bliss
Christ can fill the loving heart.
Heav'n and earth may fade and flee,
Firstborn light in gloom decline,
But while God and I shall be,
I am His and He is mine.

MAKE ME A CAPTIVE, LORD

Lyrics by **George Matheson** (see page 315), 1890

Set to the tunes *Leominster—Paradoxy—St. Bride—Llanllyfni—Diademata—Ich Halte Treulich Still—Trentham—Corona—Hosanna*

Lord Jesus, please make me your prisoner—only then will I be truly free! (Ephesians 3:1, 6:5-6) Force me to surrender to you, make me give up my sword, and then I will be a conqueror. (James 4:7) If I have to depend on my own strength to fight the battles of this life, I will sink and drown in all the terrors of this world. (Psalm 69:1-3, Ephesians 2:1-10) Jesus, please, imprison me in your arms instead, and hold me close, and *then* my hands will be strong for fighting against evil. (2 Samuel 22:35)

Make me a captive, Lord,
And then I shall be free;
Force me to render up my sword,
And I shall conqu'ror be;
I sink in life's alarms
When by myself I stand;
Imprison me within thine arms,
And strong shall be my hand.

....

On its own, my heart is weak and useless in the battle against sin. (Matthew 9:36) My heart needs a master to serve, to give it a reason to keep on when the battle is hard! Unless I have a master to serve, my sword strokes against evil will not cut where they should. If even the wind blows against me, I turn off of the path I'm supposed to be following. I don't have a master telling me where to go, and that means I'm lost. I was created to serve *you*, Jesus, so I cannot be free unless I'm chained to you. (1 Peter 2:25) Be my master, Jesus, for you love me more than anyone else does. If you make me your servant, Lord, then my heart will never die—it will reign in Heaven with you forever! (John 6:5, Romans 6:16-18)

My heart is weak and poor
Until it master find;
It has no spring of action sure—
It varies with the wind;
It cannot freely move
Till thou hast wrought its chain;
Enslave it with thy matchless love,
And deathless it shall reign.

....

All my "strength" is actually weakness until I have learned to serve a master. Without a master, my heart doesn't have the fire it needs to burn strong. I don't have anyone to tell me, "Have courage!" (Acts 23:11, 2 Corinthians 5:6-8) I cannot be the master of anything this world unless *I myself* am under a master. (1 Corinthians 9:24-26) Jesus, my battle flag against Satan and sin will do nothing at all until you breathe a wind from Heaven to make it fly.

My pow'r is faint and low
Till I have learned to serve;
It wants the needed fire to glow,
It wants the breeze to nerve;
It cannot drive the world
Until itself be driv'n;
Its flag can only be unfurled
When thou shalt breathe from heav'n.

....

I cannot be the master of my own mind until you are its master first, Jesus. If my ambition is to be a king or a ruler, I cannot rule anything until I give you the crown. There is only one way my strength will be able to stand up straight and not be wounded in the battle: I must lean on you, Jesus, and not depend on myself to be strong enough. (Psalm 121:3, Philippians 4:12-13) My strength can only be alive and active if you are its life!

My will is not my own
Till thou hast made it thine;
If it would reach a monarch's throne,
It must its crown resign;
It only stands unbent,
Amid the clashing strife,
When on thy bosom I have leaned,
And found in thee its life.

MY HOPE IS BUILT ON NOTHING LESS

Lyrics by **Edward Mote**, 1834

Set to the tunes *Solid Rock—Melita—St. Catherine—Magdalen—St. Petersburg—Stella—St. Chrysostom—Elton—Petra—Eisenach—Nashville—My Hope is Built—Admah—Filmore—Snelling—Baynard—Wavertree—Louvan—Confidence—Surrey—Connie Lynn—Saxby—Arizona*—and more

What an unshakeable reason I have for being hopeful! My hope is based on nothing other than Jesus Himself, and I refuse to trust in anything less. I know His blood that He shed for me was more than enough to pay the penalty for my sins (Hebrews 9:11-14), and He has wrapped His righteousness around me like a robe so that I can stand before God, cleaned of my sins. (Isaiah 61:10) This world will tempt me to trust in myself, or another person, but I don't dare trust anything other than Jesus. I know I am not enough, but *Jesus is*—and He is the reason I have the hope of eternal life! (Ephesians 2:8-9)

Refrain: So here I stand! I trust in Christ, my steady rock who will never change. (Matthew 7:24-25) There is no other safe place to stand. (Acts 4:11-12) To trust in anyone except Christ to save me would be like standing on deadly quicksand. (Matthew 7:26-27) I stand on Christ, my solid rock!

My hope is built on nothing less
Than Jesus' blood and righteousness;
I dare not trust the sweetest frame,
But wholly lean on Jesus' name.
(Refrain)
On Christ, the solid rock, I stand;
All other ground is sinking sand.

When the troubles in my life make Jesus feel far away and hidden from me, I will remember the grace that He showed me when He first saved me—and I'll remember that His grace is still the same. (Psalm 22:1-11) Even though I don't *feel* Him near me, I can know that He has not left me alone. So when the storms of life try to knock me over with their strong winds and toss me around on their dangerous waves, I will have an anchor to hold me upright: Jesus Christ! (Hebrews 6:17-20)

When darkness veils His lovely face,
I rest on His unchanging grace;
In every high and stormy gale
My anchor holds within the veil.

....

When I feel as if I'm drowning in an ocean of sadness and trouble, I will remember my Lord. (Jonah 2) I will remember that He swore to never leave me. (Hebrews 13:5-6, Matthew 28:19-20) I will remember that God my Father made a covenant with me and all of His children, and promised to be our God *forever,* no matter what. (Jeremiah 31:33, Hebrews 8:10) I will remember the blood that Jesus was willing to shed to pay the price that would set me free from my sins! (Romans 8:2, Hebrews 2:9-10) Remembering these things will keep me standing up, even under the heavy waves of life that crash down on my head. (Luke 21:16-18) Even if *everything* in my world is washed away, Jesus will still be there to hold on to me... and to remind me that I still have the hope of Heaven! (Philippians 4:12-13)

His oath, His covenant, His blood
Support me in the whelming flood;
When all around my soul gives way,
He then is all my hope and stay.

....

One day, Jesus will come back to this earth. Angels will blow the Heavenly trumpets to tell us, "Your King is coming!" When He comes in all His glory,

He will judge all the people who have ever been. (Romans 2:15-16, Revelation 20:11-15) Oh God, when He judges me, let Him find that I have been trusting in nothing except Him! (Philippians 3:8-11) Let it be seen that I belong to Him. Then He will bring me home to Heaven with Him, and there, wearing Jesus' perfection around me like a royal robe, clean and sinless, I will stand before the throne of God my Father. (Revelation 7:9-17)

When He shall come with trumpet sound,
O may I then in Him be found;
Dressed in His righteousness alone,
Faultless to stand before the throne.

O COME, O COME, EMMANUEL

Lyrics from Latin antiphons (short chants) of the 12th century, made into a Latin hymn in 1710

Translated by **John Mason Neale** (see page 344) in 1851

Set to the tunes *Veni Immanuel (plainsong chant)—Veni Immanuel (Goudon)—St. Petersburg—Benison—Careys—Lux Prima—The First Noel—Spires*—and more

---

Note: This hymn is written as if it is being sung by the Israelites while they waited centuries for God to send the Messiah He had promised them. Now, that Messiah has already come. We sing "O Come, O Come, Emmanuel" during Advent to remember how God's people longed for Jesus to come, and to rejoice that we don't have to wait!

....

Oh come, please come, Emmanuel, our promised Messiah! Your name means "God with us," and oh, how we long for God to be with us, to set us free from our slavery to sin. (Isaiah 7:14-15, Matthew 1:20-23) Emmanuel, we grieve because our sin keeps us separate from you. (Psalm 5:4) We cannot save ourselves... we will have to suffer this exile away from God until our Savior, the Son of God, appears on earth. (Romans 5:8-12) But Israel, rejoice! Be joyful and remember your hope, children of God: Emmanuel, our God with us, *will come.* (Isaiah 9:6-7)

O come, O come, Emmanuel,
And ransom captive Israel,
That mourns in lonely exile here,
Until the Son of God appear.
(Refrain)
Rejoice! Rejoice! Emmanuel
Shall come to thee, O Israel.

....

Please come to us, Emmanuel! You are the living Wisdom of God, and you use your wisdom and mighty hand to control everything that happens. (1 Corinthians 1:30-31, 1 Corinthians 1:22-24) Come and teach us your wisdom, and show us how to live wisely here on earth. Dear Israel, rejoice! Be joyful and remember your hope, children of God: Emmanuel, our God with us, *will come*. (Micah 5:2)

O come, thou Wisdom from on high,
Who orders all things mightily;
To us the path of knowledge show,
And teach us in her ways to go.
Rejoice! Rejoice! Emmanuel
Shall come to thee, O Israel.

....

Oh, please come, Emmanuel, descendant of Jesse! (Isaiah 11:1-10) Set your dear children free from their slavery to Satan. Save your people from falling into the deep pit of Hell because of their sins! Give us victory over death, so that we will not be forever separated from God after we die—for if you do, we will have no more reason to fear the grave. (Isaiah 25:8) Oh Israel, rejoice! Be joyful and remember your hope, children of God: Emmanuel, our God with us, will come. (Jeremiah 31:31-31, Hebrews 8:10-11, Luke 22:20)

O come, thou Rod of Jesse, free
Thine own from Satan's tyranny;
From depths of Hell thy people save,
And give them vict'ry o'er the grave.
Rejoice! Rejoice! Emmanuel
Shall come to thee, O Israel.

....

Please come to us, Mighty Lord, highest ruler of all Creation! (Psalm 2, Deuteronomy 10:14) Long ago, you gathered the tribes of Israel at Mount Sinai and taught us your law. You are too glorious for our human eyes to see, so you hid yourself in thunder and clouds that day. Yet even then, your voice, your power, and your majesty terrified us so much that we fell on our faces in awe. (Exodus 19-20) But Israel, rejoice! Be joyful and remember your hope, children of God: Emmanuel, God who will live with us, *will come.* (Matthew 1:23)

O come, O come, thou Lord of might,
Who to thy tribes, on Sinai's height,
In ancient times didst give the law
In cloud and majesty and awe.
Rejoice! Rejoice! Emmanuel
Shall come to thee, O Israel.

....

Please come to us, Emmanuel! Your coming will be like the sunrise, suddenly spilling its light on us when we had been sitting in darkness for so long. You will set us free from that darkness of sin. Cheer our sad hearts by coming to us, Messiah, Dawn of Heaven! Let your light chase away sin's clouds, which have hidden God from our eyes. We are like dead people, wandering in our sin until you come. Fill us with the light and life of Heaven, and send death and sin's shadows running! Oh Israel, rejoice. Be joyful and remember your hope, children of God: Emmanuel, our God with us, *will come.* (Jeremiah 32:39-41, Hebrews 9:15)

O come, thou Dayspring from on high,
And cheer us by thy drawing nigh;
Disperse the gloomy clouds of night,
And death's dark shadows put to flight.
Rejoice! Rejoice! Emmanuel
Shall come to thee, O Israel.

....

Come to us, Emmanuel! You will be called the Key of David, for you will be a Heavenly King descended from David, and you will hold the key that opens and shuts the doors of Heaven. (Revelation 1:17-18, 3:7) Emmanuel, open wide Heaven's doors for us, so that we may come home to you! If we have to rely on our own goodness to get us to Heaven, we are not safe at all, for we cannot keep ourselves from falling into sin. Open the road to Heaven, and keep us safely on it! (2 Timothy 4:18, Philippians 1:6) Lock the gates that lead to sin and death in Hell, so that our sin cannot drag us there again. Israel, rejoice! Be joyful and remember your hope, children of God: Emmanuel, our God with us, *will come.* (Isaiah 53)

O come, thou Key of David, come
And open wide our heav'nly home;
Make safe the way that leads on high,
And close the path to misery.
Rejoice! Rejoice! Emmanuel
Shall come to thee, O Israel.

....

Come to us, our long-awaited Messiah! Every nation who fears God knows that He has promised to send you, and we long for you to come, Emmanuel. When you come, you will have fulfilled our greatest desire! (Haggai 2:7) Come and unite our hearts, so that we will no longer bicker and be divided. (1 Corinthians 1:10, John 10:14-16) You will be our Prince of Peace (Micah 5:4-5, Isaiah 9:6), who gives us peace with God and peace with each other. Dear Israel, rejoice! Be joyful and remember your hope, children of God: Emmanuel, our God with us, *will come.*

O come, Desire of nations, bind
In one the hearts of humankind;
O bid our sad divisions cease,
And be for us our King of Peace.
Rejoice! Rejoice! Emmanuel
Shall come to thee, O Israel.

O FOR A THOUSAND TONGUES TO SING

Lyrics by **Charles Wesley** (see page 336), 1739

Set to the tunes *Azmon—Blessed Name—Lyngham (Desert)—Richmond—Antioch—Northfield—Coronation—Lydia—Nativity—Hummel—St. Agnes—Winchester Old—Ortonville—Beatitudo—Selby—St. Martin—Brown (Bradbury)—University—Miles Lane—Arlington—Evan—Tallis—Howard—Dedham—Sawley—Arabia—Halsey—Holston—Annawon—Oxford New—Expectation—Mason's Chant—Colchester—Clifford—Newbold—Mary—Jubilate—Fountain—Stracathro—Tune 419 (Gauntlett)—Groningen—Dundee—Emmanuel—Geneva—Lobt Gott, Ihr Christen—Stratford-on-Avon—Bedford—Wiltshire—York Tune—Southwark—Epworth—Azmon's Ghost—Arden—Christmas (Handel)—Belmont—Nativity—Tiverton—Mount Zion—Rochester—New Bethel*—and more

---

If only I had a thousand mouths, so that I could sing praise to God a thousand times more than I can now! I would sing praises to my Savior, my God, who bought me back when I was sin's slave. (Romans 6:16-18) I would sing of how glorious is my God, my King Jesus, and of how His grace always defeats sin! (Ephesians 1:7-8)

O for a thousand tongues to sing
My great Redeemer's praise,
The glories of my God and king,
The triumphs of His grace!

....

God, my loving master, I am not capable of worshipping you the way you deserve. Please help me, so that I can sing about your glory for the world to hear. Help me to spread the news of what you have done for your people, so that the world will know what honor your name deserves. (Psalm 71:15, 111:1)

My gracious master and my God,
Assist me to proclaim,

To spread through all the earth abroad
The honors of Thy name.

....

"Jesus!" That is the only name that reminds us we have no reason to be afraid, and tells the sadness in our hearts to be gone. (Romans 8:31-39) To a sinner who has been saved by Jesus' blood, hearing the sound of His name is like hearing lovely music. For us, His people, thinking about Jesus gives life and health to our souls and fills our hearts with peace. (1 Corinthians 1:18, John 20:30-31)

Jesus! the name that charms our fears,
That bids our sorrows cease;
'Tis music in the sinner's ears,
'Tis life, and health, and peace.

....

Jesus' blood paid the price for our sins, so they no longer count against us. (Hebrews 9:22, Matthew 26:27-28) He throws them far away from us, for sin no longer has any power over us. (Romans 6:13-15) Jesus' blood can pay for all the sins of even the filthiest sinner (1 Corinthians 6:9-11)—I know it's true, for His blood saved *me!*

He breaks the power of canceled sin,
He sets the prisoner free;
His blood can make the foulest clean,
His blood availed for me.

....

When Jesus calls their names, sinners who have been like dead men, lost in their sins, are set free and come alive. (Romans 8:29-30) When Jesus speaks to His people, all their broken hearts are filled with joy again. (Psalm 34:18) When He speaks, the ones who worried that they were too lowly to be remembered by Jesus can believe that He died to save them, too. (Matthew 5:3)

He speaks, and, listening to His voice,
New life the dead receive,
The mournful, broken hearts rejoice,
The humble poor believe.

....

All you who have been deaf, now hear Jesus' voice! All you who couldn't speak, use your healed tongues to sing His praises! You who were blind, see your Savior coming to you! You who couldn't walk, leap and dance for joy that Christ has saved you! (Luke 7:18-23, Mark 7:37)

Hear Him, ye deaf; His praise, ye dumb,
Your loosened tongues employ;
Ye blind, behold your Savior come,
And leap, ye lame, for joy.

....

If you will trust Jesus Christ as your master and Lord (Colossians 1:18), and believe that His blood is enough to save you, then you will know for certain that your sins are all forgiven. (Acts 2:38, 16:29-31, John 10:7-10) You will live here on earth knowing that everlasting life in Heaven is waiting for you—and until then, just knowing that Christ loves you as His own will be a tiny taste of Heaven here on earth. (Philippians 1:21)

In Christ your head, you then shall know,
Shall feel your sins forgiven;
Anticipate your Heaven below,
And own that love is Heaven.

....

Let all glory, praise, and love be given to God at all times, forever! (Jude 1:24-25) Let all His children on earth, and all His children in Heaven, give Him that praise. For they are all part of His Church, whether they are in Heaven or still on earth.

Glory to God, and praise and love
Be ever, ever given,
By saints below and saints above,
The Church in earth and Heaven.

....

On the day when Christ called my name and set me free from my sins, it was as if the sun rose for the first time and shone its light all through my soul, which had been sleeping in darkness till then. (Isaiah 9:2, Ephesians 5:13-14) He filled my soul with peace and rest by showing me that He was everything I needed. (Philippians 4:19)

On this glad day the glorious sun
Of righteousness arose;
On my benighted soul He shone
And filled it with repose.

....

Suddenly, all my struggling to be "good enough" was over. I understood that I didn't have to live perfectly in line with God's law in order to be saved. (Romans 3:20-26) After Christ saved me, I no longer had to grieve that I could *never* be good enough—because I didn't have to be! Christ was all I needed. Christ lived perfectly for me. (Romans 10:4, Hebrews 2:17-18) My old, sinful life died, and my new life in Christ—my first *real* life—began. (Romans 6:9-11)

Sudden expired the legal strife,
'Twas then I ceased to grieve;
My second, real, living life
I then began to live.

....

That was when my heart first believed that Jesus had saved me. (Romans 10:9) God sent the Holy Spirit to live in my heart forever, and gave me the faith I needed to believe that Jesus is my Savior. (John 20:21-22)

Then with my heart I first believed,
Believed with faith divine,
Power with the Holy Ghost received
To call the Savior mine.

....

I knew in my heart that my Lord Jesus' blood, shed on the cross to pay for sins, had been applied to *my* sins. I knew that He loves me... the Son of God Himself loves even *me!* (Romans 5:8) And for me He was willing to die, so that He could pay the punishment for my sins and set me free. (Ephesians 5:2) How wonderful it is that Jesus would even love *me!* (Psalm 8:3-5)

I felt my Lord's atoning blood
Close to my soul applied;
Me, me He loved, the Son of God,
For me, for me He died!

....

I saw in Scripture where God promised to save His people who trust in Jesus, His Son, and I believed then that it was true. (Zechariah 9:9, Isaiah 7:14, 9:6-7) God gave me the faith to be certain that Jesus came to save *me too*. (1 John 3:24) God, the Judge of all, had pardoned all my sins in the court of Heaven—and I knew this because He wrote that pardon on my heart. (Hebrews 10:15-17)

I found and owned His promise true,
Ascertained of my part,
My pardon passed in Heaven I knew
When written on my heart.

....

All you nations of the world, look to Christ! All people of this world, He is your God, so praise Him! (1 John 4:14, Mark 13:10, Matthew 28:18-20) Every one of us is born a sinner (Romans 3:23), and He is our only hope (John 14:6)—so go and be saved by Him. You can only be saved by trusting that

Christ's blood is enough to save you. (Ephesians 2:8-9) So trust in Christ, all you peoples, and His grace will cover your sins!

Look unto Him, ye nations, own
Your God, ye fallen race;
Look, and be saved through faith alone,
Be justified by grace.

....

When you trust that Jesus' blood will save you, look and see that all of your sins have been taken off of you and laid on Him. Jesus Christ was killed once, like a lamb for the sacrifice; He was the final offering that paid for every sin of God's people. (Isaiah 53)

See all your sins on Jesus laid:
The Lamb of God was slain,
His soul was once an offering made
For every soul of man.

....

For all of your life until now, you have been asleep in your sins ... now you are being awakened. (Ephesians 2:1-7) Now that you belong to Him, Christ will give you His light to guide you through life. (2 Corinthians 4:6) He will take all your sins off of you and throw them away to sink in the ocean, where they will never be remembered again. (Micah 7:19) Can a dark-skinned man make his skin turn white? Can a leopard make his spots disappear? No—and it is just as impossible for us to fix the sinful nature with which we are all born. (Jeremiah 13:23) But Christ does the impossible: He changes our nature and washes our sinful hearts clean! (Romans 8:1-4)

Awake from guilty nature's sleep,
And Christ shall give you light,

Cast all your sins into the deep,
And wash the Aethiop* white.

....

No sin is too much for Christ's blood to cover—even cheaters and thieves have been saved, and now they are winners in the war against sin because they belong to Christ. (Matthew 9:11-12) Any sinner who believes that Christ is His Savior will be saved. (Romans 10:12-13) I know that no sin is too much for Christ to wash away, because He was able to wash away *my* terrible sins! (1 John 2:2)

Harlots and publicans and thieves
In holy triumph join!
Saved is the sinner that believes,
From crimes as great as mine.

....

Murderers, sinners, all of you who have lived in Hell's ways instead of God's ways, you can be saved too. (Luke 19:9-11, Colossians 3:5-8) Christ has won the war against Satan, and we who belong to Christ join in His victory, too! (Romans 8:16-18, 37) For us to be saved, you must believe that Christ died on the cross to pay the price for your sins, and I must believe that He died to pay for mine.

Murderers and all ye Hellish crew
In holy triumph join!
Believe the Savior died for you;
For me the Savior died.

....

* "Aethiop" is an archaic term for a person from Ethiopia. This stanza is a direct reference to Jeremiah 13:23, which says, "Can the Ethiopian change his skin or the leopard his spots? Then also you can do good who are accustomed to do evil." (ESV)

I am the worst sinner of all—I'm the *chief* of sinners. So if Christ's blood can pay for my sins, He can pay for yours too! (1 Timothy 1:12-16) Come, belong to Christ with me, and then you will know in your heart that your sins have been forgiven, and that they do not count against you anymore. (1 John 2:12) We will live here on earth knowing that everlasting life in Heaven is waiting for us, and knowing that Christ loves us will be like tasting Heaven here on earth. (Hebrews 12:1-3)

With me, your chief, ye then shall know,
Shall feel your sins forgiven;
Anticipate your Heaven below,
And own that love is Heaven.

O GOD OF EARTH AND ALTAR

Lyrics by **Gilbert Keith Chesterton** (see page 290), 1906

Set to the tunes *King's Lynn—Llangloffan—Lancashire—Gilling—Willsbridge*

Oh God, Maker of this earth, and the God whom we worship (Exodus 20:24), bend down close to us and hear our cry for help! Our earthly leaders are weak. (1 Samuel 15:10-11) Our people wander away from your truth (Jeremiah 14:10), and they are walking dead men because they do not have your life in them. Our precious money and possessions are stacking up around us, and these earthly things we have loved are building our tomb! Our beloved "stuff" will be the death of us, because it has distracted us from you, God. (Luke 18:24, Psalm 39:6, Jeremiah 15:13) God, your children fight with each other, and now we are divided from our brothers and sisters in Christ. (1 Corinthians 6:7) We are full of thunder and good fighting spirit, but we use it the wrong way. God, don't take away that thunder from us, because it is from you—but God, teach us to use it *rightly* (2 Corinthians 13:10), and take away the pride in our hearts that divides us! (1 Peter 5:5)

O God of earth and altar,
Bow down and hear our cry,
Our earthly rulers falter,
Our people drift and die;
The walls of gold entomb us,
The swords of scorn divide,
Take not thy thunder from us,
But take away our pride.

....

Oh God, please save us from acting based on our fears. (2 Timothy 1:7, Romans 8:14-15) Save us from believing the lies that we hear and read. (Isaiah 10:1, John 8:44) Never let us comfort ourselves with the lie that "we're not *really* bad people" (Proverbs 30:20)—that is the lie that evil men tell themselves, so they can keep on sinning! We will not be forgiven if we do not confess our sin to you. (1 John 1:8-9) Save us from selling our honor by giving in to people's threats when we should have stood strong (Acts 4:29-30), and save us from distorting this fighting spirit that you've given us by using it to hurt our fellow men. (1 Thessalonians 5:11) Save us from getting lazy and sluggish, or else we won't see the dangers around us. (Matthew 24:42, Mark 14:38) Above all, save us from being forever separated from you in Hell, good Lord! (Revelation 20:13-15)

From all that terror teaches,
From lies of tongue and pen,
From all the easy speeches
That comfort cruel men,
From sale and profanation
Of honour and the sword,
From sleep and from damnation,
Deliver us, good Lord!

....

Lord, call all kinds of people: princes, priests, and even slaves, and tie all our lives together so that together we will be your one people. (Acts 10:34-35) Punish us when we sin against you (Proverbs 3:11-12), and save us all from our sins by washing us clean in Christ's blood. (Revelation 7:13-17) Make us one united people, full of righteous anger against evil, and victorious over sin with Christ. When you make us yours, we will burn with faith, free from our sins, and we will be like a sword in your hand, our God!

Tie in a living tether
The prince and priest and thrall,
Bind all our lives together,

Smite us and save us all;
In ire and exultation
Aflame with faith, and free,
Lift up a living nation,
A single sword to thee.

O LOVE OF GOD, HOW STRONG AND TRUE

Lyrics by **Horatius Bonar** (see page 284) 1858

Set to the tunes *Brookfield—De Tar—Martham—Ombersley—Eisenach—Jerusalem (Parry)—Wareham—Louvan—Holley—Rockingham Old—Alfreton—Merthyr Tydfil—Bow Brickhill—Dedicare—Dunedin—Maryton—Intercession Old—Abends—Herr Jesu Christ, Wahr'r Mensch—El Paran—Sweden—Via Bona*

How strong and trustworthy is God's love! God's has loved His people since before He ever made them or the world (Psalm 90:1-2), yet His love is *still* new and fresh every day. (Lamentations 3:22-23) No one can understand God's love, and no one can buy or earn it. (Ephesians 2:8-9) His love is beyond what any human mind can imagine. (Romans 11:33-36) How deep and wide is God's love for us! Find the deepest hatred on earth, and God's love will be still deeper. God's love does not depend on anyone else—it is like a torch that burns with a fire that it lit by itself. (Acts 17:24-25) God's love for His children never changes; it will never die, and it will never run out. (Romans 8:38-39)

O love of God, how strong and true!
Eternal and yet ever new,
Uncomprehended and unbought,
Beyond all knowledge and all thought!
O love of God, how deep and great,
Far deeper than man's deepest hate;
Self-fed, self-kindled like the light,
Changeless, eternal, infinite.

....

How precious is that love from Heaven when our hearts are tired and sick. When we are helpless, when there is so much trouble in life that we stay awake all night and worry, how good it is to have God's love there to heal our bodies, comfort our hearts, and bless us! (Psalm 34:17-22) God's love is like His arms stretched wide to hold all His many children! We are amazed at God's love for us. We can see God's love in the sky—He made that beautiful sky for us to enjoy. (Psalm 19:1) We see His love in the earth around us—look at this marvelous home He made for us! (Acts 14:17) We see God's love written in the seas, the streams, the rivers, and all of Creation.

O heav'nly love, how precious still,
In days of weariness and ill,
In nights of pain and helplessness,
To heal, to comfort, and to bless!
O wide-embracing, wondrous love!
We read you in the sky above,
We read you in the earth below,
In seas that swell, and streams that flow.

....

But we can see God's love *best of all* when we think of the one God sent to take the punishment of our sins for us—Jesus Christ. (Romans 5:8, 1 John 4:9) Jesus was sent to earth by our Heavenly Father so that He could live a human life without sin, and then die. He was the perfect sacrifice who was killed instead of *us*. (Hebrews 10:1-18) Through Jesus, we see that God has the power to bless and save—even to save us from eternal death! (1 Corinthians 1:18, Revelation 2:10-11) God, how much more we see your love and awesome power when we remember that one day, you will raise all your children to life again, and we will live with you forever. (Revelation 21:1-4)

We read you best in Him who came
To bear for us the cross of shame;
Sent by the Father from on high,
Our life to live, our death to die.
We read your pow'r to bless and save,
E'en in the darkness of the grave;

Still more in resurrection light
We read the fulness of your might.

....

God's love for us is the shield that protects us from Satan, and the strong arm that holds us up when we are weak and surrounded by dangers. (Psalm 18:2) God, you are eternal love itself, and we trust in you. With you we are safe and blessed, now and forever. We honor and worship you, God our King, and we will praise your name forever! Day after day, we will sing and tell this world how good you are to us (Psalm 45:17, 145:1-2), and we will spend eternity shouting your praises. (Revelation 15:3-4)

O love of God, our shield and stay
Through all the perils of our way!
Eternal love, in you we rest,
Forever safe, forever blest.
We will exalt you, God and King,
And we will ever praise your name;
We will extol you ev'ry day,
And evermore your praise proclaim.

O LOVE THAT WILT NOT LET ME GO

Lyrics by **George Matheson** (see page 315), 1882

Set to the tunes *St. Margaret (Peace)—Mallet—Consecration—Teneor—Es Ist Gewisslich—La Monte—Donna—Parker*—and more

Because He loves me, God refuses to let go of me. (Nehemiah 1:5, Psalm 136:2, Romans 8:38-39) Love of God, I rest my tired heart on you! Love of God, I will spend my life serving you, because I owe my life to you. (Ephesians 2:1-7) Without your help, the love *I* can give is weak and shallow... but God, if you will take my pitiful little stream of love, you will make it overflow with your deep *oceans* of love.

O Love that wilt not let me go,
I rest my weary soul in thee;
I give thee back the life I owe,
That in thine ocean depths its flow
May richer, fuller be.

....

God's Word is like light shining on my dark path so that I can see where to go. That light of God stays with me wherever I go, and it will never abandon me. (Psalm 119:105) Oh light of God, my life is like a flickering torch, about to blow out, but I give it to you! You gave my heart all the light it has, so here: I give it back to you. God, *your* light is brighter than the sun, and your light will rekindle my light so that my life will shine brighter and more alive than it ever has. (2 Corinthians 4:6)

O Light that follow'st all my way,
I yield my flick'ring torch to thee;
My heart restores its borrowed ray,

That in thy sunshine's blaze its day
May brighter, fairer be.

....

Even when I am in pain and suffering, the joy of God follows me. So even in hard times, I am never without joy. (Habakkuk 3:17-18, Nehemiah 8:10) Oh joy of God, I cannot close the doors of my heart when you come knocking—I can't help but let you fill me! It is when I am in the rain, the dark times of life, that the rainbow appears to remind me that God did not make an empty promise when He said that, one day, I will open my eyes and see Him face-to-face (Genesis 9:13, 1 Thessalonians 4:16-17) There will be no more sadness after *that* happy morning! (Revelation 21:4)

O Joy that seekest me through pain
I cannot close my heart to thee;
I trace the rainbow through the rain,
And feel the promise is not vain
That morn shall tearless be.

....

I take courage when I remember that Christ died on the cross to buy my freedom from sin. If Christ has saved me, what can anything on earth do to me? (John 10:27-29) Oh cross of Christ, I cannot dream of walking away from you! In my heart, I bow down on the ground at the foot of Christ's cross. All the empty glory of my old life is dead and gone. (Romans 6:11) Christ's blood there on the ground at Mt. Calvary is what paid the price of my sins (Hebrews 9:13-14), and from the blood of Christ comes my new, eternal life with God. (Romans 5:21, 6:23)

O Cross that liftest up my head,
I dare not ask to fly from thee;
I lay in dust, life's glory dead,
And from the ground there blossoms red
Life that shall endless be.

O LOVE, HOW DEEP, HOW BROAD, HOW HIGH!

Lyrics traditionally attributed to **Thomas Á Kempis**, 15th century

Originally written in Latin; translated by **Benjamin Webb** in 1854–1871

Set to the tunes *Deo Gracias (or Agincourt Hymn)—Eisenach—Puer Nobis Nascitur—Deus Tuorum Militum—Ombersley—O Amor Quam Exstaticus—Rivaulx—Zephyr—De Tar—Intercession Old—Hebron—Eden—Melcombe—Infinite Love—Rockingham Old—Russia*—and more

---

How much love our God has for us! God's love is deeper, wider, and higher than our minds are able to understand or imagine. (Deuteronomy 7:9, Nehemiah 9:17, Psalm 86:15) How could we ever understand how God could love us enough to be willing to become human for our sake? (Romans 5:8)

O Love, how deep, how broad, how high,
How passing thought and fantasy,
That God, the Son of God, should take
Our mortal form for mortals' sake!

....

God our Father didn't send an angel to us; not a low angel, and not even the highest-ranking angel. (Isaiah 63:9) Instead, God sent *Himself*. Jesus, who was God Himself, came down to earth and put on a human body, so that He could give us the salvation we desperately needed. (1 Timothy 2:5-6)

He sent no angel to our race
Of higher or of lower place,
But wore the robe of human frame,
And He himself to this world came.

....

God came to earth because He wanted to—because He loves us! (John 7:28-29) And He did not simply appear and then vanish again; no, Jesus, the God-man, chose to stay with mankind for thirty-three years. (Philippians 2:5-7)

Nor willed He only to appear,
His pleasure was to tarry here;
And God and Man with man would be
The space of thirty years and three.

....

The Son of God was baptized for our sake. (Matthew 3:13-17) For our sake Jesus endured forty days of hunger and temptation in the desert. (Matthew 4:1-11) Because He has endured temptation, He sympathizes with us when we are being tempted. But unlike us, *He* did not give in to the temptation and sin. (Hebrews 4:15) For our sake, Jesus won the test and threw Satan off the throne in our hearts, so that sin cannot rule us anymore. (Galatians 2:20, Romans 6:10-14)

For us baptized, for us He bore
His holy fast and hungered sore;
For us temptation sharp He knew,
For us the tempter overthrew.

....

Jesus prayed for us (John 17), and He taught us about God so that we could become God's children. (Matthew 4:17) Every day of His earthly life, Jesus worked miracles that helped His people. (Matthew 4:22-24) Jesus showed us in His words, His miracles, and His actions that He was not seeking what was best for *Him*, but what was best for *us*. He did all this because He loves us! (John 3:14-17)

For us He prayed, for us He taught,
For us His daily works He wrought,

By words and signs and actions thus
Still seeking not Himself, but us.

....

For our sake the Son of God was betrayed and taken captive by wicked men (Mark 14:41-49), and for our sake He suffered being whipped, mocked, and forced to wear a crown of sharp thorns on His head. (Matthew 27:26-31) He endured the incredible pain and agony of dying on a cross *for us*, so that His blood could pay the price that would set us free from our slavery to sin. (1 Timothy 1:15) In order to bring us back home to God His Father, Jesus breathed His last breath and died. (Ephesians 2:13-17)

For us to wicked men betrayed,
Scourged, mocked, in crown of thorns arrayed;
He bore the shameful cross and death,
For us He gave His dying breath.

....

But then—for us—Jesus came back to life again! (1 Corinthians 15:20-22) For our sake, He went back up to Heaven to reign forever as our King. (Philippians 2:9-11) Because He loved us, He sent the Holy Spirit into our hearts to guide us in this life, give us the strength to go on when it's hard, and cheer our hearts when we are discouraged. (John 14:26, 15:26, 16:7)

For us He rose from death again,
For us He went on high to reign;
For us He sent His Spirit here,
To guide, to strengthen, and to cheer.

....

Our Jesus, the virgin-born Son of God (Isaiah 7:14, Matthew 1:23), King of all Creation (Revelation 7:14), let *all* the honor, praise, and glory in the world be given to you! (Revelation 1:4-6) Father God, Jesus, and Holy Spirit, forever we will adore you as our triune God! (Matthew 28:18-20)

All honor, laud, and glory be,
O Jesus, virgin-born, to thee;
Whom with the Father we adore,
And Holy Ghost, forevermore.

O QUICKLY COME, DREAD JUDGE OF ALL

Lyrics by **Laurence Tuttiet**, 1854

Set to the tunes *Vater Unser—Melita—Veni Cito—St. Petersburg—Peniel—Wavertree—Eaton—St. Finbar*—and more

Oh God, righteous Judge of all Creation, please come quickly! Even though our knees tremble when we think of you coming to judge us (Romans 14:10-12), we look forward to that day because we know what it will mean: on that last day, the Day of Judgement, truth will no longer be hidden behind evil anywhere. We will be able to plainly see it, at last. All lies and evil will die at the sight your return, Judge of All. (Romans 2:6-11) Please come quickly, God, because doubts and fears will melt away like mist in the sunshine when you appear.

O quickly come, dread Judge of all;
For, awful though thine advent be,
All shadows from the truth will fall,
And falsehood die, in sight of thee:
O quickly come, for doubt and fear
Like clouds dissolve when thou art near.

....

Oh God, King of all Creation, please come quickly! Come rule this earth around us and be the only thing that our hearts worship. Do not let sin enslave our souls any longer! (Romans 8:2) On the last day, when you kill sin for good, all pain and sadness will die with it. Please come quickly, God our King, for your people are scattered all over the earth, and only you can bring us together and unite us. (Mark 13:26-27)

O quickly come, great King of all;
Reign all around us and within;

Let sin no more our souls enthrall,
Let pain and sorrow die with sin:
O quickly come, for thou alone
Canst make thy scattered people one.

....

Oh God, Giver of all Life, please come quickly! We badly need the life you give, because death hunts us here. (John 5:21, Romans 8:9-11) It is everywhere. Every home, every family, is visited by death eventually. Every heart is broken at some point by death. (Ecclesiastes 9:1-6) Please come quickly, God our Life, because we know that grief and pain will not be found anywhere once you come back to us to reign as our Eternal King. (Revelation 21:4)

O quickly come, true Life of all,
For death is mighty all around;
On ev'ry home his shadows fall,
On ev'ry heart his mark is found:
O quickly come, for grief and pain
Can never cloud thy glorious reign.

....

Oh God, our eternal Light who never fails, please come quickly! In this world, a depressing, dark night of sin covers our souls wherever we go. The darkness is causing weak souls to give up, to stop waiting for you to come and bring morning to us. (Ezekiel 12:21-23) Please come, our God who gives us Light, for when you gather us around your throne there will be no more blindness, no more waiting, and no more darkness at all! (Isaiah 9:2, John 8:12, Revelation 22:3-5)

O quickly come, sure Light of all,
For gloomy night broods o'er our way;
And weakly souls begin to fall
With weary watching for the day:
O quickly come, for 'round thy throne
No eye is blind, no night is known.

O SACRED HEAD, NOW WOUNDED

Original author is uncertain; likely **Bernard of Clairvaux** (see page 282), early 12th century

Originally written in Latin; translated from Latin to German by **Paul Gerhardt** (see page 300) in 1656; translated from German to English by **James Waddell Alexander** c.1830

Set to the tunes *Passion Chorale (Hassler)—Gerhardt—Aurelia—Munich—Crucifix—St. Christopher—Shipp—Babel—Canonbury—Webb—Memorial—Lancashire—Miriam—Kto Poda Silu—Sacred Crown—Thalberg—Redding*—and more

Oh Christ, how your godly head has been wounded! Your head hangs low because of your deep sadness and suffering. (Isaiah 50:6, 52:14) You are surrounded by enemies who mock and beat you. (Psalm 22:11-13) Jesus, you are the Son of God, the King of all! But the only crown they have given you is a mocking crown of thorns. (John 19:2-3) Oh Christ, before you left Heaven, your head wore a crown of gold—oh, what glory you used to have! Now they are treating you like a criminal. (Philippians 2:5-8) Yet though they hate you, leaving you bloody and shamed and alone, I am still glad to call you *my King*. (Matthew 10:32-33)

O sacred Head, now wounded,
With grief and shame weighed down,
Now scornfully surrounded
With thorns, thine only crown;
O sacred Head, what glory,
What bliss till now was thine!
Yet, though despised and gory,
I joy to call thee mine.

....

Christ, you chose to suffer all this just so that you could set sinners free! (Isaiah 53:3-5) They didn't kill you on the cross for anything you had done wrong, Jesus. It was *my* sin, the punishment *I* deserved, for which you died. (Hebrews 9:13-14) The sin and guilt was mine... but the pain was all yours. I did not have to take my due punishment, because you willingly took it for me. (John 10:14-18) And now Lord Jesus, I fall at your feet! Please have compassion on me, and give me your grace so that I can live my life as your servant. (Jude 1:24-25)

What thou, my Lord, hast suffered,
Was all for sinners' gain;
Mine, mine was the transgression,
But thine the deadly pain.
Lo, here I fall, my Savior!
'Tis I deserve thy place;
Look on me with thy favor,
Vouchsafe to me thy grace.

....

Men make fun of you and spit in your face—the face of the King of all Creation! You rule all this world, and the mighty nations tremble when you speak to them. (Psalm 2) So how, Jesus, has it come to *this?* How is your face pale from terrible pain and torture? How is it that the face of the King of All is sad and weak, when it used to be as mighty and glorious as the sun itself? (Matthew 17:2)

Men mock and taunt and jeer thee,
Thou noble countenance,
Though mighty worlds shall fear thee
And flee before thy glance.
How art thou pale with anguish,
With sore abuse and scorn!
How doth thy visage languish
That once was bright as morn!

....

Your kingly cheeks have lost their healthy color, and your lips are pale and cracked with pain and thirst. Death has cruelly stolen your life from you, my King Jesus! You have lost your strength because of this torture that men have put you through. (Psalm 22:14-18)

Now from thy cheeks has vanished
Their color once so fair;
From thy red lips is banished
The splendor that was there.
Grim death, with cruel rigor,
Hath robbed thee of thy life;
Thus thou hast lost thy vigor,
Thy strength in this sad strife.

....

In all your suffering on the cross, it was *my heavy sin* that weighed you down. My sin was the reason you had to suffer and die! (1 Peter 2:24) So now I bow down on my face before you, Christ Jesus, my King. I am your servant. (Galatians 1:10) I was the one who deserved to die, who deserved the anger of God because of my filthy sins! (Romans 1:18, 6:23, Colossians 3:5-6) Have mercy on me, Jesus, for you are the one who sets me free from my sins. (1 John 1:9) Do not turn me away!

My burden in thy passion,
Lord, thou hast borne for me,
For it was my transgression
Which brought this woe on thee.
I cast me down before thee,
Wrath were my rightful lot;
Have mercy, I implore thee;
Redeemer, spurn me not!

....

How can I possibly thank you with words, Jesus, my sweetest friend? What words could be enough to repay what you endured in order to save me—your pity on my lost soul which made you want to save me, and the death you died in order to buy my freedom? There is only one thing I can do now: Lord, make me your servant forever! (Luke 8:39) I know I will be weak in this life, so keep me from ever losing my love for you, Jesus.

What language shall I borrow
To thank thee, dearest friend,
For this thy dying sorrow,
Thy pity without end?
O make me thine forever,
And should I fainting be,
Lord, let me never, never
Outlive my love to thee.

....

Jesus my Shepherd, take me as your own sheep. (John 10:27-30) My Guardian, please say that I am yours! You have given me many blessings, and the true and loving words that you have spoken to me have been food that nourished my soul. You sent the Holy Spirit to live in my heart, and He has taught me about the joys that wait for me in God's Heaven. (John 14:26, 15:26)

My Shepherd, now receive me;
My Guardian, own me thine.
Great blessings thou didst give me,
O source of gifts divine.
Thy lips have often fed me
With words of truth and love;
Thy Spirit oft hath led me
To Heavenly joys above.

....

Jesus, I cannot describe the joy I feel—but it is far above any other joy in the world—when I trust that your death on the cross was enough to pay for all my sins, and I remember that I belong to you. (Romans 5:1-2) I have such joy, because I know that nothing can snatch me from you. (John 10:27-29) Jesus, Lord of my Life, I long to see your kingly glory face-to-face. I trust that your sacrifice on the cross is what has saved me, so that when I die, my soul will go to you. (1 Thessalonians 4:13-14)

The joy can never be spoken,
Above all joys beside,
When in thy body broken
I thus with safety hide.
O Lord of life, desiring
Thy glory now to see,
Beside thy cross expiring,
I'd breathe my soul to thee.

....

Jesus my Savior, please come and be with me when it is my time to die. Be there to cheer my heart if I am sad, and then never leave me for all eternity! When my soul is tired of this hard world, and my body is weak and about to give up, do not leave me alone then, dear Jesus. But in that moment, please take away all the pain in my heart by reminding me that you suffered pain *for* me—so there is nothing for me to fear. (Philippians 1:21, Romans 8:1)

My Savior, be thou near me
When death is at my door;
Then let thy presence cheer me,
Forsake me nevermore!
When soul and body languish,
Oh, leave me not alone,
But take away mine anguish
By virtue of thine own!

....

Yes, Jesus, be the one who comforts and protects me when it is time for me die. When the end of my life is near, remind me what you suffered in order to save me. After I die, my eyes will open and I will see you face-to-face, Jesus! (Revelation 22:4) I will dwell with you forever, all because you paid for my sins on the cross. You have made me trust in you, and by that faith I can hold on to you even now. (Romans 5:2) Whoever dies in Jesus, whoever dies like this, has no reason to fear! (Revelation 14:13)

Be thou my consolation,
My shield when I must die;
Remind me of thy passion
When my last hour draws nigh.
Mine eyes shall then behold thee,
Upon thy cross shall dwell,
My heart by faith enfolds thee.
Who dieth thus dies well.

O SPIRIT OF THE LIVING GOD

Lyrics by **James Montgomery** (see page 317), 1823

Set to the tunes *Melcombe (Webb)—Winchester New—Alstone—Mendon—Gonfalon Royal—Wareham—Retreat—Keble—Germany—Hursley—Come God, Creator, Holy Ghost—O Jesu Christe, Wahres Licht—Grace Church—Federal Street—Stonefield—Rockingham—St. Anselm—Song 34 (Gibbons)—Southwell—Ludborough—Mainzer—St. Bartholomew—Ernan—Canonbury—Easton—Eden*

Holy Spirit, Living Spirit of our Living God, wherever mankind may wander on this earth, we beg you to come down and be with us there. (Matthew 28:19-20, John 14:15-17) We are dirty sinners; we were made to serve God, but we have run away from Him and chosen sin instead. (Genesis 3:1-6) Holy Spirit, you have so much grace to give, and we desperately need that grace! (Psalm 51:1) Come to us, wherever we may go on this earth, and help us lost sinners.

O Spirit of the living God,
In all thy plenitude of grace,
Where'er the foot of man hath trod,
Descend on our apostate race.

....

Holy Spirit, teach us what to say so that we will be able to teach this world about you. (Luke 12:11-12) Make our hearts overflow with your love so that we will know how to love our neighbors. (Ephesians 5:2, 1 John 4:7) We long for you to say to us, "You are mine," (1 Peter 2:9-10) and for you to give us the ability to do God's work in this world wherever God sends the good news about Jesus.

Give tongues of fire and hearts of love
To preach the reconciling word;
Give pow'r and unction from above,
Whene'er the joyful sound is heard.

....

All the darkness of sin becomes light when you come near, Holy Spirit! (Isaiah 9:2, 42:16, John 1:1-5) Wherever there is confusion and chaos, if you go there, there will be calm. (1 Corinthians 14:33) A weak person finds the strength to keep going when you enter his heart, oh Spirit of our God. (Ephesians 3:14-16) Wherever you go in this world, Spirit, remind us that we are called to forgive our fellow man rather than be angry with him (John 14:26, 15:26), just as God made a way for *us* to be forgiven through Jesus, rather than punishing us for our sins as we deserved. (Matthew 6:14-15)

Be darkness, at thy coming, light;
Confusion, order in thy path;
Souls without strength inspire with might;
Bid mercy triumph over wrath.

....

Holy Spirit, prepare us and all of Creation for the day when we will meet God our Maker face-to-face. (Revelation 21:2) Spirit of our Creator, breathe a fresh breath of life into all of us, so that hearts that are as dead as stone because of sin will come to life in God. (John 6:63, Revelation 22:17, Ezekiel 11:19-20)

O Spirit of the Lord, prepare
All the round earth her God to meet;
Breathe thou abroad like morning air,
Till hearts of stone begin to beat.

....

Spirit of God, go with us to all the nations of this world, and as we baptize new believers as Christ taught us, live in their hearts and add them to God's people. (Matthew 28:19) Far and near, all over the world, spread the good news that Jesus has conquered Satan by taking our punishment on the cross! Spread this Gospel, this good news, until people from all the nations in the world call Jesus their Lord, their Master, and their King.

Baptize the nations; far and nigh
The triumphs of the cross record;
The name of Jesus glorify,
Till every kindred call Him "Lord."

....

Before He ever created the world, God decreed that people from all over this earth that He was going to make would be saved by Jesus' blood and become His people. When a person trusts that Jesus' blood has paid for their sins, you enter their heart and make them a new person. Holy Spirit, you are a gift to us, the crown of our salvation, the fulfillment of God's eternal plan! (John 14:26, 16:7, 1 John 3:24)

God from eternity hath willed
All flesh shall His salvation see:
So be the Father's love fulfilled,
The Savior's sufferings crowned through thee.

O WONDROUS TYPE, O VISION FAIR!

Lyrics from a 15th-century Latin hymn

Translated by **John Mason Neale** (see page 344), 1851

Set to the tunes *Deo Gracias—Wareham—Keble—Waltham—Ely—Aeterne Rex Altissime—Demuth—Germany—Zephyr—Erhalt Uns, Herr—Conditor Alme Siderum—Samson—Hebron—Festus—Cameronian Midnight Hymn—Overberg—Hermon—Lob Sei Dem Allmächtingen Gott*

Oh, what a wondrous hint this story is, a taste of the glory that all God's people will one day know—when we look at Christ in the story of the Transfiguration, when we see His glory there, we see what is coming for us, too. (2 Corinthians 3:18) See Him standing there on that mountaintop, shining brighter than the sun with all His kingly, Heavenly glory!

O wondrous type! O vision fair
Of glory that the Church shall share,
Which Christ upon the mountain shows,
Where brighter than the sun He glows!

....

For all the centuries since Christ left the earth, His people have read in the Bible this story of the Transfiguration, the day when Jesus, Peter, James, and John went to the top of a mountain. There Elijah and Moses came from Heaven to meet with Jesus, and the three of them spoke about the things of Heaven and shone with their Heavenly glory. (Matthew 17:1-2, Luke 9:28-31)

From age to age the tale declares
How with the three disciples there
Where Moses and Elijah meet,
The Lord holds converse high and sweet.

....

In the Transfiguration, two things of God were represented: law and prophecy. God sent Moses to represent the law which God decreed for His people, and He sent Elijah to represent the prophecies that God had spoken to His people. Then God Himself spoke from the clouds to say about Jesus, "This is my dear Son, and I am very pleased with Him. Listen to Him!" (Matthew 17:3-5, Luke 9:34-35, 2 Peter 1:17-18)

The law and prophets there have place,
Two chosen witnesses of grace,
The Father's voice from out the clouds
Proclaims His only Son aloud.

....

That day, when Moses and Elijah came to meet Jesus and He wore His Heavenly glory again for a moment, the reason was because Jesus wanted to let us glimpse the glory that waits in Heaven for us—for all those who love God, who find their joy in Him. (John 17:20-23, Isaiah 60:19, Romans 2:6-8)

With shining face and bright array,
Christ deigns to manifest that day
What glory shall be theirs above
Who joy in God with perfect love.

....

Those who are faithful to God are encouraged by thinking about this! (2 Corinthians 4:16-18) The glories of Heaven are a mystery to us (1 Corinthians 13:12), but it cheers our spirits when we remember that this glory is waiting for *us!* (Romans 8:16-18, 1 Corinthians 15:42-44) Because we know these great glories and joys will be ours in Heaven, God's people sing with joy and pray together to the God who says this is true. (Hebrews 13:14-15, Romans 8:26-29)

And faithful hearts are raised on high
By this great vision's mystery;

For which in joyful strains we raise
The voice of prayer, the hymn of praise.

....

Father God, Jesus Christ, and Holy Spirit, together you are our one beloved God. (Matthew 28:18-20) Hold your people close and teach us to be faithful to you, so that one day we will indeed see your Heavenly glory face-to-face, just as you have promised! (Jude 1:24-25, 2 Timothy 4:18, Colossians 3:3-4)

O Father, with the eternal Son,
And Holy Spirit, ever one,
Vouchsafe to bring us by thy grace
To see thy glory face-to-face.

O WORD OF GOD INCARNATE

Lyrics by **William Walsham How** (see page 308), 1867

Set to the tunes *Munich—Chenies—Aurelia—Bentley—Lancashire—Evarts—Zoan—Nyland—Magdalena—Berno—Edengrove—Missionary Hymn—Caskey—Holy Church—Albion—To Thee, O God, I Cry—Carmel—Harris—Herzlich Thut Mich Verlangen—Carlsruhe—Chebar—Whitford—Lymington—Everts—Ellacombe*—and more

Holy Scripture, you are the spoken words of God Himself, yet we can hold you in our hands. (2 Timothy 3:16-17) You are the written-down wisdom of the God of Heaven. You are *the* Truth! (2 Timothy 2:15, Psalm 119:159-160, Isaiah 8:20) No one can change what you say, and you will never change yourself. We give thanks to God because of you—the holy words on your pages shine like a lantern on our pathway, showing us where to step in the sin-darkness of this world. (Psalm 119:105) Your words have guided all of God's people who have ever lived. (Joshua 1:8, Hebrews 4:12)

O Word of God incarnate,
O wisdom from on high,
O truth unchanged, unchanging,
O light of our dark sky;
We praise thee for the radiance
That from the hallowed page,
A lantern to our footsteps
Shines on from age to age.

....

Jesus our Master gave us His Father's word as a gift from Heaven. (John 17:17) Even these thousands of years later, God's word is still shining its light on the world, as strong and true as ever! The Bibles we hold in our hands are each little golden treasure chests full of the precious jewels of God's truth. From the beginning to the end, in Scripture we see where God wove the long story of Christ (Luke 24:44-47, Psalm 40:6-8, Hebrews 10:5-7, John 5:39), who is the living, breathing Word of God Himself. (John 1:1-5)

The Church from her dear Master
Received the gift divine,
And still that light she lifteth
O'er all the earth to shine.
It is the golden casket,
Where gems of truth are stored;
It is the heav'n-drawn picture
Of Christ, the living Word.

....

Scripture is the battle flag that God's people fly when they go to battle against Satan and sin. Scripture is like the beam of light from a lighthouse, calling out into this dark world to show people the way to God. Scripture is the map that shows God's people how to find their way through life, like sailors using a chart to show them where to sail on a stormy sea. When this life feels as if we are surrounded by fog and rocks and quicksand, Scripture is there to guide us safely through the dangers and bring us home to Christ. (Proverbs 30:5)

It floateth like a banner
Before God's host unfurled;
It shineth like a beacon
Above the darkling world.
It is the chart and compass
That o'er life's surging sea,
'Mid mists and rocks and quicksands,
Still guides, O Christ, to thee.

....

Lord Jesus our Savior, make the people of your Church shine together like a golden lamp in front of the whole world. We will show them the way to your truth, just as your Church has always done. (Matthew 5:14-16, Revelation 1:12-20) Jesus, your people are strangers here, because this world is not our home. (John 15:19, John 17:14-16) So as we travel through life on our way home, teach us to use our Bibles as our map. (Psalm 119:133) Let us keep following God's word until all the clouds and darkness of this world are gone, and we see you, Jesus, face-to-face! (Mark 13:13, Revelation 2:10)

O make thy Church, dear Savior,
A lamp of purest gold,
To bear before the nations
Thy true light, as of old.
O teach thy wand'ring pilgrims
By this their path to trace,
Till, clouds and darkness ended,
They see thee face-to-face.

O WORSHIP THE KING

Lyrics by **Sir Robert Grant** (see page 302), 1833; based on William Kethe's version of Psalm 104 as found in the 1561 Genevan Psalter.

Set to the tunes *Lyons—Hanover—Haughton—Old 104th—England—Cassel*—and more

Christians, let us worship our God, the King of all glory! (Psalm 95:1-5) Let us sing out our thanks, praising Him for the mighty power and love He shows us. He is the shield who protects us, the unbeatable warrior who fights for us. (2 Samuel 22:2-4) He was God before this world was made, He is God today, and He will be God for eternity! (Psalm 90:2) God's throne room in Heaven is splendid and glorious, and He is covered by the praises His Creation sings to Him. (Revelation 4:1-8)

O worship the King all-glorious above,
O gratefully sing His pow'r and His love;
Our shield and Defender, the Ancient of Days,
Pavilioned in splendor and girded with praise.

....

People of God, tell this world how mighty is our God! (Psalm 78:4) Sing out about the grace and forgiveness He gives us. God's kingly robe is made of Heavenly light. (Psalm 93:1, 104:1-2, Revelation 22:5) The sky itself, the furthest reaches of space, is His palace. God rides on the thunderclouds as His battle chariot, and He flies on the stormy winds. (Psalm 104:3, Jeremiah 4:13)

O tell of His might, O sing of His grace,
Whose robe is the light, whose canopy space.
His chariots of wrath the deep thunderclouds form,
And dark is His path on the wings of the storm.

....

All-powerful God, it was you who built this marvelous earth long ago. You decided how it would work, and you filled it with all the wonders we see. (Psalm 24:1) When you laid the foundation of this earth (Job 38:4), you decreed once and for all that it would continue working the way you made it (Genesis 8:22), and nothing and no one can change that. (1 Chronicles 16:30) It was you, God, who built the mountains, the sea beds, the continents, and then draped the oceans over the earth like a cape. (Psalm 104:5-9, Job 38:8-11)

The earth with its store of wonders untold,
Almighty, your pow'r has founded of old;
Has 'stablished it fast by a changeless decree,
And 'round it has cast, like a mantle, the sea.

....

God, who has the words to tell about all that you do to care for your Creation? No one can even know all that you do for us! Everywhere, there is evidence that you take care of us—in the air that you gave us to breathe, and in the sunlight that shines on us to light up the world. (Psalm 104: 18-20, Job 38:19-24) Evidence that you care for us is everywhere on the earth—in the rivers, the streams, and in the dew and the rain. (Psalm 104:10-13, Acts 14:17, Job 38:28, Deuteronomy 28:12)

Your bountiful care what tongue can recite?
It breathes in the air; it shines in the light;
It streams from the hills; it descends to the plain;
And sweetly distills in the dew and the rain.

....

You are God, but we are fragile creatures made from dust. (Psalm 103:14) And we are as weak as we are fragile! (Ecclesiastes 3:19) We cannot fend for ourselves here—we depend on you, our Maker, to take care of us, and you have never failed us yet. (Psalm 104:27-29, Luke 12:24-28, Matthew 6:31-33) You are full of gentle, fatherly mercy for us (Hosea 6:6), and you will never forget to care for us. You are our Maker and our Protector. You shed your own blood to pay the price that set us free from sin, and you have made us your people. (Hebrews 9:13-15) You are our Friend who will never abandon us! (John 15:15)

Frail children of dust, and feeble as frail,
In you do we trust, nor find you to fail;
Your mercies how tender, how firm to the end,
Our Maker, Defender, Redeemer, and Friend!

....

God's strength is too much to be measured! (Psalm 147:5) His love is bigger than words can say! (Psalm 103:11) God, your angels live to sing songs of praise to you in Heaven. (Isaiah 6:1-3) We are not as glorious and noble as those angels. But even though our songs are weaker, our hearts are bubbling over with real adoration for you, our God, and we praise you with every bit of our small strength! (Psalm 104:33-34, Isaiah 6:5-6)

O measureless might! Ineffable love!
While angels delight to hymn you above,
The humbler creation, though feeble their lays,
With true adoration shall lisp to your praise.

ROCK OF AGES, CLEFT FOR ME

Lyrics by **Augustus Montague Toplady** (see page 329), 1776

Altered by **Thomas Cotterill** (see page 294), 1815

Set to the tunes *Toplady—Redhead No. 76—Rock of Ages (Dykes)—Rock of Ages (Cornell)—Rock of Ages (Gesangbuch)—Homeward—Pascal—Greenville—Graceham—Zadoc—Memorial—Sebastian—Cecil—New City Fellowship—Straf Mich Nicht—Refuge—Hodges—Cuyler—Hotham—Loraine—Harold—Würtemburg—Montagu*—and more

Jesus, you are the Rock who has sheltered all of God's people who have ever been (2 Samuel 22:2-4, Isaiah 26:3-4)—and you, the Rock of Ages, were cracked for sinners like me. (Isaiah 53:5-6) You chose to be killed on the cross so that *you* could take the punishment for *our* sins. (John 10:17-18) This life is a storm, and I need a safe place, Lord—so let me hide in you! (Psalm 71:3) Let the water and blood that flowed out of your side on the cross wash over my heart. (John 19:33-34, Matthew 26:27-28) Let it cure me in two ways: let it pay for the price of my sin so that I will not be guilty before God (Revelation 7:14, Hebrews 10:19-23), and let it wash away the root of sin in my heart and leave me clean. (Romans 6:16-18)

Rock of Ages, cleft for me
Let me hide myself in thee;
Let the water and the blood,
From thy riven side which flowed,
Be of sin the double cure:
Save from wrath and make me pure.

....

There is no "good deed" that I can do which would make me good enough for God. (Ephesians 2:8-9) I am a sinner, so I am guilty when I stand before God, the perfect Judge of the world. (Psalm 5:4) Even if I spent every hour of my life working, trying, it wouldn't be enough. If I spent the rest of my life crying and telling God how sorry I am, it would not make any difference. (Colossians 2:16-23) None of those things would pay the price of sin. Christ, *only you can save me!* (Romans 6:23, John 14:6)

Not the labors of my hands
Can fulfil thy law's demands;
Could my zeal no respite know,
Could my tears for ever flow,
All for sin could not atone;
Thou must save, and thou alone.

....

So here I am, Christ. I don't have anything to offer you; I simply trust that your death on the cross will be enough to cover my sins. (Romans 10:9) I have *nothing* good in me. (Romans 7:18) I am poor and naked when it comes to righteousness, so I am coming to you, Christ, asking you to clothe me in your goodness. I am dirty with sins, so I run to you, Christ, the fountain of God's grace, to be washed clean. Wash me clean, Jesus my Savior, or else I will die in Hell because of my sin! (Psalm 51:1-4)

Nothing in my hand I bring,
Simply to thy cross I cling;
Naked, come to thee for dress;
Helpless, look to thee for grace;
Foul, I to the Fountain fly;
Wash me, Savior, or I die.

....

Someday, it will be my day to die. I will breathe my last breath, and my eyelids will close. Then my soul will leave my body and I will go to Heaven, that world that no living person has ever seen! (Revelation 14:13) There I will see you, Christ, sitting on your throne as the King and Judge of all. (Matthew 25:21)

Oh Jesus, Rock of Ages who was broken to save me, let me be hidden in you! (Colossians 3:3)

While I draw this fleeting breath,
When mine eyelids close in death,
When I soar to worlds unknown,
See thee on thy judgment throne,
Rock of Ages, cleft for me,
Let me hide myself in thee.

SPIRIT OF GOD, DESCEND UPON MY HEART

Lyrics by **George Croly**, 1854

Set to the tunes *Morecambe—Longwood—Arthur—Ellerton—Song 22 (Gibbons)—Langran—Folkstone—Sheldonian—Emilie*

Holy Spirit, come down and touch my heart! I need you to pull my heart away from the things of this world, because I love this world too much. (Colossians 3:1-3) Spirit of God, send your life through every part of me. (John 6:63) I am weak, so bend down to me, with all your strength, and help me! (Romans 8:26-27) Teach me how to love you the way you deserve to be loved, Holy Spirit of God.

Spirit of God, descend upon my heart;
Wean it from earth, through all its pulses move;
Stoop to my weakness, mighty as thou art,
And make me love thee as I ought to love.

....

Holy Spirit, I don't want to see prophecies or visions. I don't expect to suddenly understand everything about God, all at once. I don't ask to be visited by any angels with special messages just for me, and I do not expect you to open up the skies and let me have miraculous visions of Heaven. (Colossians 2:18-19) All I ask, Spirit, is for you to take away this dullness, this sleepiness in my heart. (Acts 28:27, Hebrews 5:11) Wake me up, Spirit, and teach me how to love you as I should!

I ask no dream, no prophet ecstasies,
No sudden rending of the veil of clay,
No angel visitant, no op'ning skies;
But take the dimness of my soul away.

....

Oh God my King, have you not told us to love you? You have taught us that every bit of our heart, soul, mind, and strength should be yours. (Mark 12:30) I know that Jesus made a way for me to come to you by dying on the cross. (Colossians 1:18-20) Spirit of God, please teach me to trust in nothing except Jesus' sacrifice on that cross! (Romans 10:9, John 14:6) Make me *want* you, make me *look* for you, and let me *find* you in the story of the cross, my God. (Jeremiah 29:12-13)

Hast thou not bid us love thee, God and King?
All, all thine own, soul, heart, and strength and mind.
I see the cross—there teach my heart to cling:
O let me seek thee, and O let me find.

....

Holy Spirit, help me remember that you are always here with me. Show me how to handle the struggles and hard thoughts that my heart deals with in this life. When I am beginning to doubt that you are with me, nip that doubt in the bud! (James 1:5-8) Help me to know when I first start feeling rebellious against you, and stop that rebelliousness in my heart before it grows stronger. (Hebrews 3:7-14) Instead, teach me to be patient when it feels like you have not answered my prayers, by reminding that you never abandon me. (Romans 12:12, 2 Corinthians 1:20-22)

Teach me to feel that thou art always nigh;
Teach me the struggles of the soul to bear,
To check the rising doubt, the rebel sigh;
Teach me the patience of unanswered prayer.

....

Holy Spirit of God, teach me to love you the way your angels love you! Give me so much love for you that I am full of nothing *but* love for you. (1 John 2:4-6) Give me true baptism, the baptism of the Holy Spirit, so that I am washed clean. (Luke 3:16, 1 Peter 3:18-22) Let my heart be an altar for worshipping you, and let your love take over everything in me like a flame. (Romans 12:1, Psalm 51:17)

Teach me to love thee as thine angels love,
One holy passion filling all my frame:
The baptism of the heav'n-descended Dove,
My heart an altar, and thy love the flame.

STRICKEN, SMITTEN, AND AFFLICTED

Lyrics by **Thomas Kelly**, 1804

Set to the tunes *O Mein Jesu, Ich Muss Sterben—Hjem Jeg Laenges—Autumn—Sanctuary—Passion—Wo Ist Jesus, Mein Verlangen*

He has been slapped, beaten, wounded, and mocked. (John 18:20-23, 19:1-3) And now He is dying on that cross! (Isaiah 53:3-5) This is Jesus, the Messiah—mankind did not want Him or the truth He came to teach, so they have killed Him. (Acts 7:51-53, John 1:10-11) Yes, my soul, this is Him! This is Jesus! This dying, bleeding man is the prophet for whom Israel waited for centuries. He is the one about whom King David prophesied: Jesus is descended from David, yet David called Him his "Lord!" (Psalm 2, Luke 2:4-5, Matthew 22:41-45) God has spoken to us through this dying man, the Son of God—that is why He is called the true and faithful *Word* of God. (John 1:1-5)

Stricken, smitten, and afflicted,
See Him dying on the tree!
'Tis the Christ by man rejected;
Yes, my soul, 'tis He, 'tis He!
'Tis the long-expected Prophet,
David's Son, yet David's Lord;
By His Son God now has spoken:
'Tis the true and faithful Word.

....

All you who hear Jesus' groans and agony, tell me: have you ever seen a sadness as deep as His? It is more than the wounds on His body that are making Him suffer! Jesus' friends have all abandoned Him, because they were afraid to be punished with Him. (Matthew 26:55-56) His enemies stand around and laugh at Him while He slowly dies. (Psalm 22:6-8, Mark 15:29-32) So many people jumped at the chance to beat Him and kill Him ... but not one person stepped forward to try to save Him. But the thing that is causing Jesus the worst pain of all is the fact that He carries all the sins of God's people (Isaiah 53:6)—and that means He is facing His Father's wrath, the punishment for all that sin. (Mark 15:34)

Tell me, ye who hear Him groaning,
Was there ever grief like His?
Friends thro' fear His cause disowning,
Foes insulting His distress;
Many hands were raised to wound Him,
None would interpose to save;
But the deepest stroke that pierced Him
Was the stroke that Justice gave.

....

All you who say, "Sin isn't such a big deal," or any of you who think, "My sins aren't all that bad," here is your chance to see your mistake! Look at Jesus on the cross. That sight will show you how horrific sin really is—and it will show the cost of sin! (Romans 6:23, Luke 22:17-20, Hebrews 9:22) Think of the price that had to be paid: death! And remember who paid that price *for you*. It was the living Word of God, the King chosen by God, the Son of Man and the Son of God: Jesus Christ.

Ye who think of sin but lightly
Nor suppose the evil great
Here may view its nature rightly,
Here its guilt may estimate.
Mark the sacrifice appointed,
See who bears the awful load;
'Tis the Word, the Lord's Anointed,
Son of Man and Son of God.

....

Christ's sacrifice on the cross gives God's people the foundation on which they must stand. (Hebrews 12:1-3) Because of Christ's sacrifice, lost souls are brought safely home to God. (Hebrews 2:9-10) Christ is the Rock on which our salvation is built (Matthew 7:24-27), and the *only* thing we have to boast in is the fact that we belong to Him! (Galatians 6:14) He is the sacrificial lamb who was sent by God, who was killed in our place so that His sinless blood could pay the price of our sins and take away our guilt. (John 1:29) If anyone depends on Christ for their salvation, that person can never be shaken. (Psalm 62:2-6, 1 Corinthians 15:57-58)

Here we have a firm foundation,
Here the refuge of the lost;
Christ's the Rock of our salvation,
His the name of which we boast.
Lamb of God, for sinners wounded,
Sacrifice to cancel guilt!
None shall ever be confounded
Who on Him their hope have built.

TEN THOUSAND TIMES TEN THOUSAND

Lyrics by **Henry Alford**, 1867

Set to the tunes *Alford (Dykes)—Komm Seele—Eastham—St. Catharine*—and more

Imagine that it is the end of time. Christ has come back, and the world as it has always been is no more. Look! Here are ten thousand *times* ten thousand people, each dressed in shining, glorious clothes—they are the army of God (Revelation 9:16), made up of all His children who were saved by Christ's blood. (Revelation 7:9-10) Together they climb the stairs to God's throne room. Their struggles are all finished. Sin, pain, and death, all the hardship of life on earth, is over forever. (Revelation 21:1-4) So open wide the gates of Heaven, and let in God's people! Because they belong to Christ, they are winners in the war against Satan—because they were faithful until the very end. (Daniel 7:9-14, 1 Corinthians 15:57, Matthew 10:21-22, Revelation 2:10)

Ten thousand times ten thousand
In sparkling raiment bright,
The armies of the ransomed saints
Throng up the steeps of light:
'Tis finished, all is finished,
Their fight with death and sin:
Fling open wide the golden gates
And let the victors in.

....

How loudly they all sing, "Praise the Lord!" Their joyful shouts fill the whole sky. A voice comes from Heaven, with a sound like a thousand harps playing at once, to tell all of Creation that today is the day: the end of the war, the victory of Christ's people, is here. (Revelation 14:1-3) This glorious day is the reason that Creation and all mankind were made in the first place. What joy! The joy of this day of victory makes up for all the sadnesses of earth a thousand times over. (Revelation 7:13-17)

What rush of alleluias
Fills all the earth and sky!
What ringing of a thousand harps
Bespeaks the triumph nigh!
O day, for which Creation
And all its tribes were made;
O joy, for all its former woes
A thousandfold repaid!

....

Then what happy reunions we will see when we reach the New City of God! (1 Thessalonians 4:13-18) There, we will meet old friends and family who died long ago, and this time we know we will never be separated from them again. As much as our eyes used to be full of tears on earth, now our eyes will sparkle with joy. (Psalm 30:5) Here in the everlasting city of God, orphans will never be fatherless and widows will never be lonely again—they have God Himself to protect and comfort them. (John 14:18-20, Psalm 68:5)

O then what raptured greetings
On Canaan's happy shore;
What knitting severed friendships up
Where partings are no more!
Then eyes with joy shall sparkle,
That brimmed with tears of late;
Orphans no longer fatherless,
Nor widows desolate.

....

How we long for that day! Christ, the Lamb who was killed to save sinners, please come soon to bring this deliverance to us. Before the earth was ever created, you knew who would be yours. (Ephesians 1:3-6, Romans 8:29-31) So gather all of your people whom you have called, and then take your rightful throne and be our King for all eternity! (Mark 13:24-27, 2 Peter 1:10-11) Come soon, dear Christ. Your people are strangers in this world, and your people in every nation long for you to come back to us and call us to our Home. (John 14:3) Show us the signs that you are coming soon, and come quickly, Christ our Prince and Savior! (Revelation 22:20)

Bring near thy great salvation,
Thou Lamb for sinners slain;
Fill up the roll of thine elect,
Then take thy pow'r, and reign:
Appear, Desire of nations,
Thine exiles long for home;
Show in the heav'n thy promised sign;
Thou Prince and Savior, come.

THE CHURCH'S ONE FOUNDATION

Lyrics by **Samuel John Stone**, 1866; based on this article of the Apostles' Creed: "I believe in ... the holy catholic* Church, the communion of saints."

Set to the tunes *Aurelia—Lancashire—If God Himself Be for Me—Llanfyllin—Somerstown—Webb—Greenland*—and more

There is only one foundation on which the Church can stand, only one thing on which she can depend—Jesus Christ, her Lord and Master. (Isaiah 28:16, 1 Corinthians 3:11) The Church is all the brothers and sisters in Christ from all places in all times, the people to whom Christ has given new hearts, the ones He washed clean by baptizing them with the Spirit and teaching them God's Word. (1 Corinthians 12:13) All together, the Church is Christ's bride—He came down from Heaven to win her heart, and chose her to be His bride. (Ephesians 5:25-32) He shed His blood to pay the price that would set her free from slavery to sin. Christ loved His Bride so much that He gave up His life, so that she could live with God.

The Church's one foundation
Is Jesus Christ, her Lord;
She is His new creation
By water and the Word:
From heav'n He came and sought her
To be His holy bride;
With His own blood He bought her,
And for her life He died.

....

* The word *catholic* comes from the Greek word *katholikos*, which means "universal." It refers to all of Christ's people, from all places, in all times. It does not refer to Roman Catholicism.

People from every nation on earth are a part of the Church. (Galatians 3:8) But even though they are so many different people, they are united together as one: the Church, Christ's Bride. (Colossians 3:11, 1 Corinthians 12:12-27) They are united because they all believe the same thing: that we have only one Lord, Jesus; we can only be saved by faith in God, and not by anything we do; and that when Christ saves each one of us, He makes us a new person. (Ephesians 4:4-6) The whole Church worships the same name: *Jesus Christ.* (Philippians 2:9-11) The whole Church depends on one spiritual food to keep her alive: the body and blood of Christ. (1 Corinthians 11:23-26) The whole Church hopes in the same thing: that we are saved because of what Christ did for us, and we will belong to Him forever! (1 Peter 1:13, Titus 2:11-14)

Elect from ev'ry nation,
Yet one o'er all the earth,
Her charter of salvation
One Lord, one faith, one birth;
One holy name she blesses,
Partakes one holy food,
And to one hope she presses,
With ev'ry grace endued.

....

The outside world looks at the Church and wonders why we continue to worship Christ even when it brings trouble on us. They laugh at us, because we say we are all united in Christ; yet the world sees that we are divided up into groups and denominations that argue with each other (1 Corinthians 1:10-13), and we are constantly having to deal with false teachings. (2 Peter 2:1-2) Still, the *true* Church is united, and the Christians are watching for Christ. (1 Corinthians 11:18-19, Philippians 1:27-28, Hebrews 10:36-39) While we wait in this hard world, suffering all these divisions and tests, we call, "How long until you come for us, Christ?" The Church knows that though the dark and sad night *seems* to be lasting forever, morning *will come* when Christ comes back for us—and then Christ's bride will have such joy! (Psalm 30:5)

Though with a scornful wonder
Men see her sore oppressed,
By schisms rent asunder,
By heresies distressed,
Yet saints their watch are keeping,
Their cry goes up, "How long?"
And soon the night of weeping
Shall be the morn of song.

....

The Church will never die! (Luke 12:4, Philippians 1:21) Her dear Lord Jesus will be with her to defend her, guide her, and love her dearly until the end, when He comes to take her home. (Matthew 28:19-20) Even though the Church has many enemies in this world, and though there may be liars hidden like spies in her midst (Galatians 2:4-5, Matthew 7:15-16), the Church will always conquer, because Christ is with her. (1 Corinthians 15:57-58)

The Church shall never perish!
Her dear Lord to defend,
To guide, sustain, and cherish,
Is with her to the end;
Though there be those that hate her,
And false sons in her pale,
Against or foe or traitor
She ever shall prevail.

....

When she is living in hard times and trouble, and when the world is at war against her, the Church still waits patiently. (1 Peter 4:12-13, Matthew 10:21-22) She knows that Christ will keep His promise to come back for her, and then she will live in peace forever. (John 14:1-3) She will keep on waiting patiently until her tired eyes see Heaven. Then, because of Christ, the Church will be the winner in the war against sin, and she will be able to rest forever after. (James 1:12, 2 Timothy 4:7-8, 1 Peter 5:4, Revelation 2:10)

'Mid toil and tribulation,
And tumult of her war,
She waits the consummation
Of peace forevermore;
Till with the vision glorious
Her longing eyes are blest,
And the great Church victorious
Shall be the Church at rest.

....

Even while she waits here on earth, the Church already belongs to the Triune God—Father, Son, and Spirit. (1 Corinthians 3:21-23, Galatians 4:4-7) The saints on earth now are family with the saints who have already gone to Heaven. Oh, how happy are those Christians in Heaven, Jesus' humble, faithful servants of the past! Lord Jesus, give us grace so that we can someday go to live with you forever, just as they have. (1 Peter 5:8-11)

Yet she on earth hath union
With God the Three in One,
And mystic sweet communion
With those whose rest is won:
O happy ones and holy!
Lord, give us grace that we,
Like them, the meek and lowly,
On high may dwell with thee.

THE DYING BELIEVER

Lyrics by **Augustus Montague Toplady** (see page 329), mid-18th century; altered in 1860

Set to the tunes *Manifestation—Mercy*

To the child of God who is about to leave this world—remember that only your *body* will die. *You* are a soul, which can never die! (Ecclesiastes 12:7) So go on, deathless soul, leave this world; it was never your home. Christian, fly away to Heaven, where you came from, and where you will live forever with your Maker. Dear one, your soul is as precious as a pearl, for Jesus shed His precious blood to make you His. (John 3:14-16, 11:25-26) Ever since He saved you, God has been making you more and more like Jesus—and once you leave behind your earthly body, the change will be complete. (Romans 8:29, 1 Thessalonians 5:23) So fly away, precious soul, and stand before Jesus throne, shining in the perfection that He has given you! (Revelation 7:9-17) You are one of His children, one more precious jewel in Jesus' priestly crown. His people in Heaven are singing the praises of Jesus' victory over sin—go now, Christian, and add your own voice to the song. You were created for God, and now you are going back to Him.

Deathless principle! arise;
Soar, thou native of the skies;
Pearl of price, by Jesus bought,
To His glorious likeness wrought,
Go, to shine before His throne;
Deck His mediatorial crown;
Go, His triumphs to adorn;
Made for God, to God return.

....

Listen, Christian—Jesus, your King and Savior, is calling you! So don't be afraid; leave this world behind, and fly away to be with Him. With His blood, Jesus paid the price of sin, and then He gave that forgiveness to you. (Ephesians 1:3-10) He is perfect, and He has given his perfection to *you*. (Isaiah 61:10) So even as you are lying here on your deathbed, your earthly body sick and weak, there are angels waiting all around you, dear Christian. They are eagerly waiting to hear your last breath, the moment your soul leaves this earth—and then they will immediately carry you home to Heaven. (Luke 16:22)

Lo! He beckons from on high,
Fearless to His presence fly;
Thine the merit of His blood,
Thine the righteousness of God.
Angels joyful to attend,
Hovering 'round thy pillow bend;
Wait to catch the signal given,
And escort thee quick to Heaven.

....

Christian, don't be afraid to cross the boundary between this world and Heaven. If you are afraid, give all your fears to Jesus, who keeps your soul safe forever. (John 10:28) Remember His love for you: He was willing to *die* in order to make you His! When Jesus died and then rose back to life, His power conquered death forever. (Hosea 13:14, 1 Corinthians 15:54-56) There is no reason for His people to fear dying anymore. (Matthew 10:28) Death used to seem like an angry ocean that you would have to cross someday, but now, because of Jesus, death is smooth sailing, as calm as a glassy lake on a summer evening. Not once has death kept one of Jesus' people away from Him. He always brings His people safely to Heaven. (Romans 8:38-39)

Shudder not to pass the stream;
Venture all thy care on Him;
Him whose dying love and power
Stilled its tossing, hushed its roar:

Safe is the expanded wave;
Gentle as a summer's eve:
Not one object of His care
Ever suffered shipwreck there.

....

Look, and you will see Heaven ahead of you. Because God loves you as His own child, He will make sure you get there safely. So trust that God is able to get you there, then lift up the anchor that is holding you to this world, and let God sail your spirit away to Heaven! All of God's people in Heaven, who have already been made complete, are waiting for you to join them. Look, dear Christian, and see them waiting for you on the shores of Heaven—they are eagerly looking for your arrival.

See the haven full in view;
Love divine shall bear thee through.
Trust to that propitious gale;
Weigh thy anchor, spread thy sail.
Saints in glory, perfect made,
Wait thy passage through the shade;
Ardent for thy coming o'er,
See! they throng the blissful shore.

....

So fly away and join them, Christian! Make their songs of praise even louder by adding your own voice to them, and sing with the Heavenly choir of God's people forevermore. Don't hold on to this evil world—go to them now, and you will make the joy in Heaven even greater, because one more child of God is home! (Psalm 116:15) These are the things your eyes will see, dear Christian, when it is your time to die. Because you have had faith in Christ, death will pull the curtains back and you will finally see the glories of Heaven! (Acts 7:56-60)

Mount, their transports to improve;
Join the longing choir above;
Swiftly to their wish be given;
Kindle higher joy in Heaven.
Such the prospects that arise
To the dying Christian's eyes;
Such the glorious vista, Faith
Opens through the shades of death.

THE SON OF GOD GOES FORTH TO WAR

Lyrics by **Reginald Heber** (see page 304), 1827

Set to the tunes *All Saints New—Crusader—St. Ann—Lambeth—Ellacombe—Brigade—Lawton—De Koven—Hummel—St. Nicholas—Bristol—Old 81st—Ladywell—Fight of Faith—Old 44th*—and more

---

Jesus Christ, the Son of God, is marching to war against Satan and sin. He will win, and when He does, God will crown Him as the King of all. (Revelation 19:11-16) See His blood-red battle flags flying in the wind—who will follow Jesus when He marches to Heaven as a triumphant, conquering King? When Jesus was on the earth, He did not have a comfortable, easy life. He was poor and rejected, and He suffered a terrible death. (Isaiah 53:3, Matthew 8:20) If our Lord suffered on this earth, how can we expect to be any different? (John 15:20) The ones who continue to follow Jesus no matter how hard it gets, the ones who are patient and faithful even through suffering, *those* are the ones who get to march behind triumphant King Jesus. (Matthew 10:21-22, Revelation 2:10)

The Son of God goes forth to war,
A kingly crown to gain;
His blood-red banner streams afar:
Who follows in His train?
Who best can drink his cup of woe,
Triumphant over pain,
Who patient bears his cross below,
He follows in His train.

....

The first man to follow Jesus was the first martyr, Stephen. (Acts 7:54-60) When he was about to be killed, Stephen saw more than just the danger in front of him—he looked past the danger and remembered that Jesus, his Master, was waiting for him on the other side of death. Just as Jesus did when evil men killed *Him*, Stephen prayed that God would forgive his attackers, even while he suffered the pain of death. (Luke 23:34) Who else will follow Stephen's example? Who will follow him in Jesus' glorious army?

The martyr first, whose eagle eye
Could pierce beyond the grave,
Who saw his Master in the sky,
And called on Him to save;
Like Him, with pardon on his tongue
In midst of mortal pain,
He prayed for them that did the wrong:
Who follows in his train?

....

The next group to follow Jesus into victory were the ones whom Jesus had specially chosen, the ones to whom the Holy Spirit came first. They were the twelve apostles, the twelve brave servants of Jesus. (Matthew 19:28) They were not afraid to suffer. They laughed in the face of even being crucified or burned, because they knew their hope in Jesus was not for nothing! (Acts 5:40-41) They were faithful to Jesus even when soldiers hunted them down to kill them. They were faithful even when they were thrown to hungry lions. No matter what happened, they did not deny Jesus—they willingly gave up their lives for their Lord's sake. (Acts 21:13) Who will follow their example? Who will follow them in King Jesus' glorious army?

A glorious band, the chosen few
On whom the Spirit came,
Twelve valiant saints, their hope they knew,
And mocked the cross and flame:
They met the tyrant's brandished steel,
The lion's gory mane;

They bowed their necks the death to feel:
Who follows in their train?

....

All the Christians of the past together make up Christ's noble army. Men, boys, women, and girls, all the servants of Christ who have ever lived—they all stand around Christ's throne in Heaven now, dressed in shining white robes. (Revelation 7:9-17) They are the faithful ones who followed Christ on the steep, rocky road to Heaven, through hard work, danger, pain, and sadness. (Revelation 12:11) Oh God, please give us grace so that we can follow their example! Let us follow behind them in King Jesus' army! (Revelation 14:12-13)

A noble army, men and boys,
The matron and the maid,
Around the Savior's throne rejoice,
In robes of light arrayed:
They climbed the steep ascent of heav'n
Through peril, toil, and pain:
O God, to us may grace be giv'n
To follow in their train.

THE SPACIOUS FIRMAMENT ON HIGH

Lyrics by **Joseph Addison** (see page 276), 1712

Set to the tunes *Creation (Haydn)—Addison's (London)—Peterborough—Firmament—Stockbridge—Cephas—Samson—St. Serf—Kickapoo—El Paran—Cantate Domino—Creation (Hopkins)—Carelle—Angels' Song—Grove—The Voice of Nature—Tallis' Canon—Bristol*—and more

All of space above us, the airy blue sky, the spray of stars that shine in the night—all of them are meant to remind us about the One who made them, the original Star of Heaven. (Psalm 19:1, Jeremiah 31:35) So is the sun, which never gets tired of making its trip across the sky day after day after day. The sun's brightness is an example of the power of God, who created it. (Psalm 84:11, Revelation 1:16, 21:23) As it travels around and around the earth, the sun is telling all the people on whom it shines, "The all-powerful God made me!" (Psalm 19:4-6, 104:19)

The spacious firmament on high,
With all the blue ethereal sky,
And spangled heav'ns, a shining frame,
Their great Original proclaim.
Th' unwearied sun, from day to day
Does his Creator's power display,
And publishes to ev'ry land
The work of an almighty hand.

....

When the sun has passed by and darkness comes, the moon takes it turn telling about its Maker. (Psalm 19:2) Every night, the moon shines and reminds the people of this earth who it was that made her. (Psalm 8:3-4) Meanwhile, all the stars around her, and all the planets whirling around in space say, "It's true!

God who made the sun and moon made us, too!" (Psalm 147:4) From the North Pole to the South Pole, the night sky reminds the entire earth that God is the one who made all of this.

Soon as the evening shades prevail,
The moon takes up the wondrous tale,
And nightly to the list'ning earth
Repeats the story of her birth;
Whilst all the stars that 'round her burn,
And all the planets in their turn,
Confirm the tidings as they roll,
And spread the truth from pole to pole.

....

"How do they do that?" you might ask. "The sun, moon, and stars don't speak." True—they are silent as they float above the earth. We do not hear a voice, or any sound from them at all. (Psalm 19:3) This is how they remind you that God made them: seeing them makes you ask yourself, "How could anything *except* God have made things like the sun, moon, and stars? How could anything so perfect and incredible have just happened on its own? God must have made them!" (Job 9:1-12, Psalm 136:7-9) That is how the sky will go on singing God's praises day after day, reminding you that, "It is God who made us and put us here!" (Psalm 74:16)

What, though in solemn silence all
Move 'round this dark terrestrial ball?
What, though no real voice nor sound
Amidst their radiant orbs be found?
In reason's ear they all rejoice,
And utter forth a glorious voice;
Forever singing, as they shine,
"The hand that made us is divine."

THIS IS MY FATHER'S WORLD

Lyrics by **Maltbie Davenport Babcock** (see page 278), 1901

Set to the tunes *Terra Beata—Mercer Street—Diademata*—and more

This world belongs to God my Father, because He is the one who made it. (Psalm 24:1-2) When I walk out in the world, my ears hear music—nature around me, and the planets and stars of the sky above, are all singing about the God who made them and me. (Psalm 19:1, Luke 19:40) This world belongs to my Heavenly Father, and it calms my heart to sit and think about all the wondrous things He has created: rocks, trees, skies, seas, and so much more. (Psalm 92:4)

This is my Father's world,
And to my list'ning ears
All nature sings, and 'round me rings
The music of the spheres.
This is my Father's world:
I rest me in the thought
Of rocks and trees, of skies and seas;
His hand the wonders wrought.

....

This world belongs to my Heavenly Father. The birds each sing the songs that God taught them to sing when He made them. The pale sunlight in the early morning, the perfect whiteness of flower petals, all of it is there to glorify God, the Maker of it all. (Matthew 6:28-30) Yes, this world belongs to my Heavenly Father! You can see examples of His glory in every good thing on the earth. When the grass rustles, it's as if His Spirit is walking there. Wherever I go, God tells me about Himself by showing me the things He has made. (Acts 14:17)

This is my Father's world;
The birds their carols raise,
The morning light, the lily white,
Declare their Maker's praise.
This is my Father's world:
He shines in all that's fair;
In the rustling grass I hear Him pass;
He speaks to me everywhere.

....

This world belongs to my Heavenly Father. Oh God, please don't ever let me forget that even though the evil in this world seems so strong, you, my God, are still the Ruler of all. (Psalm 37:9-15, Psalm 2) This world belongs to my Heavenly Father! Jesus has already defeated Satan, but the battle against evil is not over quite yet. Nevertheless, Jesus is still the winner of this war! He will certainly come back to claim this earth as His rightful kingdom someday (Revelation 22:12-13), and then earth and Heaven will not be separate any longer.

This is my Father's world.
O let me ne'er forget
That though the wrong seems oft so strong,
God is the Ruler yet.
This is my Father's world:
The battle is not done:
Jesus who died shall be satisfied,
And earth and Heav'n be one.

....

This world belongs to my Heavenly Father! Sometimes I close my eyes and daydream that I can see His face. Then I open my eyes and see His world around me, and I am surprised all over again to realize that He is *here!* I don't have to imagine it—the Lord is really here among us. From Heaven, God sent His only, dear Son to be here with us, to prove how much He loves us. (1 John

4:9) And that love will never die, for Jesus Christ is always with His people. (Matthew 18:20, 28:20)

This is my Father's world,
Dreaming, I see His face.
I ope my eyes, and in glad surprise cry,
"The Lord is in this place."
This is my Father's world!
From the shining courts above,
The Beloved One, His only son,
Came—a pledge of deathless love.

....

This world belongs to my Heavenly Father—so what reason could I ever have to be sad? (Romans 8:31) My Lord Jesus is the King of this world, so let all of Heaven be filled with joyful singing! My God rules over the entire universe—let everything on earth be glad at this good news! (1 Chronicles 29:10-12) This world belongs to my Heavenly Father. Jesus came and paid the price that makes the earth new again, and washes it clean from sin. (Revelation 21:5) God loves this earth because it is His, and His dear Son once walked here. There is no place on earth that is not made clean by Christ.

This is my Father's world,
Should my heart be ever sad?
The Lord is King—let the Heavens ring.
God reigns—let the earth be glad.
This is my Father's world.
Now closer to Heaven bound,
For dear to God is the earth Christ trod.
No place but is holy ground.

....

Oh yes, this world belongs to my Heavenly Father. Even when it seems like this world is a desert and I am in it all alone, even then will God show me something wonderful for which to thank Him—just as He showed Moses the burning bush in the wilderness, a spectacular thing in a dead, dry place. (Exodus 3:1-3) The *whole* world belongs to my Heavenly Father, so wherever I wander on the earth, and whether I'm poor or rich or sick or healthy, it makes no difference. (Philippians 4:11-13) If this whole world belongs to my Father, then no matter where I am, my heart is at home. (Romans 8:38-39)

This is my Father's world.
I walk a desert lone.
In a bush ablaze to my wondering gaze
God makes His glory known.
This is my Father's world,
A wanderer I may roam;
Whate'er my lot, it matters not,
My heart is still at home.

THOU ART THE WAY

Lyrics by **George Washington Doane**, 1824

Set to the tunes *St. James—Dundee—Lambeth—Arlington—Heber—Beatitudo—Faith (Dykes)—London New—Redhead No. 66—Godre'r Coed—Pollock—Downs—St. Bernard—Dedham—Vulpius—Richmond—Nun Danket All' (Gräfenberg)—Walke—Twenty-Fourth (Chapin)—Cherith—New Castle—Nannie—Selby—Falmouth—Manoah—Aspurg—Medfield—St. Peter—Holy Trinity—Melody (Cole)—Coventry—Groningen—St. David—Stracathro—St. Flavian—Johnville—Eversley—Bliss—Cambridge—Haight—St. André—Boston—Ruthwell—Hyde Park—Evan—Nicolaus—Shanti—Vernal Day—Morning Song*—and more!

Jesus, you are the Way, the only road to God. (John 14:6) Only to you, Jesus, can we run to escape sin and eternal death, separated from God forever. (Psalm 2:12) Anyone who wants to find God the Father has to look through you, Lord Jesus, for there is no way to reach God without you. (Acts 4:11-12)

Thou art the Way: to thee alone
From sin and death we flee;
And he who would the Father seek
Must seek Him, Lord, by thee.

....

Jesus, you yourself are God's Truth. (John 1:17) Wisdom comes only from your teaching—there is no way for us to be wise without you. (1 Corinthians 1:30) Only you can make our minds truly understand God and His Creation. (Luke 24:45, Matthew 11:27) And only you can wash our hearts clean from our filthy sin! (Hebrews 10:4-7)

Thou art the Truth: thy Word alone
True wisdom can impart;
Thou only canst inform the mind,
And purify the heart.

....

Jesus, you are the Life that God gives us. (John 1:4, 6:33-35, 11:25-26) That empty tomb that sits broken open outside of Jerusalem is the proof that you have defeated sin and death. (John 20:1-9) If you had not defeated Satan, you would still be dead in that tomb—but it is empty, Lord, and you are alive! (John 10:17-18, Luke 24:4-7, 1 Corinthians 15:3-8) Anyone who trusts *you* to save them, instead of relying on themselves, can never be harmed by death or Hell. (Revelation 2:11) Their body's death will only send their soul to be with you forever! (Luke 23:39-43)

Thou art the Life: the rending tomb
Proclaims thy conquering arm,
And those who put their trust in thee
Nor death nor Hell shall harm.

....

Jesus, you are the Way to God, you are God's Truth, and you are the Life that God gives our dead, sinful hearts. (John 14:6) Oh Jesus, please, let us walk in that Way, that path to God, all our lives. Teach us to believe that Truth, and to *act* like we believe it. And let us win that eternal Life at the end of our earthly lives, so that we will have the joy of living forever with you, Jesus! (Acts 20:32, 1 Peter 5: 10, Jude 1:24-25)

Thou art the Way, the Truth, the Life:
Grant us that Way to know,
That Truth to keep, that Life to win,
Whose joys eternal flow.

THRONED UPON THE AWFUL TREE

Lyrics by **John Ellerton** (see page 295), 1875

Set to the tunes *Arfon—Redhead No. 76 (Petra)—Spanish Hymn—Sebastian—Ouseley—Gethsemane—La Trobe—Rossal*

This is the King of all, but His only throne is this cross where they have nailed Him. Jesus, my suffering King, I will stay here with you. Your face is dark and sad, and twisted in pain. We might imagine the pain your body is feeling, Lord, but none of us can ever understand how deep your sadness really is. (Matthew 26:36-46) Oh Jesus, the pain of your wounded body is not the worst pain you are feeling! But no one but you and God can understand the weight you are carrying, so you are forced to suffer alone. (Isaiah 53:3-5)

Throned upon the awful tree,
King of grief, I watch with thee.
Darkness veils thine anguished face:
None its lines of woe can trace:
None can tell what pangs unknown
Hold thee silent and alone.

....

You are silent as you hang on that cross for three awful hours. (Luke 23:44-46) Our eyes cannot see it, but as you hang there, Jesus, you are wrestling with Satan, and you are carrying all the sins of God's people on your shoulders, with no one to help you! (1 Peter 2:24) There is darkness in the air around you, and there is darkness in your heart. (Matthew 27:45) You must suffer like this until it is over—until it is time for you, the chosen Lamb of God, to die.

Silent through those three dread hours,
Wrestling with the evil pow'rs,

Left alone with human sin,
Gloom around thee and within,
Till th' appointed time is nigh,
Till the Lamb of God may die.

....

Listen, everyone! Hear Jesus calling up at the clouded sky, saying "Why have you abandoned me, Father God?" (Matthew 27:46, Psalm 22:1-2) Jesus, you are God's only Son, and you are the one He chose to send, to pay the price that would set His people free from sin. (John 1:29) How has it come to this, that the only, dear Son of God is hanging here in pain, crying, "Oh God, why have you left me?"

Hark, that cry that peals aloud
Upward through the whelming cloud!
Thou, the Father's only Son,
Thou, His own Anointed One,
Thou dost ask him—can it be?
"Why hast thou forsaken me?"

....

So when my own heart feels as if it is drowning in fear and pain, help me remember that you once suffered too, Jesus—and that you did it *willingly*, to bring your people home to God. (John 15:20, Hebrews 12:1-3) So when I am crying and calling out, "Where are you, God?" because of the trouble in my life, remind me that you are there with me, Lord! (2 Corinthians 1:5, Psalm 34:18)

Lord, should fear and anguish roll
Darkly o'er my sinful soul,
Thou, who once wast thus bereft
That thine own might never be left,
Teach me by that bitter cry
In the gloom to know thee nigh.

TILL HE COME!

Lyrics by **Edward Henry Bickersteth**, 1861

Set to the tunes *"Till He Come!" O, Let the Words (Bliss)—Guide—Wells—Eltham—Reynoldstone—Tichfield—Redhead No. 76—Nassau—Aletta—St. Sebastian—Jesu, Mein Zuversicht (Ratisbon)—Grace (Chwatal)—Moravia—Till He Come—St. John—Reliance—Dykes—Cromer—Patience (Foxwell)—Toplady*—and more

"Only until Christ comes back!" Even as our voice is shaky and our eyes are full of tears because of the sadness of this life, let us remember what those sweet words mean! It seems so long to us, but the time between when Christ went back to Heaven and when He will come to earth again is really only a short time. (Revelation 22:20) Let those words, "Until Christ comes back," remind us of that sweet truth: Christ's return will be here before we know it. Let us think about those words and remember that Heaven, our true home, will be ours as soon just as Christ comes back for us. (John 14:1-3)

"Till He come!" O let the words
Linger on the trembling chords;
Let the little while between
In their golden light be seen;
Let us think how heav'n and home
Lie beyond that "Till He come."

....

Christian, when your loved ones die, when they go to rest with Jesus before you do, does this earth seem big and empty without them? Does your life seem to be cloudy now, with no more joy and sunshine? Hush those thoughts, my friend! Do not complain about God taking your loved ones to Heaven. Instead, remember that all death, sadness, and separation will only last until Christ comes back. (1 Thessalonians 4:13-18, Revelation 21:4)

When the weary ones we love
Enter on their rest above,
Seems the earth so poor and vast,
All our life-joy overcast?
Hush, be ev'ry murmur dumb:
It is only till He come.

....

Trouble and fighting surround us in this life. But tell me: if you could, would you really ask God to take away any of these sadnesses in your life? (1 Peter 4:12-14, Acts 5:41, Matthew 5:10-12) All of these hard times are exactly what Jesus told us we would go through if we followed Him. He told us we would have to "take up our cross" too. (John 15:20, Luke 9:23) After all, Jesus *Himself* suffered a horrible death in order to save us, didn't He? His death was a terrible sadness for His friends, but now look at that darkness, death, and tomb! (John 20:11-13) The sadness is gone, and Christ is alive! Whenever some sadness reminds us how evil this world is, Christ's *empty* tomb is there to remind us, "Death and sadness won't last forever—only until Christ comes back." (1 Corinthians 15:50-56)

Clouds and conflicts 'round us press:
Would we have one sorrow less?
All the sharpness of the cross,
All that tells the world is loss,
Death and darkness, and the tomb,
Only whisper "Till He come."

....

Look and see God's love—it has been laid out like a feast for you and me at Communion. (Luke 22:19-20) Drink the wine and break the bread! It is there to remind us that Christ's blood, flowing from His broken body, has defeated Satan and death forever. (1 Corinthians 11:26) The Lord's Table is our memorial, our constant reminder of what Christ has done, until He calls us to eat this same feast with Him in Heaven. (Luke 22:14-15, Revelation 19:6-9) Then He will call every one of His people—some from the earth, and some who are already in Heaven. We are separate from our brothers and sisters in Heaven now... but only until Christ comes back!

See, the feast of love is spread,
Drink the wine, and break the bread:
Sweet memorials, till the Lord
Call us 'round His heav'nly board;
Some from earth, from glory some,
Severed only till He come.

'TIS NOT THAT I DID CHOOSE THEE

Lyrics by **Josiah Conder** (see page 292), 1836

Set to the tunes *Calcutta—Savoy Chapel—O Du Liebe Meiner Liebe—Elwin—Aulé—Offertorium—Wieisse Flaggen—Conder—Miriam*

I am yours, Lord Jesus, but it is not because I chose you. I did not go looking for you. My heart was born sinful, so how could I ever decide on my own to come to you? (Matthew 11:27) My heart would still be ignoring you, Jesus, if *you* had not chosen me. (John 15:16) You are the one who washed my heart clean and set me free from my slavery to sin. (1 Corinthians 6:9-11) Before this world was ever created, you decided that I would follow you—that I would be yours! (Romans 8:29-30, Ephesians 1:4)

'Tis not that I did choose thee,
For, Lord, that could not be;
This heart would still refuse thee,
Hadst thou not chosen me.
Thou from the sin that stained me
Hast cleansed and set me free;
Of old thou hast ordained me,
That I should live to thee.

....

It was God's sovereign mercy that found me when I was lost in my sin. I was not looking for you, God, but you came and opened my blind mind so that I could understand your ways. (Luke 24:45) Until you changed my heart, I was perfectly happy to be a slave to this sinful world. (Romans 6:16-18) I was unable see the beauty of Heaven. But you made me want you, God, and that is why I will never serve any master above you, Lord. (Luke 16:13) My heart is thirsty for the grace that you give! (Psalm 42:1-2) How could I ever think that

I am saved because I went looking for you? I was helpless and sin-blind, and I did not even know it! (Ephesians 2:1-9) I am only saved because *you* chose *me.* (Romans 5:8) This is all I know: if there is any love in my heart for you at all, my God, it is only because *you loved me first.* (1 John 4:19, Ephesians 2:10)

'Twas sov'reign mercy called me
And taught my op'ning mind;
The world had else enthralled me,
To heav'nly glories blind.
My heart owns none before thee,
For thy rich grace I thirst;
This knowing, if I love thee,
Thou must have loved me first.

TO JORDAN CAME OUR LORD, THE CHRIST

Lyrics by **Martin Luther** (see page 310), 1541
Originally written in German; translated by **Richard Massie** in 1845
Set to the tune *Christ Unser Herr Zum Jordan Kam*

One day, our Master Jesus Christ walked down to the shore of the Jordan River to do something that God had sent Him to do: to be baptized by John the Baptist. Jesus told John that He had to be baptized in order for God's plan to be carried out completely, because, by being baptized, Jesus was creating a new sign for His people. (Matthew 3:13-14) He was going to shed His blood to pay the price for our sins, and we were going to become His people, so He gave us *baptism* to make a picture of our sins being washed off of us. (1 Peter 3:21-22) The old, sinful man dies with Christ, and the new man comes up out of the water with the new life that Jesus has given him, with all his sins washed away. (Colossians 2:11-12)

To Jordan came our Lord, the Christ,
To do God's pleasure willing,
And there was by St. John baptized,
All righteousness fulfilling;
There did He consecrate a bath
To wash away transgression,
And quench the bitterness of death.
By His own blood and passion,
He would a new life give us.

....

So listen, all of you, and understand what God means by baptism. Whatever God says about it is what Christians should believe—no more, no less. We must be careful not to either believe something wrong, or divide from other Christians because they don't believe exactly what we do. (1 Corinthians 1:10-17) So what does God's Word say? Our Lord Jesus made it clear that He wants us to use water. But Jesus also taught that it is not only about water. When we baptize each other in water, Jesus Himself baptizes us in His Words and His Spirit, and *that* is our true baptism. (Acts 2:38, Matthew 3:11, Ephesians 5:25-27)

So hear ye all, and well perceive
What God doth call a baptism,
And what a Christian should believe
Who error shuns, and schism:
That we should water use, the Lord
Declareth it His pleasure,
Not simple water, but the Word
And Spirit without measure—
He is the true Baptizer.

....

To teach us these things, God has given us His Word, full of signs and symbols that help us understand Him. On that day when Jesus was baptized in the Jordan, everyone around clearly heard God's voice calling out from Heaven, saying, "This is my dearly loved Son, and I am very pleased with Him. Listen to what He says to you!" (Matthew 3:17) Yes, every one of you, listen to Jesus when He calls to your heart! *Hear* His words, and then *do* what He teaches you. (John 13:17, James 1:22, Romans 2:13)

To show us this, He hath His word
With signs and symbols given;
On Jordan's banks was plainly heard
The Father's voice from Heaven:
"This is my well-beloved Son,
In whom my soul delighteth;
Hear Him!" Yea, hear Him, every one,

When He Himself inviteth;
Hear and obey His teaching!

....

So God the Father spoke from Heaven, and Jesus the Son of God stood as a young man in the water of the Jordan River. Then down from Heaven flew the Holy Spirit of God, and He looked like a dove. (Luke 3:21-22) So no one could deny what we see here: all three Persons of the Trinity were there that day, when Jesus was baptized in the Jordan. Each time a child of God is washed clean by baptism, God the Father, Jesus the Son, and the Holy Spirit all enter into that believer's heart, too. (Acts 2:37-39)

In tender manhood God the Son
In Jordan's water standeth;
The Holy Ghost from Heaven's throne
In dove-like form descendeth;
That thus the truth be not denied,
Nor should our faith e'er waver,
That the Three Persons all preside
At baptism's holy laver,
And dwell with the believer.

....

When Jesus sent His disciples out into the world, He told them, "Go to every nation in this world. Tell them to turn away from their sins and come to me in order to be saved from God's anger and the punishment of their sins. Then, if anyone believes in Me, *baptize them.* (Matthew 28:19-20) They will become a brand-new person in Me. They will be free from the kind of death that lasts forever, safe from being separated from God for eternity. (Revelation 2:11) That person will be with me in Heaven forever." (Luke 23:42-43)

Thus Jesus His disciples sent:
"Go, teach ye every nation,
That, lost in sin, they must repent,

And flee from condemnation;
He that believes and is baptized
Shall thereby have salvation,
A new-born man he is in Christ,
From death free and damnation,
He shall inherit Heaven."

....

If there is anyone who does not trust in Christ's mercy to save him, that person is still living in their sin, and they are doomed to spend eternity separated from God, in the fire that will never go out! (2 Thessalonians 1:5-10) That person's "good deeds" make no difference if he does not trust Christ to save him. (Galatians 2:16) His sin has not been washed away, and all of his "goodness" is worthless. (Matthew 6:22-23) The sin in that person's heart will bring him eternal death, because he is completely incapable of saving himself!

Who in this mercy hath not faith
Nor aught therein discerneth,
Is yet in sin, condemned to death
And fire that ever burneth;
His holiness avails him not,
Nor aught which he is doing;
His inborn sin brings all to naught,
And maketh sure his ruin;
Himself he cannot succor.

....

If we rely on our eyes and our own mind to understand baptism, it will make no sense. Our eyes only see some water—"And how does water wash our *souls* clean?" we might ask. But if we trust what Christ has taught us, our faith will show us that baptism is a picture of Christ's sacrifice on the cross. Christ is the Lamb whose blood paid the price for our sins. (Romans 6:3-5) The water of baptism washing over us is a picture of Christ's blood washing over us, washing away all our sin with it—all the sins we inherited from Adam, and all the sins we have committed ourselves. Christ's blood sets us free from *every* sin! (1 John 1:7, Hebrews 10:12-18)

The eye of sense alone is dim,
And nothing sees but water;
Faith sees Christ Jesus, and in Him
The Lamb ordained for slaughter;
It sees the cleansing fountain, red
With the dear blood of Jesus,
Which from the sins, inherited
From fallen Adam, frees us,
And from our own misdoings.

WELCOME, HAPPY MORNING!

Lyrics by **Venantius Honorius Clementianus Fortunatus**, 6th or early 7th century

Originally written in Latin; translated by **John Ellerton** (see page 344) in 1868

Set to the tunes *Fortunatus—Festa Dies—Hermas—St. Alban—Noel Nouvelet—Sei Du Mir Gegrüsset—Laus Tibi, Christe—Eventide—Salve, Festa Dies—Prince Rupert—Baptiste*—and more

As long as this world goes on, people of every generation will be glad to welcome this morning when it comes each year, because we know that Easter is the anniversary of the day when Hell was defeated and Heaven was opened up to God's people. (Colossians 1:13-14, Revelation 3:21) How did all of this happen? Look and see: one dead man, Christ, is not dead anymore! He is alive, and He rules with God now and forever. (1 Corinthians 15:20-22) Christ is our Maker, and all His Creation adores Him, because He has ended sin's curse, which held us prisoner. (Colossians 1:15-20)

"Welcome, happy morning!"
Age to age shall say:
Hell today is vanquished;
Heav'n is won today.
Lo! the Dead is living,
God forevermore!
Him, their true Creator,
All His works adore.

....

Jesus Christ, you are the one who made us, and you paid the price to buy us back from sin. Our soul's eternal life, and even our earthly life, is all thanks to you! (Romans 8:10) From your home with God in Heaven, you saw how mankind fell into sin and became Satan's slaves. So, even though you are the Son of God, you chose to come to earth—you became a man in order to save mankind. (John 1:14, Hebrews 10:4-7)

Maker and Redeemer,
Life and health of all,
Thou, from heav'n beholding
Human nature's fall,
Of the Father's God-head
True and only Son,
Manhood to deliver,
Manhood didst put on.

....

How can this be? You are the one who created life itself (Acts 3:14-16, 17:24-25, John 1:1-5), Christ, yet you chose to come down to earth and *die!* You, the Son of God, were the only one strong enough to save us. You walked through the darkness of Hell and death so that we would not have to. You told your disciples that you would be killed on a cross to pay the price for our sins... but you also told them what would happen next. (Matthew 20:17-19) Christ, you are the one God calls True and Faithful (Revelation 3:14, 19:11), and you were faithful to do just what you promised. On the third morning after you died, you walked out of the tomb, alive! (Matthew 28:1-10)

Thou, of life the author,
Death didst undergo,
Tread the path of darkness,
Saving strength to show;
Come then, True and Faithful,
Now fulfill thy word,
'Tis thine own third morning;
Rise, O buried Lord.

....

And now, Christ our *living* King, find your lost people and set their souls free! (John 10:7-15) Until now they have been chained up as Satan's prisoners. You will find all your people who have fallen into sin's death, Christ, and bring their souls back to life just the way *you* came back to life. (Romans 5:10, 6:4-5) Show them your victorious, kingly face, Christ! (Revelation 1:12-18) Tell all the nations of this world, "See, I was dead, and now I am alive, and I have bought this world with my blood!" This world has lived in the darkness of sin for so long. So come to us, Christ, and your life will come like a sunrise chasing away the darkness! (Colossians 3:4)

Loose the souls long prisoned,
Bound with Satan's chain;
Thine that now are fallen
Raise to life again;
Show thy face in brightness,
Bid the nations see;
Bring again our daylight;
Day returns with thee.

WHATE'ER MY GOD ORDAINS IS RIGHT

Lyrics by **Samuel Rodigast**, 1675

Originally written in German; translated by **Catherine Winkworth** (see page 346) in 1863

Set to the tunes *Was Gott Tut*—*Rodigast*—*Armstrong*—*I Jesus Søger Jeg Min Fred*—and more

---

Whatever my God orders for my life is right. He is holy and perfect, so I can rest easy knowing that whatever *He* decides will happen is what will happen (Isaiah 43:11-13)—and it will be good for me. (Jeremiah 29:11) No matter what He sends my way, I will follow Him. I will not grumble, because I know that it is from Him. He is my *God*, after all! (Isaiah 55:9) However dark my life seems to be, I know He is holding me, and will not let me fall. (Psalm 116:8-9) I know He sent me this darkness because it is what I need, so I leave it all in His hands. (Philippians 4:11-13)

Whate'er my God ordains is right:
His holy will abideth;
I will be still whate'er He doth
And follow where He guideth;
He is my God; though dark my road,
He holds me that I shall not fall:
Wherefore to Him I leave it all.

....

Whatever my God orders for my life is right. He will never lie to me! He has promised to bring me home to Himself, and He will do it. (Numbers 23:19) No matter how it looks to me, I know that any path He is leading me on is the right path for me. (Psalm 23:3, 139:3) He will never leave me to walk it alone! (Deuteronomy 31:8) So no matter what He sends me in life, I will take it gladly. (1 Thessalonians 5:16-18) He will not leave me in that darkness forever, I know. (Psalm 30:5) My God's hand led me here, and it will be His hand that leads me back out of this sadness, so I will patiently wait for Him to move me when He decides it is time. (1 Peter 5:6-7)

Whate'er my God ordains is right:
He never will deceive me;
He leads me by the proper path:
I know He will not leave me.
I take, content, what He hath sent;
His hand can turn my griefs away,
And patiently I wait His day.

....

Whatever my God orders for my life is right. I know beyond doubt that He loves me, so how could I worry that something He sends would hurt me? (Psalm 103:11) It may be bitter, but He knows what I need better than I do, so I will take what He gives me! (Matthew 26:39) My God is faithful! Every morning, I will make sure I am truly trusting Him, and I will offer my life to Him all over again. (Romans 12:1)

Whate'er my God ordains is right:
His loving thought attends me;
No poison can be in the cup
That my Physician sends me.
My God is true; each morn anew
I'll trust His grace unending,
My life to Him commending.

....

Whatever my God orders for my life is right. My God is also my friend (John 15:15), and my loving Father! (Matthew 7:11) No matter how many storms are casting their shadow on my life, He will never allow them to hurt my soul. (2 Samuel 22) In this life I will have both joys and sadnesses, and sometimes

I may wonder if my God really *does* love me. But someday, when I see His face in Heaven, I will know for certain that it was true: He loves me more than I can imagine! (1 Corinthians 13:12)

Whate'er my God ordains is right:
He is my friend and Father;
He suffers naught to do me harm,
Though many storms may gather,
Now I may know both joy and woe,
Some day I shall see clearly
That He hath loved me dearly.

....

Whatever my God orders for my life is right. The things God has sent to my life now might feel like a cupful of bitter medicine, but I will drink it all anyway, because I know He would not have sent it to me if I didn't need it. (1 Thessalonians 5:23-24, Matthew 20:22-23) My God is faithful, and He will not abandon me! Every morning, my God, you fill up my heart with comfort and peace all over again, and you send the sadness and pain running. (Lamentations 3:22-24)

Whate'er my God ordains is right:
Though now this cup, in drinking,
May bitter seem to my faint heart,
I take it all, unshrinking.
My God is true; each morn anew
Sweet comfort yet shall fill my heart,
And pain and sorrow shall depart.

....

Whatever my God orders for my life is just right! That is the truth I will stand on. Even if sadness, poverty, sickness, or even death is what God has for me, I will still know for certain that He has not left me alone. (Romans 5:2-5) My Heavenly Father is taking care of me; the proof of that is everywhere! I know

He is holding me up so that I do not fall, so I trust Him to bring me safely through my life—all the way home to Heaven, with Him. (Jude 1:24-25)

Whate'er my God ordains is right:
Here shall my stand be taken;
Though sorrow, need, or death be mine,
Yet I am not forsaken.
My Father's care is 'round me there;
He holds me that I shall not fall:
And so to Him I leave it all.

WHEN I SURVEY THE WONDROUS CROSS

Lyrics by **Isaac Watts** (see page 333), 1707–1709

Set to the tunes *Hamburg—Rockingham—Eucharist—Duke Street—O Waly Waly—Doncaster—Vicaria—McCabe—Carey—Lacrima—St. Cross—Louvan—Mildred—Breslau—All Saints—Retirement—Constance—Wondrous Cross—Kingsley—Eden—Heber—Belville—Ward—Missionary Chant—We Thank Thee, Lord Jesus Christ—Windham—Uxbridge—Rockingham New—Genevan 100—Zephyr—Morte Christe—Erhalt Uns, Herr, Bei Deinem Wort—Hebron—Effingham—Sutheran—Crucifixion—Sessions—Mohr—Bethany*—and many more!

Whenever I think about the cross on which Jesus Christ, the Prince of Heaven, died, worldly things always seem far less important to me. (Colossians 3:1-2) The cross makes me realize that any gains I might get in this life—education, money, friends—are actually a *loss* to me if they distract me from Jesus. (Philippians 3:3-11) I can only be grateful for what Christ did for me, and that gratefulness chases all the worldly pride out of my heart. (1 Corinthians 1:18)

When I survey the wondrous cross
On which the Prince of glory died,
My richest gain I count but loss,
And pour contempt on all my pride.

....

Lord Jesus, never let me boast about anything *except* that you died to save me, my Lord and my God! (Galatians 6:14) All these worldly things that my heart loves ... here, I let them all go. I sacrifice them to Christ. (Romans 12:1) Nothing in the world means more to me than His blood that saved me!

Forbid it, Lord, that I should boast,
Save in the death of Christ, my God;

All the vain things that charm me most
I sacrifice them to His blood.

....

When Jesus sacrificed Himself to save me, they wounded His head, His hands, and His feet. (Mark 15:17, Psalm 22:16, John 20:24-29) Imagine how that must have looked—see the blood flowing from His wounds! That blood represents both His *grief* over sin and His *love* for us, mixing together, flowing down to the ground. Has anyone ever seen so much sadness and so much love together? They made fun of Jesus, and crowned the King of kings Himself with a crown of *thorns.* (Matthew 27:29) But remember what His death on the cross means! Have thorns ever been made into a more meaningful and honorable crown than this one?

See, from His head, His hands, His feet,
Sorrow and love flow mingled down!
Did e'er such love and sorrow meet,
Or thorns compose so rich a crown?

....

Imagine how Jesus' blood flowed out of His wounds, covering His body like a robe as He hung there on the cross. When I think of His blood and how it paid the price that set me free from sin (Ephesians 2:13, 1 John 1:7), how can I help but give my whole self to Jesus in thanks? (Hebrews 12:28) Since Christ has given me a new heart, I no longer belong to this world, and this world's "treasures" mean nothing to me. (Romans 6:11)

His dying crimson, like a robe,
Spreads o'er His body on the tree;
Then I am dead to all the globe,
And all the globe is dead to me.

....

Even if all of earth and space belonged to me, if I offered it all to Jesus, it would not come *near* being enough to repay what Jesus did for me. When I have been given a love as amazing as Jesus' love for me—a love which only God can give—then I owe Him my soul that will live forever, and my time and my work here on earth; everything I have, and nothing less! (Luke 10:27)

Were the whole realm of nature mine,
That were a present far too small;
Love so amazing, so divine,
Demands my soul, my life, my all.

WHY SHOULD CROSS AND TRIAL GRIEVE ME?

Lyrics by **Paul Gerhardt** (see page 300), 1653

This hymn is *cento* poetry, meaning the author put together verses and bits of writing from various other authors to make a new poem.

Originally written in German; translated mainly by **John Kelly** in 1867

Set to the tune *Warum Sollt' Ich Mich Denn Grämen*

Why should I be downhearted when I go through hard times? Christ said that if anyone wanted to follow Him, they would have to go through troubles just like He did. (Luke 9:23, John 15:18-19) He also promised that when I do walk through hard times, He is *constantly* near me to comfort me. (Matthew 5:4, 28:19-20, 2 Corinthians 1:3-5) He will never abandon me! With the Son of God as my Savior, what reason do I have to fear anyone else? (Romans 8:31) Who could possibly stop God from bringing me safely to Heaven, to the home that Christ Himself has given me? (Philippians 1:6, John 10:27-29)

Why should cross and trial grieve me?
Christ is near with His cheer,
Never will He leave me.
Who can rob me of the Heaven
That God's Son for my own
To my faith hath given?

....

Even though I am carrying a heavy trouble right now, and my heart is weak under the pain and the weight of it, do I have any reason to think that God has forgotten me? (Psalm 42) God has made Himself my helper. (Psalm 54:4) He Himself *sent* this trouble to teach me and make me more like Christ. (Romans 8:28-30, Hebrews 12:5-6, Isaiah 45:5-7) He understands it better than I do!

He also knows, far better than I do, when it will be time to end my trouble. (Psalm 69:13)

Though a heavy cross I'm bearing
And my heart feels the smart,
Shall I be despairing?
God, my Helper, who doth send it,
Well doth know all my woe
And how best to end it.

....

God often sends me times of happiness in my life. Do I have a right to complain if He sometimes sends me a time of sadness? (Job 2:9-10) I know beyond a doubt that *God is good.* (Psalm 31:19, 84:11) And when He decides I must walk through a hard time, He walks through it with me (Hebrews 4:15), and He even makes the pain He sends easier to bear. He will never leave me—never! (Hebrews 13:5)

God oft gives me days of gladness;
Shall I grieve if He give
Seasons, too, of sadness?
God is good and tempers ever
All my ill, and He will
Wholly leave me never.

....

If you look, you can find them everywhere: people who are truly hopeful, cheerful, and not discouraged no matter what happens to them. (2 Thessalonians 1:4) *Those people are trusting in Christ*—and that means nothing can shake them! Even if they have to face death itself, they only feel joy because they hear the voice of Jesus their Savior and Master calling them home. (Acts 5:40-42, 7:54-60, 21:13)

Hopeful, cheerful, and undaunted
Everywhere they appear
Who in Christ are planted.
Death itself cannot appall them,
They rejoice when the voice
Of their Lord doth call them.

....

Death is not *just* a destroyer. If we belong to Christ, when we die, that means we are freed forevermore from all the fear, worry, and sadness of earth! (Revelation 14:13, Psalm 116:15) Yes, death will be the last chapter in the story of our lives on earth, but death is also the doorway into Heaven—our eternal, glorious home.

Death cannot destroy forever;
From our fears, cares and tears
It will us deliver.
It will close life's mournful story,
Make a way that we may
Enter Heavenly glory.

....

All of the "treasures" of this earth ... what is it really worth, in the end? Nothing more than a handful of sand—and think of all the trouble it brings us, too! Yet we all worry so much about our precious "stuff," even though it will fade away in the end and leave us empty again. (Ecclesiastes 5:10-12) The gifts that Christ gives to all His people are something very different: His Heavenly gifts will never fade away, and we will never regret or get tired of them. (Matthew 6:19-21)

What is all this life possesses?
But a hand full of sand
That the heart distresses.
Noble gifts that pall me never

Christ, our Lord, will accord
To His saints forever.

....

Lord Jesus, my Shepherd, please bring me home to you! You have given yourself to me, and I belonged to you before I ever even knew you. Yes, I am yours, because you bought me. (1 Corinthians 7:23) I was doomed to spend eternity in death, away from my God, but you paid the price of my sin with your blood, Christ, and now I am saved! (John 5:24)

Lord, my shepherd, take me to thee.
Thou art mine; I was thine
Even ere I knew thee.
I am thine, for thou hast bought me;
Lost I stood, but thy blood
Free salvation bought me.

....

Not only am I yours because of what you did, but you are *mine,* Jesus! I love you because you have loved me (1 John 4:19), and I will gladly tell this world that I am yours. (Matthew 10:32, 2 Timothy 1:12) You are the light that shines on my path, and all my joy is from you, Christ, so forevermore you will be the One most important to me. You will sit on the throne as King of my heart, and nothing will ever replace you. My dear Savior, please let me come to you soon, so that I will finally see you face-to-face! (1 Corinthians 13:12) Hold me tight in your grace, so I that I will be yours forever. (Jude 1:24-25)

Thou art mine; I love and own thee.
Light of joy, ne'er shall I
From my heart dethrone thee.
Savior, let me soon behold thee
Face-to-face—may thy grace
Evermore enfold me!

HYMNWRITERS

Meet some of the poets who wrote the hymns in this book. They read in Scripture how wonderful our God is, then helped the rest of us find the words to sing about it.

JOSEPH ADDISON

1672–1719

On May 1, 1672, in Milston, a tiny parish in Wiltshire, England, a baby boy named Joseph Addison got started on his busy life. When he grew up and went to Magdalen College in Oxford, his plan was to become a minister, like his father. But he quickly discovered two things that changed his plans: one, he was fascinated by diplomacy (the way different countries deal with each other); two, he had a talent for writing. He began to look for a career that would use these two new interests—yet he didn't forget about his faith.

In 1700, three years after he graduated from Magdalen College, Joseph was offered a traveling scholarship. He set out to tour Italy, Switzerland, Vienna, Germany, and the Netherlands in order to study foreign countries and get ideas for his writing. He did not come home to England until his father died in 1703.

In 1704, Joseph wrote a poem called "The Campaign" to celebrate the victory that the British Army and its allies had won at the Battle of Blenheim. The poem was so appreciated by the people that in 1706 Joseph was made Under Secretary of State. He was given a seat in Parliament in 1708 (which he kept until he died), and he also eventually served as Secretary of State, Commissioner of Appeals, Secretary to the Lord Lieutenant of Ireland, and Chief Secretary of Ireland.

But Joseph Addison is best remembered for his writing. His tragedy play Cato was very popular—it was George Washington's favorite play—and he often published essays in English magazines such as *The Spectator, The Tatler, The Guardian,* and *The Freeholder.* Joseph crafted his own style of writing which was simpler than the old, usual style, and the people loved it. Occasionally, he included a poem at the end of his essays in *The Spectator.* When he saw how people loved those poems, he wrote more. Eventually, five of those poems would become hymns.

Like so many others of his time, Joseph Addison suffered bad health. The story goes that when he lay on his deathbed, he did not pray for himself—instead, he prayed for his brother-in-law, the Earl of Warwick, who was not a believer. When the Earl came to see him, Joseph said to him, "See in what peace a Christian can die!" In that peace, Joseph Addison died at age 47 on June 17, 1719.

....

The Spacious Firmament on High (page 241)

MALTBIE DAVENPORT BABCOCK

1858–1901

Maltbie Davenport Babcock was born at 708 East Fayette Street in Syracuse, New York on August 3, 1858. He was the great-grandson of Henry Davis, the second president of Hamilton College, and he got his first two names from his grandfather, Reverend Ebenezer Davenport Maltbie, an influential minister with Puritan ancestors.

Maltbie was a tall, handsome, broad-shouldered young man who played baseball in college and graduated from Syracuse University with highest honors. He married Katherine Eliot Tallman on October 4, 1882, the same year that he graduated from Auburn Theological Seminary. Maltbie and Katherine had two children, but both of them died as infants.

The first church Maltbie pastored after seminary was First Presbyterian Church in Lockport, New York. In 1887 he moved to Brown Memorial Church in Baltimore, Maryland, where he was dearly loved by his congregation. During his three years there, Maltbie gained a reputation for being a powerful speaker. He raised funds to help Jewish refugees who were fleeing to America from the "pogroms" (riots against Jews) in Russia at the time.

Maltbie was skilled at playing the piano, organ, and violin, and he wrote several hymns. People said that Reverend Babcock "lived or sung his thoughts."

He loved to go for runs in the early mornings—"I'm going out to see my Father's world," he would tell his wife.

In 1900, he was asked to be the pastor of Brick Church in New York City. But the next year, on May 18, 1901, Maltbie Davenport Babcock died in Naples, Italy, on his way home from a trip to the Holy Land. He was only 42 years old. The *New York Times* wrote an article about his funeral: there was no special memorial address—just as Maltbie had wanted. No address was needed, said Maltbie's friend, Dr. Henry Van Dyke. "We do not need a candle to show a sunbeam. The work our brother has done—the life he lived speaks for him. This is not a black funeral—it is a white one—and we are going to thank God for what He has given, but has taken unto Himself."

....

This Is My Father's World (page 243)

BEDE THE VENERABLE

673–735

Bede (also spelled Beda, or Baeda) was born in 673 in the Kingdom of Northumbria, very near where a monk named Benedict Biscop would build a double-monastery called Monkwearmouth-Jarrow Abbey a few years later. Today, the area is called Tyne and Wear, in northeast England.

Bede got his schooling at the twin monasteries of Monkwearmouth and Jarrow. Books were rare and incredibly expensive in the 7th century, but Benedict Biscop of the monasteries, and his successor, Ceolfrith, both adored learning and literature. The books they collected (and made!) at the twin monasteries formed one of the best libraries in Britain at the time. Monkwearmouth-Jarrow Abbey was a fortunate place for a boy to grow up in the Middle Ages, and young Bede made the most of it—in fact, he never left the abbey.

By the age of 19 Bede had a reputation of being well-educated and devout in his faith. So, the bishop of Hexham, named John of Beverly, ordained Bede to be a deacon. Ten years later, he made Bede a priest. Bede was also a scholar, philosopher, poet and hymnwriter, grammarian, historian, biographer, and preacher. Monkwearmouth-Jarrow was a place of book-making, and Bede did his part by writing volumes on all sorts of topics. His book *Historia Ecclesiastica* is a valuable record of early English Church history. Though Bede did not write many hymns—probably no more than 12, if even that many—his hymns are a fascinating example of Church poetry in its earliest days. Bede was fond of directly quoting Bible verses in his hymns.

Bede the Venerable died in the monastery of Jarrow on May 26, 735. Monkwearmouth-Jarrow Abbey had been the only home he'd ever known, and together he and his beloved abbey had made a mark in England's literary history.

....

A Hymn of Glory Let Us Sing (page 18)

BERNARD OF CLAIRVAUX

c. 1090–1153

Bernard of Clairvaux was born in his father's castle in Les Fontaines, Burgundy (which is now in France) sometime in 1090–91. His father, Tesselin, was a knight of Burgundy and a friend of the Duke of Burgundy, so Bernard grew up with the charmed life of a nobleman's son. But his mother, Aleth, raised him to also be a Christian, and when he went to school at Châtillon-sur-Seine he gained a reputation for being a studious, sober-minded boy. Bernard's mother died in 1105, but Bernard said he saw visions of her at night, urging him to be a faithful Christian. So in 1113, Bernard and 12 of his friends (including his uncle and two brothers) became monks at a Cistercian monastery called Citeaux.

But Citeaux was a crowded place. In about 1115, when he was 25 or 26, Bernard was sent with a group of monks to start a new monastery. They settled in the Valley of Wormwood in Burgundy. Hounded by raiders, Bernard and his monks nearly starved before they could finish building their new home, but they finished at last, and Bernard named their new home Clara Vallis, meaning "clear valley"—the name that would eventually morph into Clairvaux.

Even as the busy abbot (leader) of a monastery, Bernard didn't lose his old studiousness: he spent regular time studying Scripture. His knowledge of the Bible made him one of the most influential churchmen of his century. Due to his nobleman's education he was an eloquent preacher, and over the course of his life the people relied on Bernard to settle several huge controversies in the

Church. It was Bernard's delight to teach people about the hope of Christ, and by doing so he brought light and hope to a dark time in history.

Bernard of Clairvaux died in 1153. Over three hundred years later, Martin Luther—a fellow monk—wrote, "Bernard was the best monk that ever lived, whom I love beyond all the rest put together."

....

Jesus, Thou Joy of Loving Hearts (page 142)
O Sacred Head, Now Wounded (page 200)

HORATIUS BONAR

1808–1889

On December 19, 1808 in Edinburgh, Scotland, Horatius Bonar was born into a family that had been growing their sons into pastors for two centuries. So, though his own father was a lawyer, Horatius and his brothers were raised to join the family business—preaching the Gospel.

After Horatius graduated from the University of Edinburgh, he spent four years ministering to the people who lived in the poorest parts of Edinburgh. While teaching there, Horatius noticed that the children did not care for the music of the old psalter—so he wrote new hymns for them. He began to write more and more hymns for both children and adults. Even his hymns for children were full of deep meaning.

When he left the mission work in Edinburgh, Horatius assisted Reverend John Lewis for a time at St. James' Church in Leith, Scotland, until he became the minister of North Parish in Kelso in 1837. In 1843, Horatius married Jane Lundie, who also wrote hymns. In 1866, Horatius became the minister of Chalmers Memorial Church, and in 1883 he was chosen to be the Moderator of the General Assembly of the Free Church of Scotland. He was described as a highly energetic man—if he wasn't preaching, he was writing. Horatius published numerous books containing his own hymns, Jane's hymns, and hymns he had translated from other languages.

His 40-year marriage to Jane was full of suffering—five of their children died young. Jane died in 1884, and Horatius suffered bad health for the last two years of his life. But even through his troubles, he was known for constant prayer and a gentle nature. A revival came to Scotland under the preaching of Horatius, his brothers, and their friend Robert Murray McCheyne. By his death in 1889, Horatius Bonar had written around 600 hymns, and hymn-singers all over the world mourned him.

....

O Love of God, How Strong and True (page 189)

JOHN BUNYAN

1628–1688

John Bunyan was a rascal, born to a tinker and his wife sometime in November 1628, in Elstow, England. He received very little schooling. Though he grew up to be a tin-smith like his father, John was more dedicated to using foul language and running wild than he was to his work. Occasionally, something would happen to make John Bunyan think about the wicked way he was carrying on. In those moments, the idea of God's anger at his sin terrified John so much that he decided there was no hope for him anyway—so why bother changing his lifestyle? But God's warnings were getting harder for John to shrug off.

As a teen, John fought in the English Civil War under Oliver Cromwell. After the war, when he was 20, John met a godly girl, from a godly family, and decided she was a good reason to reform himself. When she and John married, her father gave them two books: *The Plain Man's Pathway to Heaven* and *The Practice of Piety*. Through the influence of his wife's godliness and those Christian books, John became interested in salvation. He cleaned up his life on the outside—but in his heart, he was still torn up by fear of God's punishment for his sins. He saw how wicked he had been, and he did not see how Christ could save a rogue like him.

The Bunyans' first daughter, Mary, was born blind. They had three more children, and then John's wife died. John was certain this was punishment for his sins. Still worried that he was unforgivable, John was introduced to a pastor named John Gifford, who told John that he too had once lived a wild life. But Gifford had discovered the truth: that Christ's blood is enough to pay for all sins. It took time, but one day John Bunyan found 2 Corinthians 1:9, which says, "My grace is sufficient for you"—and he finally believed it was true.

John began preaching the Gospel to his customers who came to have their tin pots fixed. He used ordinary, easy-to-understand words when he preached, and the people loved him. When his friend John Gifford died, Gifford's congregation asked John Bunyan to be their new pastor.

Then there came a new king in England... and new laws about who was allowed to preach. Noy being a licensed minister, John was kicked out of his church. But his people still wanted to hear him, so he took to preaching under an enormous oak outside of town. This was "unauthorized" preaching, against the law—and John was arrested for it in November 1660, along with thousands of other "unauthorized" preachers like him. He could have been released at any time if he promised to stop preaching, but that he would never do.

John spent a total of twelve years in prison. He used that time to write *Grace Abounding to the Chief of Sinners, The Pilgrim's Progress, The Life and Death of Mr. Badman, The Holy War,* and more. When the laws finally changed, John Bunyan was released on May 17, 1672, and spent the rest of his life preaching, writing, and enjoying being with his family again. He died on August 31, 1688, two weeks after preaching his last sermon in Whitechapel, London.

....

He Who Would Valiant Be (page 108)

JOHN CENNICK

1718–1755

On December 12, 1718, John Cennick was born in Reading, an old market town in Berkshire, England. His family came from Quaker ancestors, but John was raised in the Church of England. As a young man, John worked as a land surveyor in his hometown. That changed when he met the Wesley brothers in 1739.

John Wesley hired 21-year-old John Cennick to be a teacher in his school for coal-miners' children in the town of Kingswood. John taught there for a year, and then he began preaching like the Wesley brothers. The partnership didn't last long, however; in 1740, John left the Wesleys because of doctrinal differences and took to preaching under George Whitefield instead.

John began to write hymns during his time at Kingswood, and asked his hymnwriter friend Charles Wesley to edit them. John published four different collections of his original hymns in the 1740's, as well as some prose books and a few of his sermons.

John worked with Whitefield until 1745, when he joined a group of Moravian Christians from Germany. In London, in 1749, John became a deacon in the Moravian Church, and that job gave him the opportunity to travel twice to Germany and once to the north part of Ireland, where many other Moravian Christians were living. John spent the rest of his life spreading the Gospel in England and Ireland.

Back home in Chelsea, London, John came down with a fever and died on July 4, 1755. He was only 36 years old, but he had already helped to start at least 40 churches. He left a wife and two children. Years after John's death, his son-in-law, Reverend John Swertner, published more of his hymns in the 1789 *Moravian Hymn Book.* Still more of John Cennick's hymns appear in the famous *Sacred Harp* hymnal also.

....

Lo! He Comes, with Clouds Descending (page 155)

GILBERT KEITH CHESTERTON

1874–1936

Gilbert Keith Chesterton (commonly known as G.K. Chesterton) was born on May 29, 1874 in Kensington, England. As a boy he went to school at St. Paul's in London. He was a talented artist, so he studied art at the Slade School of Art in London, but he never finished earning a degree.

In September 1895, at age 21, Gilbert began working for Redway, a publishing house in London. He worked there until the next October, when he starting working for the T. Fisher Unwin publishing house. He married Frances Blogg in 1901, and she would be Gilbert's devoted companion for the rest of his life. Though he been baptized as a toddler, Gilbert had not grown up as a Christian, and he afterwards said that Frances helped to lead him back to the Church. He remained a committed Christian for the rest of his life.

Gilbert had begun writing for newspapers occasionally, and in 1902 he got a job writing a column each week in the *Daily News*. Three years later he switched to writing a column for the *Illustrated London News*, and he did so until just before his death. In 1925, Gilbert founded his own newspaper, *G.K.'s Weekly*, and kept that going until his death, too.

Gilbert was 6'4" tall, weighed nearly 300 pounds, and had a tendency to forget where he was going—he occasionally had to telegraph his wife from a railway station to ask her where he was supposed to be. When Gilbert wrote his autobiography, he claimed that he and his friend George Bernard Shaw had once acted as cowboys in a silent film that was never released. Some of Gilbert's stories were mysteries, so he served for six years as the president of a group of British mystery writers called the Detective Club.

Gilbert also found time to write hundreds of poems, roughly 200 short stories, a few thousand essays, a handful of plays, a few hymns, and almost 100 books including novels, mysteries, biographies, theology, and books to defend Christianity. And for the last four or five years before his death, Gilbert gave an average of 40 radio talks per year on BBC radio. It is said that Gilbert's book, *The Everlasting Man,* helped convince young C.S. Lewis to become a Christian; his novel, *The Napoleon of Notting Hill,* inspired Michael Collins to fight for Irish independence; and one of his essays in the *Illustrated London News* inspired Mahatma Ghandi to work for India's independence! Whether these stories are true or not, G.K. Chesterton's writing certainly did heavily influence the people of the early 20th century. He died of heart failure on June 14, 1936, in Beaconsfield, England, at 62 years old.

....

O God of Earth and Altar (page 186)

JOSIAH CONDER

1789–1855

On September 17, 1789, Josiah Conder was born in his father's bookshop on Falcon Street in London. He was the fourth son of Thomas Conder, a Nonconformist engraver and bookseller. As a child, Josiah came down with smallpox and lost vision in one eye, so his family sent him to Hackney, north of London, for treatment. His eye recovered, and he was schooled in Hackney. He began to work with words at a young age: his first essay was published in the *Monthly Preceptor* when he was ten.

At 15, Josiah began working in his father's bookshop in London. He took over the business when he was 21, in 1810. That same year, Josiah befriended a young woman named Joan Elizabeth—they worked together to write a contribution for a magazine, and then they got married. Together they had four sons and a daughter. The Conders were a family of Christians and wordsmiths: Josiah and Joan were both writers and hymnwriters, and their son Eustace would be as well.

In 1819, Josiah left the bookshop to become the proprietor and editor of *Eclectic Review* magazine, a job he kept for 20 years. He also spent 23 years editing the *Patriot*, a Christian and political magazine. He and Joan both worked diligently for the abolition of slavery. Josiah published six books of his own poetry, but he also wrote more than nine prose books on theology and geography, and even a biography of John Bunyan. As a hymnwriter, Josiah admired Isaac Watts, and wrote an article about him. In the 1830's Josiah edited *The Congregational Hymn Book: a Supplement to Dr. Watt's Psalms and Hymns.* It contained fifty-six of Josiah's original hymns. *The Congregational Hymn Book* was his most popular book—about 90,000 copies sold in the first seven years!

All told, Josiah Conder wrote about 60 original hymns. He died suddenly in Hampstead, England on December 27, 1855.

....

'Tis Not That I Did Choose Thee (page 254)

THOMAS COTTERILL

1779–1823

Thomas Cotterill was born on December 4, 1779, the son of a wool-stapler (a wool-seller) in Cannock, England. In 1801, when he was 22, he graduated from St. John's College, Cambridge and became a minister in the Church of England. In June, 1803 Thomas got his first position as a curate (pastor's assistant) at the church in Tutbury. He worked there for five years before he was moved to the Incumbency of Lane End in Staffordshire, where he stayed from 1808–17, and then served as the Perpetual Curate of St. Paul's Church in Sheffield for the rest of his life.

Thomas published several books, and his most well known was his *Selection of Psalms and Hymns,* first published in 1810. But when he tried to publish a new edition of his *Selection* in 1819, he ran into problems. In Thomas' time, the Church was not certain whether it was right to sing hymns in worship—some Christians believed that the Psalms, as inspired Scripture, were the only songs we ought to sing to God.

But at last the Church of England allowed Thomas to write a new edition of his hymnal and publish it. So, with the help of hymnwriter James Montgomery, Thomas made a new version of his *Selection* and published it in 1820. It became the first official hymnal of the Anglican Church in his region.

Thomas wrote about 25 hymns of his own and made new versifications of certain Psalms. He also created some *cento* hymns by putting together pieces of other hymns to make new ones. But the hymnwriting Thomas liked best (and is most remembered for) is the alterations he made to old hymns from other writers.

Thomas Cotterill died at only 44 years old on December 29, 1823 in Sheffield, England.

....

Lo! He Comes, with Clouds Descending (page 155)
Rock of Ages, Cleft for Me (page 218)

JOHN ELLERTON

1826–1893

John Ellerton was born in Clerkenwell, near London, on December 16, 1826. Growing up, he went to school at King William's College on the Isle of Man, and when he was grown he went to Trinity College, Cambridge.

In 1850, John became a curate (pastor's assistant) at the church in Easebourne, England. Two years later he was the curate at Brighton. Then, in 1860, John was given his own church in Crewe Green, a congregation full of farmers and steelworkers. He stayed at Crewe Green longer than anywhere else. John moved to be the rector of Hinstock in 1872, then the rector of Barnes in 1876. He had a huge congregation to care for in Barnes, and eventually John's health broke from exhaustion. He lived for one year, from 1884–85, in Italy, then came home to be the rector of White Roding in 1886.

Aside from his pastoring work, John Ellerton was an expert hymnologist. In 1871, he helped fellow hymnwriter William Walsham How edit *Hymns for Schools and Bible Classes*, a hymnal from the SPCK (Society for Promoting Christian Knowledge). John wrote at least two prose books, but he is remembered now for his hymns and translations—he wrote at least 50 of his own hymns, and translated at least ten from Latin. By the time John Ellerton died in Torquay, England, on June 15, 1893, all of his hymns were being regularly sung by churches.

. . . .

God the All-Terrible! (page 100)
Throned upon the Awful Tree (page 249)
Welcome, Happy Morning! (page 261)

JOHANN FRANCK

1618–1677

Johann Franck was born in Guben, Germany on June 1, 1618—the same year the Thirty Years' War began. Johann's father died when he was only two years old, so his uncle, the Town Judge of Guben, adopted him. Johann was sent to a Latin school in Guben, and later to other schools in Cottbus, Stettin, and Thorn.

In 1638 he went to study to be a lawyer at the University of Königsberg—the only German university not destroyed in the Thirty Years' War. Though many of his fellow students lived wild and foolishly, Johann did not join in their behavior—his faith, his love for nature, and his good choice of friends kept him on the straight and narrow. Two of those good friends were hymnwriters, like himself: Simon Dach, and Heinrich Held.

During the Thirty Years' War, Johann's hometown of Guben was frequently filled with German and Swiss soldiers. For this reason, at Easter in 1640, Johann chose to leave the University to be with his mother in Guben. But though felt the need to leave school and protect his mother, Johann did eventually complete his law studies and began working as a lawyer in Guben in May 1645. A few years later Johann became a city councillor, then the burgermeister (mayor) of Guben in 1661. Finally, Johann became a member of the Landtag, representing his region in the government.

But Johann wasn't just a politician; he was a Christian, and a hymnwriter. In all, he wrote around 110 hymns, which were published by his friend, Johann

Crüger, a fellow hymnwriter and the organist at St. Nicholas' Church in Berlin. Johann's hymns appeared in the first Guben hymnbook in 1648. Johann had certainly left his mark on his hometown! Of German hymnwriters from his time, Johann Franck is considered to be second only to Paul Gerhardt. He died in his beloved Guben on June 18, 1677.

....

Jesus, Priceless Treasure (page 145)

BENJAMIN FRANCIS

1734–1799

Benjamin Francis was born in Pen-y-gelli, Wales in 1734. His parents died when he was only six, and afterwards he was raised in Swansea, Wales. He was baptized at age 15. A few years later he began studying at Bristol Baptist Academy in England. Around the age of 20, Benjamin began preaching as an assistant minister at a church in Broadmead, Bristol, England. Shortly afterward he moved to be the pastor of his own congregation in Chipping Sodbury, England, but very soon after he moved again to be the pastor in Horsley (a town now known as Shortwood). There Benjamin stayed, and had a very fruitful and happy ministry for 42 years. Several times he was invited to be the pastor of bigger churches in London and elsewhere, but Benjamin turned them all down—he wanted to stay with his beloved congregation in Horsley.

He was a very busy hymnwriter, as well as pastor. When fellow hymnwriter John Rippon published his *Selection of Hymns*, it contained five of Benjamin's hymns. But you likely couldn't read Benjamin Francis' most famous hymns—he wrote them in Welsh! His native Welsh culture was dear to Benjamin for all his life. He preached 14 times for the Welsh Association, and published 194 hymns written in Welsh.

Benjamin Francis died on December 14, 1799, in Horsley. One hundred years later, all of his hymns—English and Welsh alike—were still being commonly sung by Christians in the British Isles.

....

Jesus, and Shall It Ever Be (page 128)

PAUL GERHARDT

1607–1676

On March 12, 1607, Paul Gerhardt was born in Gräfenhainichen, Germany, the son of the mayor. His growing-up years were shaped by the tumult of Thirty Years' War. When Paul was fifteen he went to a strict Christian school in Grimma. The plague came in 1626 and nearly shut down the school, but Paul stayed, studied, and graduated at age 20.

The next year, in 1628, he went to the University of Wittenburg, where Martin Luther had been a professor a hundred years before. Two of his professors, Paul Röber and Jacob Martini, first taught him to deeply love hymns. Paul continued studying at Wittenburg until 1642. But when he finally left the University, the troubles of the long war kept him from finding a church to pastor.

So Paul moved to Berlin, and began to write hymns. His hymns were noticed by Johann Crüger, a fellow hymnwriter and the organist at St. Nicholas' Church in Berlin—and Crüger liked Paul's hymns very much. By 1648, Paul had found a job, tutoring the children of Andreas Barthold in Berlin. About this time he began preaching often, and on November 18, 1651 he became the chief pastor of Mittenwalde, near Berlin. Paul's nine years at Mittenwalde were probably his happiest, and he wrote most of his hymns there. In 1655, at 48 years old, Paul married Andreas Barthold's daughter, Anna Maria.

In 1657 he and his family moved back to Berlin, where Paul served as a deacon in St. Nicholas's church, the same church where his friend Crüger played the organ. One year later, Paul's hymns were published in the Brandenburg hymnal. From the first, Christians loved Paul's hymns!

But trouble came in 1666. There was enormous tension between different church denominations in Berlin, and because of this the government made Paul, a Lutheran, leave his position as deacon. The people of Berlin begged the government to let Paul come back. After a time the government did invite him back, but there were conditions. Those conditions went against Paul's conscience, so he refused. During this same time, Paul's wife, Anna, died. Only one of their five children had lived past childhood, so Paul was now left alone with one son.

At last, in autumn of 1668, he was invited to be an archdeacon in Lübben, a city beside the River Spree in Germany. Paul spent the last few years of his life there. Shortly before he died, Paul wrote out his testimony for his son. He ended by writing: "Pray diligently, study something honorable, live peacefully, serve honestly, and remain unmoved in your faith and confessing. If you do this, you too will one day die and depart from this world willingly, joyfully, and blessedly. Amen."

Paul Gerhardt died in Lübben in the spring of 1676. His last words were a line from one of his hymns: "Us no death has power to kill!" After his death, his grateful congregation in Lübben had a portrait painted of him. As a memorial of Paul's faithfulness through his hard life, the inscription below the painting describes him as "A Theologian Sifted in Satan's Sieve."

Paul Gerhardt's hymns have made him perhaps the most popular German hymnwriter besides Martin Luther. The theme of his hymns is the massive, unchanging love God has for His people. Paul also translated some hymns from hymnwriters before him, and his own hymns have been translated to English by Catherine Winkworth, John Wesley, and others.

....

SIR ROBERT GRANT

c. 1779–1838

Robert Grant was born in Bengal, India, but his parents were Scottish. The Grant family was in India because Robert's father, Charles, was serving in the British Army and the East India Company. Charles Grant was no good example to his boys. But after two of Robert's younger siblings died of smallpox in India, Charles Grant found Christ and became a new man.

The family moved back home to Britain when young Robert was about ten years old. There, his father was elected as a Member of Parliament to represent Inverness, Scotland, and also became a devoted member of William Wilberforce's anti-slavery Clapham Sect. His father's drastically changed life must have had a significant impact on Robert!

The family's move to Britain also launched a glittering political career for both Robert and his older brother, Charles, Jr. Robert went to Magdalen College, Cambridge, and graduated in 1806. On January 30, 1807, both Robert and his brother Charles became lawyers. In 1818 Robert was elected to Parliament to represent the Elgin Burghs, and in the following years he would also represent the Inverness Burghs, Norwich, and then Finsbury. In 1829 Robert married Margaret Davidson, a girl from the Scottish Highlands, and they had two sons and two daughters. He became a Privy Councillor to the king in 1831, and the king knighted him in 1834.

And all the while as he was climbing the ranks, Robert was writing hymns.

In 1835, he moved back to India to serve as the Governor of Mumbai. He served there for five years before he suffered a stroke and died in Dapodi, India, on July 9, 1838. Grant Medical College, the oldest medical school in India, was named in his honor.

A year after Robert died, his brother Charles published twelve of his poems and hymns. The world then discovered what a gifted hymnwriter Sir Robert Grant had been! One of the hymns in the collection was "O Worship the King"—Robert probably knew several kings and rich rulers in his lifetime, and this hymn shows that he saw King Jesus as the King of kings, the most glorious of them all.

....

O Worship the King (page 215)

REGINALD HEBER

1783–1826

Reginald Heber was born in Malpas, Cheshire, England on April 21, 1783. He showed both his faith and his brilliance at a very young age—by the time he was five, he could read the Bible easily. His well-educated and well-to-do family sent him to Brasenose College, Oxford, and there he befriended another up-and-coming poet named Sir Walter Scott. While at Brasenose, Reginald won the Newdigate prize for his poem "Palestine," and this sparked his fame as a poet.

In 1807, Reginald became a minister in the Church of England. His first position was as the vicar of Hodnet, a farming village in Shropshire, England. His congregation in Hodnet loved him dearly. Reginald understood how important it is for the whole congregation to sing praise together, and that inspired him to write hymns. Heber wrote 57 hymns during his 16 years at Hodnet, and a few of them were published at that time in a magazine called *The Christian Observer*.

In 1822, he moved to be the preacher at Lincoln's Inn in London, but that same year he was invited to become the Bishop of India—a place he had a special fondness for. He accepted, moved to India with his wife Amelia and their two children, and leapt into the immense job ahead of him. It was now his responsibility to oversee the church in India, Ceylon, and all of Australia. After only three years the hot climate of India and over-exhaustion from his work broke down his health. On April 3, 1826, Reginald Heber died suddenly in his room in Trichinopoly, India, leaving Amelia and his two children behind. He had just finished preaching a service that welcomed 42 new Christians into the Church.

The rest of Reginald Heber's hymns did not meet the public until after his death, but they have been well-loved ever since. Alfred, Lord Tennyson—another famous poet—once described "Holy, Holy, Holy" as one of the world's greatest hymns.

....

Holy, Holy, Holy (page 110)
The Son of God Goes Forth to War (page 238)

JOHANN HEERMANN

1585–1647

Johann Heermann was born in a German town called Raudten (modern-day Rudna, Poland) on October 11, 1585. He was his parents' fifth baby, but the first one to survive. When he was a young boy, he became very sick, and his mother promised God that if he lived she would have him trained to become a pastor. Johann recovered, and his mother kept her promise—even though she had to beg for the money to do it.

She sent Johann to schools in Wohlau, Fraustadt, Breslau, and Brieg. When he was grown, Johann became a tutor to the two sons of Baron Rothkirch in Brieg. Being with the Baron's boys gave Johann the chance to travel with them through Europe, and during this time people began to see what a gifted poet Johann was—to the point that on October 8, 1608, Johann was crowned Poet Laureate in Brieg!

In 1609, Baron Rothkirch's sons went off to the University of Strassberg, and Johann went with them. But his old, frail health caught up with him, and in 1610, he had to leave the University because of illness in his eyes. Johann moved to Köben (modern-day Chobienia, Poland) and fulfilled his mother's dream by becoming a pastor there in 1611.

But his time as a pastor would not be easy. The dreaded plague came to Köben one year, and another year a massive fire swept through the city. In 1623, twelve years into preaching, Johann contracted an infection in his nose and throat. He never fully healed, and in 1634, his disease forced him to stop preaching. About the same time Johann retired, the Thirty Years' War came to his doorstep. Catholic soldiers raided Köben four times in the next decade, and robbed Johann and other citizens in the process. Johann and his family lost all of their worldly possessions on multiple occasions. The war even forced Johann to flee the city several times—once, as he was escaping in a leaky boat over the Oder river, Johann was in such danger that he could hear the bullets whistling over his head.

Eventually Johann moved to Lissa (modern-day Leszno, Poland) and died there on February 17, 1647. Johann Heermann had a tumultuous life, but it shaped his hymns in a great way. Johann's hymns show how deep his trust in Christ was, and the peace that he felt even in sickness and war.

He wrote over 150 hymns in German. Some consider Johann Heermann to be the best German hymnwriter from the time between Martin Luther and Paul Gerhardt.

....

Ah, Holy Jesus, How Hast Thou Offended? (page 31)

WILLIAM WALSHAM HOW

1823–1897

William Walsham How was born in the market town of Shrewsbury, England, on December 13, 1823. He got his early schooling from Shrewsbury School and graduated from Wadeham College, Oxford, in 1845.

William became a minister soon afterward: starting in 1846, he served as the curate (pastor's assistant) of St. George's in Kidderminster, then two years later moved to be the curate at Holy Cross in his hometown of Shrewsbury. In 1851, he was given a church of his own, as the rector of Whittington. It was during his time at Whittington that William wrote his many hymns. He published many of his sermons, and also several books, including *Commentary of the Gospels, Plain Words, Plain Words for Children, Pastor in Parochiâ, Lectures in Pastoral Work,* and *Three All Saints' Summers and Other Poems.* When Reverend Thomas Morrell published his *Psalms and Hymns* collection in 1854, the collection featured several of William How's hymns. So did *Church Hymns,* a hymnal which William edited with his hymnwriter friend, John Ellerton, in 1871. He believed that a good hymn is "something like a good prayer—simple, real, earnest, and reverent."

In 1879, the Queen made William How the Bishop of Bedford. His new responsibility was to preach at St. Andrew Undershaft, a tiny stone church in London, and to look after East London—a dirty, cramped part of the city where the very poor lived. William rolled up his sleeves and got busy making East London a better place.

In William's era, most bishops lived in large, rich houses and traveled in their own private coaches. William How did no such thing. He lived with the poor, and got around on public transportation like the poor did. For this he was known as "the poor man's bishop"—but as he especially enjoyed being with children, he loved it best when people called him "the children's bishop."

In 1886, he collected his hymns and poems and published them together in his book *Poems and Hymns*. William Walsham How died eleven years later on August 10, 1897.

....

O Word of God Incarnate (page 212)

MARTIN LUTHER

1483–1546

Martin Luther was born in Eisleben, Germany, on November 10, 1483. He was abused and nearly starved at boarding schools as a boy, and took to going door-to-door to sing for money or food to survive. Martin's father insisted that he become a lawyer, so Martin studied at the University of Erfurt from 1501–1505.

But on July 2, 1505, he was caught in a terrible thunderstorm on the road between home and the university. Martin was terrified of dying—he knew he was a sinner, and deserved God's anger—so in a panic he vowed that if God let him survive the storm, he would become a monk and spend the rest of his life making himself good enough for God.

It made his father furious, but Martin kept his vow fifteen days later by joining a monastery in Erfurt. He spent the next two years torturing himself and confessing every sin he could imagine, doing his best to make himself good enough for God. It ruined his health, but it did not fix his sinful heart. Martin could find no peace with God.

In a time when most common people never even saw a Bible, being a monk meant that Martin had access to the Bible owned by the monastery. He began to read it. After he was chosen to pastor the *Stadtkirche* (church) in Wittenberg in 1507, and also to be Professor of Theology at Wittenburg University in 1508, he studied the Bible even more. From it, Martin slowly began to understand that it was *only* God's grace that saved him, and not his own goodness! He found peace for the first time in his life.

But Martin also learned that the Roman Catholic church was teaching things that Scripture did not. Over the next ten years, he became more convinced. He particularly didn't like the popular "Indulgences" that the Roman church was selling as forgiveness of sins. Martin wrote a paper giving 95 reasons why Indulgences were unbiblical, and on October 31, 1517 he nailed his paper to the door of All Saints' Church in Wittenburg for the people to read. Soon all Germany was talking about this monk who dared to disagree with the Roman church ... and whether maybe he was right.

In summer 1521, the Pope wrote a document called a *bull* condemning Martin Luther's teaching. It was delivered to Martin on October 10, 1520. In the bull, the Pope offered Martin 60 days to recant, or else he would be excommunicated.

Martin answered the Pope by publicly burning the canon law, Roman Catholic theology books, and the Pope's bull. The Pope excommunicated him in January 1521, and Martin was ordered to come before Emperor Charles V at the Diet of Worms.

He did so on April 17 and 18 in 1521, and was told would be forgiven if he would admit he was wrong. Martin Luther told the Diet that he would only recant if they could prove from Scripture that he *was* wrong. "To go against conscience is neither honest nor safe," he told them. "Here I stand; I cannot do otherwise. God help me. Amen."

Charles V declared Martin Luther to be outlaw and gave him 21 days to return safely to Wittenburg. But on the road, in the dark forest near Wittenburg, a passel of horseman suddenly surrounded Martin Luther's wagon, threw a hood over his head, and carried him off into the forest.

When they unhooded him, Martin found himself at Wartburg Castle. His kidnapper explained that he was hired by the Duke of Saxony (who secretly supported Martin Luther) to "kidnap" Luther and keep him safe in hiding for a time. Going along with the plan, Martin stopped wearing his monk's habit, grew a beard, and pretended to be a knight named "Junker Jörg." He spent his ten months at Wartburg Castle translating the New Testament into German, and he also began writing hymns.

Martin secretly slipped back into Wittenburg on March 6, 1522, and got right back to preaching, teaching, and writing an unbelievable number of books. He used the singing voice that had saved his life as a boy to teach the hymns he wrote to his congregation. On June 13, 1525, Martin renounced his monastic vows and married Katharina von Bora—a former nun! The Duke of Saxony gave Martin and his dear Katie the empty Augustinian monastery in Wittenburg to be their home. In "Lutherhaus," as the monastery began to be called, Martin and Katie raised their six children and four adopted orphans and boarded many of Martin's University students.

Martin Luther wrote 37 hymns in all, and he compiled and published nearly 60 hymnals. His love for music helped to make good music a theme of the Reformation. He died on February 18, 1546, at his birthplace in Eisleben.

....

A Mighty Fortress Is Our God (page 28)
All Praise to Thee, Eternal Lord (page 40)
To Jordan Came Our Lord, the Christ (page 256)

HENRY FRANCIS LYTE

1793–1847

On June 1, 1793, Henry Francis Lyte was born in Ednam, a small village in Scotland. Both of his parents died by the time he was nine, and he was raised as an orphan afterward. But his schoolmaster saw Henry's poetry, and realized that this orphan boy had talent. He encouraged Henry to write more. Even though he was poor, Henry saved enough to attend Trinity College, Dublin and graduated in 1814. He won three prizes for his poetry while he was there. He went to school intending to become a doctor, but something changed his mind, and after college he became a minister in 1815.

First, Henry served as the curate in Wexford, Ireland. Two years later he moved to Marazion in Cornwall, and there, in 1818, he saw something happen to a friend which changed him. His friend, a fellow minister, knew he was sick and going to die soon... but he did not feel prepared to meet God. So Henry and his dying friend took to studying the Bible together, especially Paul's letters, and his friend finally came to understood the true Gospel. He trusted that Christ was enough to save him, and when he died, he was at peace. Watching this change come over his friend moved Henry, and he later said that it changed his own heart, and even the way he preached. He began to study the Bible more.

The next year Henry moved to preach in Lymington, England, and there he wrote poetry again. In 1823, he became the Perpetual Curate of Lower

Brixham, England, where his congregation was mostly made up of sailors and fishermen. Henry diligently cared for his congregation, educated his five children, and wrote constantly. He was never famous during his life, but he published several books of his own poetry, and those poems have become his hymns.

Henry contracted tuberculosis, so beginning in the 1840's Henry and his family spent their winters on the Continent (especially France and Rome), where the air was healthier for Henry's sick lungs. But Henry never neglected to come back to his congregation when the summer air of England allowed him to return. Back and forth he went, for years. By September 1847, Henry remarked that he was now so weak that he felt he was only able to crawl—but still, he was determined to preach a farewell sermon to his church in Brixham before he left for Europe again. His friends urged him not to, saying he was too weak, but he told them, "It is better to wear out than to rust out."

After that sermon he left for Europe with his wife and son, knowing he would never see Brixham again. When Henry Lyte died in Nice, France, on November 20, 1847, his last words were "Peace! Joy!"

....

Jesus, I My Cross Have Taken (page 131)

GEORGE MATHESON

1842–1906

George Matheson was born in Glasgow, Scotland on March 27, 1842, the firstborn of eight children. He had very poor eyesight as a boy, but that did not stop him from going to Glasgow University when he was 15 years old. He graduated with a master's degree in 1862—only one year after earning his bachelor's degree! But study had worsened his bad eyesight, and by the time he was 20 he could only see shadows and outlines. Nevertheless, George had a reputation for being joyful, high-spirited, and not easily discouraged.

After college he became an assistant minister in Sandyford for a short time, before he was made the pastor of a bigger congregation in Innellan, Scotland in 1868. During this time his eldest sister was his closest helper. She guided him around, wrote his sermon notes, and helped him with his pastoral work. George's 18 years of preaching at Innellan began to make him famous. People now traveled from all over Scotland to hear him—but many of the people who heard him never realized that he was almost completely blind. When he preached, George acted as if he was frequently glancing at his sermon notes... but actually, he had memorized his entire sermon and large passages of Scripture.

Late at night in Innellan on June 6, 1882, 40-year-old George was hit with a sudden attack of depression. He never told what the reason for his sadness was, but that night he sat down and poured out what is probably his most famous hymn: "O Love That Wilt Not Let Me Go." This hymn was peculiar to George. He said about it, "I had the impression of having it dictated to me by some inward voice rather than of working it out myself. I am quite sure that the whole work was completed in five minutes, and equally sure that it never received at my hands any retouching or correction. I have no natural gift of rhythm... .this came like a dayspring from on high."

In 1885, Queen Victoria invited George to come preach for her at Balmoral, her home in Scotland. She loved his sermon so much that she asked for it to be published. George also published a single book of hymns, and wrote several prose books—first with the help of his sister or a secretary, then by himself with braille and a typewriter.

In 1886 he moved to pastor St. Bernard's Church in Edinburgh. Thirteen years later, at age 64, George Matheson died of a stroke on August 28, 1906.

....

Make Me a Captive, Lord (page 168)
O Love That Wilt Not Let Me Go (page 192)

JAMES MONTGOMERY

1771–1854

On November 4, 1771, James Montgomery was born to a Moravian missionary couple in Irvine, an ancient town in North Ayrshire, Scotland. In 1776, his family joined other Moravian families at a settlement in Gracehill, Northern Ireland, but in 1778, James parents sent him to the Moravian-run Fulneck School in England.

About five years later both of his parents sailed away to be missionaries in the West Indies, and that is where they both died soon after. James suffered depression after being orphaned so young. But he was a very devout Christian, and was already discovering that he had a knack for poetry.

James was also a very daydreamy boy who couldn't keep a schedule. His caretakers in Fulneck decided he needed stiffening up, so in 1787 they sent him to work with a baker. The work wasn't challenging enough, so James took to composing poetry behind the bakery counter. He moved to a similar job in Wath, England, but didn't like it any better. So he gave up baking and traveled to London to find a publisher for his poems. He was ignored.

In 1792, he became assistant to Mr. Gales, an auctioneer, book seller, and printer of *The Sheffield Register*. Within two years, James took over the newspaper and renamed it *The Sheffield Iris*. He would serve as its editor for 31 years. In 1835, he moved into a grand mansion in Sheffield called The Mount, and he was able to spend the rest of his life writing and lecturing about poetry at Sheffield and the Royal Institute in London.

Yet James Montgomery is best remembered for his hymns—about 400 of them! He never forgot his parents, and the theme of his hymns was his love for missionary work. He had a remarkable knowledge of the Bible and was a devout Christian all his life. He died in his sleep at The Mount on April 30, 1854. Fifty years later, about 100 of his hymns were being regularly sung in churches. As hymn scholar John Julian wrote, "[James Montgomery's hymns] come from a true genius and a sanctified heart."

....

Angels, from the Realms of Glory (page 53)
In the Hour of Trial (page 122)
O Spirit of the Living God (page 206)

GEORG NEUMARK

1621–1681

Georg Neumark was born in Langensalza, Germany, on March 16, 1621. He was the son of a cloth-merchant and grew up attending schools in Schleusingen and Gotha. When he was 20, Georg was ready to go to college. To get there, he set out in the autumn of 1641 with a group of merchants who were traveling to the Michaelmas Fair in Leipzig. From the fair, Georg traveled on with another group to Lübeck. Then he set out with another group, intending to eventually arrive at the University in Königsberg.

But he and his group were attacked by robbers on the road. Georg was robbed of everything he had with him ... except his prayer book and a little money which he had sewn into his clothes. His plans to go to the University were ruined, and now he had nothing to live on. So Georg now headed to Magdeburg, where he hunted for a job, but he could not find one. He tried looking in Lüneberg. Then in Winsen. Then in Hamburg. Nothing. It was almost winter now.

In December Georg went to Kiel, and stayed with a friend there for a short time before—finally—a job opened up for him as a tutor to a judge's son. Twenty years old and extremely grateful that God had provided a job for him, Georg wrote one of his first hymns that winter. He saved his earnings for two years and then was able to go to the University after all. He graduated as a lawyer in 1643, and stayed in Königsberg to tutor again and study some more.

But in 1646, a fire caused Georg to lose everything he owned... again. He traveled around Germany for a few years after this, and in 1651 he moved back to the region where he was born. During all these years, he had continued to write poetry, and in 1652 Duke Wilhelm II made Georg Neumark his Court Poet! Georg would spend the rest of his life writing and working in Weimar. He went blind in 1681, but kept working until he died that same year on July 18.

Georg Neumark wrote at least 34 hymns in German. Several have been translated to English. The hymn that he wrote in the winter of 1641–42, when he was deeply thankful to have finally found a job, was so lovely that two German composers—Johann Sebastian Bach and Felix Mendelssohn—later used it in their own musical work.

....

My Hope Is Built on Nothing Less (page 171)

JOHN NEWTON

1725–1807

John Newton was born in London on July 24, 1725. His father, a sea captain, was rarely around. His mother was a devout Christian who diligently taught her son Scripture, catechisms, and hymns. But when John was seven years old, his mother died, and he was largely left to raise himself. He starting running with a bad crowd, and became interested in atheism. When he was 11, he quit school—after only two years of education—and joined the crew on his father's ship. When his father retired in 1742, he wanted John to go work on the sugar plantations of Jamaica, but instead John hopped aboard a trading ship.

One year later, when he was 16, John Newton was kidnapped by a conscripting gang and forced to serve in the English Navy. He was made a midshipman on the HMS *Harwich*. After a while he tried to desert the ship, but he was caught, whipped, and demoted. He considered taking revenge by murdering the captain and then committing suicide, but he changed his mind.

Eventually he was allowed to move to a slave ship that was bound for Africa. John did not get along with that crew, either. They left him behind in Africa, where he became the servant of another slave dealer named Amos Clowe. Clowe treated John as badly as he treated his slaves. John nearly starved, but the slaves around him pitied him and gave him some of their own measly food, and he survived until he managed to catch a merchant ship and left Africa.

On board, he stumbled across a book by Thomas à Kempis. He read it, and the deeply-buried Christian teaching his mother had given him began to wake up in John's heart again. In 1748, when he was 23, the ship sailed through a tremendous storm off the Irish coast. Stuck on that flooding ship which he knew could sink any minute, John cried out to God to save him. After that experience, he repented of his sins and claimed to be a Christian, journaling that "on March 10th, the Lord came from on high and delivered me out of deep waters."

John went home and married his long-time sweetheart Mary Catlett in 1750, adopted his two orphaned nieces, and cleaned up his life. But it wasn't long before he was back on the sea as the first mate—and eventually, the captain—of a slave ship. John carried on until 1754, when he had a stroke at age 29, which prompted him to leave the sea.

He finally began to understand the slave trade for what it truly was, and repented of ever having been a part of it. John wrote later that his *true* conversion happened during this time. He became a tide-surveyor in Liverpool, England, and diligently studied the Bible in its original languages. He met John Wesley and George Whitefield and was greatly moved by their preaching. In 1758, John Newton asked the Church of England for permission to be a pastor, but—presumably because of his history—he was not allowed, at first. But at last, in 1764, he became the curate (pastor's assistant) of Olney, and later a full-fledged minister. He wrote his books *Omicron's Letters* and *Cardiphonia* at Olney. He invited hymnwriter William Cowper to move there, and when Cowper did, he and John became great friends. They spent four days a week together, writing new hymns for every Tuesday prayer meeting. Later, Cowper and John Newton published their collection of *Olney Hymns*.

In 1780, John Newton moved to be the rector of St. Mary Woolnoth, a tall stone church in London. He preached there for the rest of his life, and befriended and counseled several influential people, including Hannah More and William Wilberforce. John's eyesight started to fade, but he refused to stop preaching while he still had his voice. In his old age he said, "My memory is nearly gone, but I remember two things: that I am a great sinner, and that Christ is a great Savior." John Newton lived to be 82 (a rare old age for his time) and died on December 21, 1807, leaving his life story as evidence that Christ can save any sinner.

....

Amazing Grace (page 45)
Come, My Soul, Thy Suit Prepare (page 82)
Glorious Things of Thee Are Spoken (page 97)
Let Us Love and Sing and Wonder (page 151)

RAY PALMER

1808–1887

Ray Palmer was born on November 12, 1808, in Little Compton, Rhode Island, the son of Judge Thomas Palmer. His family was so poor that, Ray had to quit school when he was 13 and get a job as a dry-goods clerk in Boston for two years. During that time, he struggled back and forth with the idea of religion, but in the end Ray decided to become a Christian and joined Park Street Congregational Church. Eventually, he was able to go back to school. He attended Phillips Academy in Andover, Massachusetts for three years to finish high school, and then was able to graduate from Yale College in 1830.

But Ray spent the year after his college graduation struggling with illness and loneliness. When he couldn't bear it any longer, he poured his troubles into a poem. The next year, that poem would become the hymn "My Faith Looks Up to Thee." It is probably Ray's most famous hymn (as its first tune writer, Lowell Mason, predicted it would be), and he was only 22 when he wrote it.

In 1835, Ray became the pastor of Central Congregation Church in Bath, Maine. He had the chance to visit Europe in 1847. He moved to pastor First Congregational church, in Albany, New York, in 1850, and then served as the Corresponding Secretary to the American Congregational Union from 1865–1878. When Ray retired he moved to Newark, New Jersey, where he died on March 29, 1887.

In the midst of his busy pastoring work, Ray Palmer also actively supported education, wrote for Christian newspapers, and published 11 books of his own. He was the first American writer to translate Latin hymns into English, and wrote at least 31 hymns of his own—most of which have been widely used in churches in both America and Great Britain.

....

Jesus, Thou Joy of Loving Hearts (page 142)
Lord, My Weak Thought in Vain Would Climb (page 159)

JOHN RIPPON

1751–1836

John Rippon was born in Tiverton, Devon, England on April 29, 1751. He attended the Baptist College in Bristol. After he graduated at age 22, in 1773, he became the pastor of the Baptist Church on Carter Lane, Tooley Street, London, and later on New Park Street, after the congregation moved to another church building. John pastored that church for 63 years—only death made him stop.

He published a magazine called the *Baptist Annual Register* from 1790 to 1802, but John's most famous work is his hymnal, *Rippon's Selection of Hymns,* which he first published in 1787. We know that John Rippon wrote some hymns of his own, and we know they are included in his *Selections*—however, he did not attach his name to them, so no one knows for certain which hymns are his. But besides writing his own, John frequently altered or added on to several other writer's hymns, and a number of his altered versions are still used today. *Rippon's Selections* was very popular, and John enlarged and republished it every few years. By the time he died, his hymnal had been through 27 editions! It gives us a tremendous record of hundreds of the hymns of John Rippon's day.

John Rippon died on December 17, 1836, at 85 years old.

....

All Hail the Power of Jesus' Name (page 36)

CHARLES HADDON SPURGEON

1834–1892

Charles Haddon Spurgeon was born on June 19, 1834, in Kelvedon, England. He was the firstborn of 17 children—though only 8 of them would live to adulthood. Charles' father was a minister, and Charles was very fond of *The Pilgrim's Progress* as a boy, but still he grew up with only a head-knowledge of Christianity. His heart had not yet been changed by Christ.

When Charles was 15, in January 1850, a blizzard caught him outside. He ducked into a church for shelter, and listened to the sermon being preached on Isaiah 45:22—"Turn to me and be saved, all the ends of the earth! For I am God, and there is no other." (ESV) Though Charles thought the sermon was rather badly preached, God used it to convict his heart. That day, Charles finally "looked to Christ," and it set the course of his life.

Shortly after being saved, he moved to Cambridge, joined a church, and became a traveling preacher. In October 1851, he was asked to come be the pastor of a small Baptist congregation in Waterbeach, and that is where Charles Spurgeon began to be famous for his gifted preaching—at only 17 years old.

In 1854, he moved to London to pastor the same church that hymnwriter John Rippon had pastored before him, on New Park Street. But so many people began coming to hear Charles preach that he had to move his congregation to Exeter Hall, and then to the Surrey Music Hall. His popularity grew over the next few years until he often preached to congregations of 10,000 people. He was 22 years old.

In 1856, Charles married Susannah Thompson and founded The Pastor's College. He and Susannah had twin baby boys in 1857. His congregation continued to grow so much that Charles decided a whole new church building was needed, and he himself donated over one third of the money needed to build the massive new church. On March 18, 1861, he and his congregation officially moved into their new London church: the Metropolitan Tabernacle, which offered seats for 5,000 people, and room for 1,000 more to stand up!

Aside from preaching, Charles also taught at the Pastor's College one morning each week and wrote books of all sorts. In 1866, he gathered hymns to make a new hymnal for his congregation, including 20 hymns which he himself had written.

Charles preached in London for 38 years. By the time he resigned on October 28, 1887, his ministry had resulted in the founding of 66 new ministries. Charles had baptized over 15,000 new Christians with his own hands, preached over 3,600 sermons (and published them weekly), and published 49 books: Bible commentaries, devotionals, an autobiography, and more.

Both he and his wife suffered from bad health late in life, so they frequently went to stay in Menton, France, to recuperate, and that is where Charles Spurgeon died on January 31, 1892.

....

Amidst Us Our Beloved Stands (page 48)

AUGUSTUS MONTAGUE TOPLADY

1740–1778

On November 4, 1740, a boy named Augustus Montague Toplady was born in Farnham, an incredibly old town in Surrey, England. He never got to meet his father, Major Richard Toplady, who was away with the British Army and died in 1741. When Augustus was a boy his wise mother sent him to Westminster School in London—the same school where the hymnwriters John Dryden, Charles Wesley, and William Cowper had graduated.

By and by, the Toplady family moved to Ireland, and that is where 16-year-old Augustus found himself sitting with a crowd one evening, in a barn, to hear preacher James Morris give a sermon on Ephesians 6:13. Augustus, who had recently become a student of Trinity College, Dublin, met Christ that night.

Augustus graduated from Trinity College in 1760, and just two years later he became a minister in the Church of England. About a year after being ordained as a minister, he was walking through the Burrington Combe gorge in the Mendip Hills of England when a storm suddenly blew up. Augustus quickly hid in a crack in the massive limestone walls of the gorge for safety. While he sat there, he pondered on the way that crack in the cliff was protecting his body in the same way Jesus protected his soul ... and by the time the storm passed,

Augustus had the stirrings of an idea for a hymn that would begin, "*Rock of Ages, cleft for me / Let me hide myself in thee.*"

Some said that Augustus was bad-tempered, and his constant ministry work wore out his health. But till the end of his life, he remained a faithful servant of God who depended only on Christ's perfection and God's mercy to save him, not his own goodness—"A debtor to mercy alone," as he put it. Augustus Toplady died at age 38 on August 11, 1778, saying, "I enjoy Heaven already in my soul. My prayers are all converted into praises."

....

A Debtor to Mercy Alone (page 16)
The Dying Believer (page 234)
Fountain of Never-Ceasing Grace (page 93)
Hail, Thou Once-Despised Jesus! (page 103)
Rock of Ages, Cleft for Me (page 218)

RALPH WARDLAW

1779–1853

Ralph Wardlaw was born in Dalkeith, Scotland, on December 22, 1779, but his family moved to Glasgow when he was six months old, and the rest of his life would center around that city.

Ralph went to grammar school as a boy and then began studying theology at the University of Glasgow at age 12. After he graduated in 1800, people began to notice that young Ralph Wardlaw was a gifted preacher. Some tried to get him to move to Perth to pastor a church there. But his friends and family had already been trying to build a new chapel in Glasgow, in the hopes that Ralph would stay and preach there—so that is what he did.

The year 1803 was an eventful one for Ralph Wardlaw. On February 16, 1803, he became the pastor of North Albion Street Chapel in Glasgow, the chapel his friends and family had built for him. His little congregation was made up of 61 people, but his preaching quickly made him popular, and the church's numbers began to grow. Also that year, Ralph married Jane Smith (with whom he would eventually have eleven children) and worked with a Dr. Charles Stuart, from Dunearn, to compile a new hymnal for his new congregation. He himself wrote twelve hymns for the hymnal.

But aside from being a preacher and hymnwriter, Ralph was also a gifted writer—in fact, he was probably most famous for his books on theology. He published at least 15 books in his life, and they were loved in both Britain and

America. In 1811, he helped to found a Congregationalist Seminary—the first one in Glasgow. By 1819, Ralph Wardlaw's popularity as a preacher had grown so much that he had to move his congregation to West George Street in Glasgow, into a bigger church which could seat 1,500 people! One of the thousands who heard him speak was David Livingstone, the great missionary to Africa, who was living in Glasgow in the 1830s to study medicine and theology. David Livingstone and his missions in Africa were greatly shaped by Ralph Wardlaw.

Ralph pastored only that one congregation in his entire ministry, and he did so from when he was barely 23 until his death. When he died, he passed away in his own home, Provan Hall, in a suburb of Glasgow called Easterhouse. It was December 17, 1853, five days before he would have turned 74.

....

Christ, of All My Hopes the Ground (page 67)

ISAAC WATTS

1674–1748

Isaac Watts was born on July 17, 1674, in Southampton England. His father was not home to see it, however—much like John Bunyan, Mr. Watts was a "Nonconformist" who was in prison (and would be imprisoned again while Isaac was an infant) because his particular Christian beliefs were not popular in England at that time. Isaac's mother came from Huguenots (persecuted French Christians), and it is said that she often stood outside her husband's prison, singing psalms and holding baby Isaac. Isaac and his eight younger siblings grew up in a household that stood firm in their faith.

Isaac's father schooled his children himself, but Isaac also studied Latin, Greek, and Hebrew under Mr. Pinhorn, the rector of the local All Saints' Church and the headmaster of a Southampton grammar school. Isaac experimented with poetry early. One of his earliest was written on the fly, after he watched a mouse climb the bell rope beside the fireplace. Isaac laughed out loud—though it was in the middle of family prayers—and when his parents asked him why, he quipped, "A mouse, for want of better stairs, / ran up a rope to say his prayers."

Seeing young Isaac Watt's talents, some wealthy friends offered to send him to a university to become a minister. Isaac turned them down. Instead, in 1690, he went off to the Dissenting Academy (*Dissenting* meaning Nonconformist) in Stoke Newington, near London.

Two years later, when Isaac was 18, he remarked to his father that he did not care for the church music that was being sung: haphazardly-translated versions of the psalms, set to tunes that didn't quite match. His father told him that if he didn't like them, he should write something better. Isaac did. His very first hymn, "Behold the Glories of the Lamb," was sung by his church the very next Sunday! His church asked him to write more hymns, so he did. Isaac wrote a new hymn each week for the next two years. At age 20, he left Stoke Newington and came home to Southampton for two years, where he wrote most of the hymns which he would later publish in his collection, *Hymns and Spiritual Songs*, in 1707.

All grown up, Isaac Watts was only five feet tall. His head was too big for his body and his eyes were small. His awkward looks were the reason a lovely girl once refused his proposal of marriage. "I like the jewel, but not the setting," she explained... bluntly. In about 1696, Isaac moved back to Stoke Newington to tutor Sir John Hartopp's son. He filled this position for six years. Some say that the heavy studying he did during this time is what first caused his health to chip.

When Isaac was 24, after he had been tutoring for two years, he preached his first sermon. He preached more frequently over the three years after that. In 1702, he became the pastor of Mark Lane Congregational Chapel in London and lived with a Mr. Hollis in Minories, an area of London. One year later, Isaac's health cracked and he had to take on a preaching assistant, Mr. Samuel Price. In 1712, Isaac suffered a fever that ruined what was left of his health, so his friend Sir Thomas Abney invited him to stay with him at Abney House to regain his strength. Isaac went, but his health did not improve very quickly, so the Abney family urged him to stay longer. He did—and ended up spending the 36 remaining years of his life with them. Isaac wrote more hymns and books during this time. One of his favorite places to find inspiration was where Hackney Brook flowed across the Abneys' land.

Isaac's bad health gradually became worse until he died on November 25, 1748. He had written at least ten books, in addition to his hymns—and of those hymns, over 450 were still being regularly sung 150 years after his death. Isaac Watt's hymns set the template for traditional English hymns.

Many of them are paraphrases of Scripture (especially the psalms), and they helped prepare England for the revivals that happened under John Wesley's and George Whitefield's preaching.

....

Alas! and Did My Savior Bleed (page 33)
Come, We That Love the Lord (page 85)
When I Survey the Wondrous Cross (page 268)

CHARLES WESLEY

1707–1788

Charles Wesley was born in the rectory in Epworth, England on December 18, 1707—several weeks too early. He was the eighteenth child of Samuel and Susannah Wesley.

Their family suffered one hardship after another: Samuel, the rector of Epworth, struggled to provide for his family and ended up in debtor's prison the year Charles was born. Then the family's barn blew over. When Charles was 17 months old, half of the rectory burned down in the middle of the night—it might have been an accident, but Samuel suspected the fire was started by some parishioners who were angry with him. Then the flax crop burned. Samuel lost his job as the chaplain of a regiment. Someone murdered the family's three cows.

But Susannah Wesley managed to hold the family together, and every week she set aside time for each of her children to teach them about God. Her methodical way of life shaped the way Charles and his older brother, John, would live their own lives.

Charles was homeschooled at first, then attended Westminster School in London in 1716. He lived with his oldest brother in town until he was chosen as "King's Scholar" in 1721, and was allowed to board at school for free. In 1726, he earned another scholarship and went to Christ Church, Oxford, the same college his brother, John, had graduated from. At college Charles continued to be studious and respectable, and he collected friends who were, too. He, his brother, John, and their friends—including a young man named George Whitefield—were teasingly called the "Holy Club," and eventually the "Oxford Methodists."

Sometime in 1735–36, James Oglethorpe invited Charles and John to sail with him and a group of Moravian Christians to Georgia, Oglethorpe's new colony in the New World. Charles was to be Oglethorpe's secretary, and John was to be a missionary to the Indians. The trip was a disaster. Both Charles and John had been raised to live religiously, but their time in Georgia showed them they only had a head-knowledge of the Gospel—their hearts had not been changed by it. Both Charles and John were awed at the peace that filled their Christian Moravian friends, and they wanted the same peace and certainty of salvation.

Charles very soon returned home from his failed mission. John came home later in February, 1738, defeated as well. Still looking for peace with God, both brothers made friends with the Moravian Christians around them. On May 21, 1738—Pentecost Sunday—Charles journaled that at last the Holy Spirit had "chased away the darkness of my unbelief," and his soul found rest. The same thing happened to John three days later.

Charles wrote a hymn to praise God for his salvation—exactly which hymn is not certain, but it might have been "And Can It Be, That I Should Gain?" Charles once heard his friend, the Moravian preacher Peter Böhler, remark, "If I had one thousand tongues, I'd praise Christ with them all." Charles took the phrase to heart, and a year after his true conversion he wrote the hymn, "O for a Thousand Tongues to Sing."

Charles began preaching at St. Mary's Church in Islington, but certain leaders did not like his preaching, and he was asked to leave. So he and John took to the open air. Though John is usually remembered as the preaching brother, Charles Wesley was a tireless and gifted field-preacher too. He married Sarah Gwynne on April 8, 1749 (one of the only happy marriages in the Wesley family) and settled in Bristol. When Charles traveled with John through Britain, preaching the gospel to all and sundry, Sarah often went with him.

Charles stopped traveling in 1756 and moved to London in 1771, where he spent much time ministering to the prisoners of Newgate Prison in London. He spent entire nights with those who had been sentenced to death, praying with them before their executions. In the prison, Charles saw both the physical and spiritual filth of London. It depressed him, but some of his best hymns came from his thoughts during that time.

It is said that Charles Wesley wrote *at least* 6,500 hymns. His hymns deal with every type of situation, and he carried the torch after Isaac Watts in writing hymns specifically for children. Charles Wesley died on March 29, 1788, and is buried in Marylebone churchyard in London.

....

And Can It Be, That I Should Gain? (page 50)
Christ the Lord is Risen Today (page 70)
Hark! the Herald Angels Sing (page 106)
Jesus, Lover of My Soul (page 135)
Lo! He Comes, with Clouds Descending (page 155)
O for a Thousand Tongues to Sing (page 178)

CHRISTOPHER WORDSWORTH

1807–1885

In Lambeth, England, on October 30, 1807, one last son was born to the rector and his wife. They named him after his father: Christopher Wordsworth. His father, the rector of Lambeth, was the younger brother of William Wordsworth, making baby Christopher the nephew of one of England's most famous poets. The poetic family talent ran in his veins, too.

As a boy Christopher went to school in Winchester, where he showed himself to be a good student and a talented athlete. In 1826, all grown up, he headed for Trinity College, Cambridge and his reputation as a scholar only grew. Christopher Wordsworth won more of Trinity College's prizes for poetry-writing than any one student ever had.

After he graduated in 1830 Christopher taught at the college for a time, and went on a long tour of Greece. In 1836, he became the Headmaster of Harrow School, a boys' school in London. It is said that great moral reform happened among the boys while Christopher was in charge, and his students respected and loved him.

In 1844, Christopher changed professions and became a minister in Westminster. Five years later, he moved to also be the priest in the country villages of Stanford-in-the-Vale and Goosey. For the next nineteen years,

Christopher spent four months every year in Westminster, and the rest of the year in the two villages.

And he was writing books all the while (just like other members of his famous family!) Christopher Wordsworth published at least 12 books, including a history of the Church, a commentary on the entire Bible, a Latin grammar, memoirs about his uncle William Wordsworth, and a collection of his sermons. Another of his books was a hymnal called *The Holy Year*, a collection of 127 hymns which Christopher had written for different seasons of the year. Christopher did not haphazardly throw his hymns together; he took his job as a hymnwriter seriously. His favorite place to find material for his hymns was Scripture itself.

He was promoted from priest to bishop of Lincoln in 1869, and that is where he served for the last fifteen years of his life. Christopher Wordsworth resigned as bishop just a few months before he died on March 20, 1885. He is buried in Lincoln Cathedral, where he had served as a bishop.

....

Alleluia! Alleluia! (page 42)

TRANSLATORS

Meet the men and women who took hymns from other languages and gave them to English-speaking Christians. The ideas in these hymns come from the original authors, but the words we know and love come from *these* special hymnwriters.

ROBERT SEYMOUR BRIDGES

1844–1930

In Walmer, England on October 23, 1844, Robert Seymour was born the eighth child in the Bridges family. His father died when he was eight years old. A year later Robert's mother married again, to a minister, and the family moved to Rochdale. When he was just nine years old, Robert was sent to school at Eton. He proved himself to be a good athlete—he especially loved batting in cricket. At 19, he headed to Corpus Christi College in Oxford, where he kept up his athletics. Then, in 1869, Robert set off to become a doctor, studying at St. Bartholomew's Hospital in London. He graduated in 1874, when he was 30. Robert's plan was to work as a doctor until he was 40 years old, then retire and write poetry.

But he began working on his poems long before he retired. His first volume of poetry was published in 1873. After developing lung disease, Robert was forced to retire from medicine two years earlier than intended—so his beloved poetry became a main part of his life even sooner than he had hoped.

He moved to a little brick house in the country village of Yattendon. There, he married Mary Monica Waterhouse in 1884, when he was 40 years old. A great part of Robert Seymour Bridges' poems show a common thread—his Christian faith—and while in Yattendon, his love of poetry turned to poetry set to music: hymns.

Robert took charge of the church music in Yattendon, and in the late 1890's he worked with his pastor and another friend, Harry Ellis Wooldridge, to put together a new hymnal for their church. It was published in 1899, and featured 48 hymns which Robert had translated into English (several of which are still used today). Later the same year, Robert published a book about hymn-singing.

In his later life, Robert and his wife moved to another country village, Boar's Hill, near Oxford. where Robert spent the rest of his life. As a writer, Robert did not only write poems. He published a handful of prose books, and during WWI he worked as one of the writers in the War Propaganda Bureau. He was chosen as the Poet Laureate of the United Kingdom in 1913—but even so, he and his poems were not well-known until shortly before his death.

However, a few British composers found his poems, and loved them so much that they wrote music to turn those poems into hymns.

Robert Seymour Bridges died on April 21, 1930, at 85 years old.

....

Ah, Holy Jesus, How Hast Thou Offended? (page 31)

ELIZABETH RUNDLE CHARLES

1828–1896

Elizabeth Rundle Charles was born in Tiverton, England, on January 2, 1828. She showed her talent and spark for poetry early in life. The famous poet Lord Alfred Tennyson himself once read a few of her early poems, and thought they were very good indeed. Elizabeth married Andrew Paton Charles in 1851.

She was a musician and painter, but above all, she was a busy writer. She published about 50 books in her life, including books about Martin Luther, the Wesley brothers, the English Civil Wars, and other subjects. She was also a poet, and contributed a good deal to English hymnology. Elizabeth wrote several hymns of her own, and translated others from Latin and German—at least 50 hymns, all told. In her later life she lived in a house on Oak Hill Way in Hampstead, London. She died in Hampstead on March 28, 1896, at 68 years old.

....

A Hymn of Glory Let Us Sing (page 18)

A Lamb Goes Uncomplaining Forth (page 21)

JOHN ELLERTON

See page 295

PAUL GERHARDT

See page 300

JOHN MASON NEALE

1818–1866

John Mason Neale was born on Conduit Street in London on January 24, 1818. He was named after the accomplished hymnwriter John Mason, who was his ancestor on his mother's side. Both of his parents were devout Christians and very well-educated, and it seems John inherited their faith and their brilliance… except in math.

John's father was a minister, and died when John was five. His mother was his teacher when he was a boy. When he went to Trinity College, Cambridge, John developed a reputation as a busy writer and poet. He wrote numerous articles for *The Ecclesiologist* magazine, and his poetry won the college's Seatonian prize *eleven times*. While at college, John befriended fellow hymnwriter Benjamin Webb. John was a dedicated student and a devoted Christian, and almost everyone loved him—he was bold and steadfast in his convictions, but also gentle with those who disagreed with him.

In 1842, after college, John married Sarah Webster. That same year he published the first of his six collections of original hymns. In 1843, he became a minister in Crawley, England, but he had to resign shortly afterward because of bad health. John moved to the island of Madeira for a year to recover, and he did improve, but his sick lungs would plague him for the rest of his life.

Back in England, in 1846, John became the warden of Sackville College in East Grinstead. The job did not pay much, but it also didn't take much of his time, so John continued to write constantly. He also founded the Society of St. Margaret (where women cared for the sick), an orphanage, and a girls' school. As a writer, John published some sermons and a devotional, but he is most famous for his books on the history of the Church and its hymns.

John wrote a fair number of original hymns, but he is most remembered for being a hymn-*translator*. He knew about 20 languages, and was especially expert in medieval Latin. His translations made ancient Greek and Latin hymns available to the English-speaking Church. Plenty others had translated Latin hymns before him, but John was the first to translate Greek hymns into English.

On one occasion, John showed what a brilliant mind he had for translation by playing a prank on his hymnwriter friend, John Keble. One day, when they were working on a new hymnal together, Keble left the room for a while to find paper. When he came back, John handed him a Latin hymn. "I thought you said *you* wrote this hymn, 'The Christian Year,'" he said. "But if it's new, how is there an old Latin version of it?" Keble was very confused—the hymn *was* his own writing, he declared, and he'd never seen this Latin version in his life! After a laugh, John confessed that he had simply translated Keble's hymn into Latin during the few minutes Keble was out of the room.

John wore himself out with his charitable work and writing. Eventually, his sick lungs got the better of him, and his health suddenly crumbled in the spring of 1866. Five months later, after much suffering, John Mason Neale died on August 6. He was not even 50 years old, but he had made an enormous impact on English hymnody.

....

Christ Is Made the Sure Foundation (page 64)
Christian, Dost Thou See Them? (page 73)
Let Our Choir New Anthems Raise (page 148)
O Come, O Come, Emmanuel (page 174)
O Wondrous Type, O Vision Fair! (page 209)

RAY PALMER

See page 324

CATHERINE WINKWORTH

1827–1878

Catherine Winkworth was born in London on September 13, 1827. Her mother died when she was very young, but her father (who loved art and music) had a deep influence on her. She spent her early life in Manchester, and later, Clifton.

Catherine was a smart little girl, but often sick. When illness kept her in bed, she used her downtime to soak up all the learning she could. She became an expert in languages. Her teacher was William Gaskell, and Catherine was friends with his wife, Elizabeth Gaskell, the writer of *Cranford.*

When Catherine was a teenager, she and her family traveled to Dresden, Germany. After that trip, Catherine fell completely in love with all things German—especially German hymns. She took to translating some German hymns into English, just for herself to use privately.

But it did not take long for her to realize what treasures the old German hymns were! After all, the incredible music of the Reformation had started in Germany, under Martin Luther—but these rich hymns were not available to English-speaking Christians. So Catherine translated more of them into English and published over 100 in a collection, *Lyra Germanica,* in 1853. English-speaking Christians loved it. She published more collections in the following years, and wrote *Christian Singers of Germany,* a book of biographies of German hymnwriters. In all, Catherine translated nearly 400 German hymns into English.

She continued to battle bad health all her life; but still, she traveled to France and Germany several more times in her last few years. When Catherine was 50, she was traveling back to France to care for her sick nephew when she had a heart attack and died on July 1, 1878. She is buried in Monnetier, a tiny, out-of-the-way village in France, not far from Geneva.

....

If Thou But Suffer God to Guide Thee (page 115)
Jesus, Priceless Treasure (page 138)
Whate'er My God Ordains Is Right (page 264)

CPSIA information can be obtained
at www.ICGtesting.com
Printed in the USA
LVHW030826260222
712052LV00001B/49